To Wendy,

Cooking becomes a joy when made with ease and confidence and served with love to family and friends.

Bon Appétit

[signature]

Le Kitchen Cookbook:

a workbook

everything you need to know to be a good cook

Le Kitchen Cookbook

a workbook

ADELINE M. OLMER

ISBN: 978-0-578-94197-4 (Paperback)

Library of Congress Control Number: 2021913799
Front cover image by Adeline M. Olmer
Book design by Adeline M. Olmer Design.
Photographs of Adeline M. Olmer Quentin Bacon

First printing edition 2021.

Maxi Var Publishing
Sleepy Hollow Rd.
Briarcliff, NY, 10510

www.french-secrets.com

"Recipes tell you nothing. Learning techniques is the key."

– Tom Colicchio

DEDICATION

I would like to dedicate this book to all the people whose love for food has inspired me. Some I remember and some I don't, but their influence is undeniable and I am grateful to each and every one of them for their extraordinary inspiration. They are also the reason I wrote this book. I was given the gift of knowledge and passion and I knew I wanted to pass it on.

"A cookery book should be there for inspiration. Recipes should be a guideline, and they shouldn't be cast in stone."

—Marco Pierre White

ACKNOWLEDGMENTS

If it weren't for my parents, Monique and Francis Olmer, who taught me the importance of food—not only how to appreciate it but they took the time to show me how good it could really be—this book would not exist. That combined with the joy of eating together and good conversation allowed for a lifetime of exploration and joy that led to my writing this book. Without that pleasure, I would have missed out on a lot.

To my children, Tyler and Olivia, who never hesitated to tell me what they liked and what they didn't, thank you. "Please make this, it's my favorite" was what I named my first blog. It was what they would say when they asked me to make a dish they really liked and I understood that I had created something that would be carried on to their families.

My husband, Mark, thank you for your continued support and love. His enjoyment of the everyday pleasures of life always somehow end up in the kitchen as we create something to eat. Though not always perfect, more often than not we both utter, "Wow, this is really good!" I am grateful for his passion for food and family as well as his continued ability to make me laugh. These have turned ours into an extraordinary partnership. And thank you for your final go through of the book. I needed that.

Jane Hamill, without you I might not have gone full force into this project but when I did, you never questioned my commitment and were always there when I needed to think outside the box. Both as coach and friend you've been wonderful.

Betsy Robinson, thank you for your quick and impeccable editing. And your friendship over the years.

To The Briarcliff "Virtual Wine & Supper Club": John, Judy, Peter, Gindy, John, and Lisa. All dear friends who have supported my ventures and were willing to test my recipes and listen to my endless talk about cooking and the book. Peter thank you for the early support, John, for the edit.

Lynn and Tulis, without your support over the last decades, my life wouldn't have been nearly as wonderful as it has been.

Thank you, my sister Audrey, who loves to cook and eat as much as I do and has been a real partner in the kitchen over all the holidays and times we gather. It's always been fun. I've missed you over this past year of isolation.

There are so many people to thank for being in my life and always supporting my crazy ideas.

Elissa, Ellie, Arlene, Tony, Theo, Pat, Barbara, Jordan, Allison, Jim, Seth, Luke, Dana, Adrisse, David, Tristan, and that's not all.

I love you all!

TABLE OF CONTENTS

TABLE OF CONTENTS

"Cooking is one of the greatest gifts you can give to those you love."

—Ina Garten

"The web is no substitute for cookbooks."

"It will, provide you every imaginable variety and conception of 'peanut butter,' 'jelly,' and 'sandwich,' . . . but in the end it will still only be offering you a list; it will not have a viewpoint. It will not assist you in evaluating this massive compilation of what happens when these three food ideas intersect."

"He argued that recipes should serve as directional cues that encourage creative detours rather than being mimicked precisely, like a road map. . . . coddled by the printed recipes that encourage obedience and conformity at the expense of knowledge and understanding, we have become a generation of cooks that do not know how to cook."

—Nack Waxman

Quote from Sam Roberts for the New York Times

INTRODUCTION

Discover the fun of cooking.

WHY DID I WRITE A COOKBOOK?

When I was learning to cook, I looked for a book that would explain procedures in a way that allowed me to learn to do more than just follow a recipe. What I wanted was to understand basic techniques and what made some dishes exceptionally good and others not so much.

I didn't find the book I was looking for. There were plenty of cookbooks that explained techniques but no book that explained what made food flavorful, how to create sauces, or how to change the ingredients in a dish to what I actually had in the refrigerator. I didn't just want recipes; I wanted to learn how to cook!

When our children started to ask questions about how to make the recipes they had grown up eating, I decided it was the right time to write the book I wished I had had when I was learning how to cook. As it turns out, it is also the book I'm glad I have access to when I'm cooking now.

WHAT MAKES THIS BOOK DIFFERENT?

To begin with, the way the book is divided and what is included is different than other cookbooks. It is not just filled with good recipes, but with how these recipes are made.

Instead of being divided by ingredient—chicken, beef, fish, etcetera—the chapters are divided by cooking techniques such as baking, grilling, or roasting. The beginning of each chapter explains the technique and the steps and ingredients necessary to make the dish. Recipes follow, demonstrating each method of cooking so that you can experience how it is made as well as taste the flavor possibilities.

THE BOOK CONTAINS A SECTION THAT EXPLAINS WHAT I CALL "THE BASICS"

The power of the five basic flavor categories: salt, sweet, bitter, acid, and umami and how they play against each other to build levels of interest for your pallet. The importance of thickeners for transforming liquids into sauces that stay on the food instead of sliding off. What herbs and spices are used to develop the tastes we like so much—including lists of the spice combinations necessary to build up the seasonings used in recipes from different countries, such as Italy, France, Mexico, India, or China. Types of ingredients such as dairy and the many different ways they are used in creating recipes.

Other sections are devoted to setting up your kitchen—explaining what you need as opposed to the items that are tempting but not necessary. What is in a working pantry? One that has what you need when you need it. What all those cooking terms really mean and a section where you will have access to all the charts you'll need to understand measurements used in your recipes, what temperature meat needs to be cooked at, or how to tell if your meat is well done or rare by the touch.

THIS BOOK ISN'T THE ONLY RECIPE BOOK YOU WILL EVER NEED.
But it is a good place to start. You'll learn the basic components necessary for you to actually cook and not just follow a recipe.

THE BASIC COMPONENTS YOU NEED TO COOK:

INGREDIENTS
Including fats, vegetables, fruits, grains, nuts, meat, fish, eggs and dairy.

AROMATICS—FLAVORS
All the ingredients used to add different flavors to food: herbs, spices, carrots, celery, garlic, ginger, onions, peppers, shallots, tomatoes.

COOKING TECHNIQUES
The science that alters the ingredients through heat energy: baking, braising, grilling, roasting, searing, steaming, stewing.

THE POWER OF SAUCES
How sauces can transform ordinary dishes into spectacular ones. It is often said that a good cook is defined by the sauces they make. Once you learn how they are made you'll realize they're not hard but the impact they have is huge.

I improvise as I cook, I sometimes get great results, sometimes not. Problems occurred when friends asked me for the recipe of a great dish or could I make it again? "Sure," I'd reply, "can you remind me what I made?" The tricky part was I couldn't remember how I made it. That's when I realized I needed to write everything down. The fun of a good recipe is being able to savor it. It seems a shame not to be able to repeat it, and so *Le Kitchen Cookbook* was born.

This book has become one of the most essential tools in my kitchen. I hope you will find it as useful as I.

DO YOU NEED TO LEARN HOW TO COOK?

You don't, but you do have to eat so why not learn?

Cooking isn't hard once you understand the basics. I don't mean just learning how to follow a recipe. Though that is important and a good place to start, that doesn't really teach you how to cook or give you the freedom or ease to cook on your own.

When you are learning a new skill, you first need to master the basic techniques. For instance, when you learn to ski, you start with the basics: how to stop, turn, use your edges and your poles. And then you practice over and over again until you've mastered those skills. Then you challenge yourself by moving from the beginner slope to harder trails and mountains. Before you know it, your skills are second nature and you've forgotten to think about all the steps you needed to learn to get to that point.

The goal of this book is to teach you to cook the same way: one step at a time. Remembering that like everything else, it takes time and practice.

The fun happens when, like skiing, you no longer focus only on technique and begin to play with the flavor, texture, and ingredients you use—that's when cooking really gets to be exciting!

I'm so glad you bought the book! This is the place to sign up to get access to the online book extras: french-secrets.com/pages/book

"Good food is the foundation of genuine happiness."

—Auguste Escoffier

1.

HOW TO USE THIS BOOK

This book is more than a cookbook; it is a workbook.

> **"Once you have mastered a technique, you hardly need look at a recipe again and can take off on your own."**
>
> **—Julia Child**

This is a book that is meant for you to write notes in—do it wherever you find space. If you decide to alter a recipe, write it down; make an addition, write it down; something didn't work, write it down. That's how you learn and how you can repeat what you did.

There is a section that is blank called *It's Your Turn* for you to write down the recipes you create. More than anything, this book is a place for you to record your experiences in the kitchen.

The place to start is on the cover by adding your name and the date. Own the book. It's yours.

I hope that it will be the type of book you will pass on to your children so they'll have access to all the gems you have fed them and taken the time to write down in your own hand. My intention is that you will create a book that is a gift truly worth passing on.

QUESTIONS
and answers

Why is the book divided by cooking methods instead of types of food?
The book's focus is to explain how to cook not what to cook. If you want to find specific types of recipes, you can find them in the index.

Why does the book cover have a spot for your name and the date?
The book is intended to be customized by the owner. That's what makes it special.

Why are some recipe sidebars full of information and others empty?
They won't be empty once you fill them with your notes.

Why does it say READ PREPARE ADJUST (RPA)at the top of every recipe?
It is a reminder that you need to start by reading the recipe, then prepare all the ingredients, and finally, as you are cooking, you need to adjust the flavors.

Why are some recipes so long, especially when you say they are easy?
The steps are explained in detail so they seem long but that is only to make them easy to follow.

Why are stories included?
Stories are part our lives and the memories that inspire us.

Why is there space to write your recipes? Aren't cookbooks suppose to provide recipes rather than leave room for you to write yours?
This isn't just a cookbook; it is a workbook meant to become your recipe book where you can add your own flavors.

Do you have a website where I can get more information from you?
Yes, we have a special section available just for you to get more information about recipes, tools, methods, and a place you can ask questions. french-secrets.com/pages/book

Are you planning to write other books?
Yes, the next in the series will be *La Dinner Party.*

"I have loved to cook since I was a child in my mother's kitchen. If I don't have time to cook, I'll just read a cookbook."

—Kamala Harris

2.

in your kitchen

KITCHEN SUPPLIES

What do you really need to stock a good kitchen?

PROBABLY A LOT LESS THAN WE THINK.

Kitchen tools are fun, generally inexpensive, and often unnecessary. They end up stuffed in drawers taking up space and never really used. Never discarded because what if it turns out to be the perfect tool one day—I have a drawer full. My experience is if they aren't there you won't miss them and you'll be glad for the extra space in your drawers.

My advice is buy tools that are multi-functional and look to see how you can use what you already have in different ways. Flexibility is always optimal.

POTS AND PANS

CAST-IRON FRYING PAN

10" to 12"

These last forever. They often can be purchased at reasonable prices at flea markets. They are well worth the purchase.

To season the cast-iron pan: Scrub the pan clean, let it dry, coat it with vegetable oil, and rub it in. Place in 400° oven, bottom up with foil on the lower shelf to catch any drippings. After 30 minutes, remove the hot pan from the oven. Rub oil all over the pan again and place back into the oven for another 30 minutes. Repeat this process 4 or 5 more times. The result will be a well seasoned pan. To clean the pan, use a paste of salt and water to scrub the pan clean. Remove the salt and rub a little oil back on the pan.

In order to preserve the coating you created do not wash the cast-iron pan with soap and water.

SET OF STAINLESS PANS.

10" frying pan
3 qt sauté pan plus lid
2 qt saucepan plus lid
8 qt stock pot plus lid

My favorite are All-Clad but that doesn't mean they are the ones you have to purchase. There are a lot of different brands available; do your research to decide the ones that are right for you. Here is what you are looking for: 18/10 stainless steel that is 3 to 5 ply. The bottom plate should extend the entire length of the pot and it needs to be comfortable when you pick it up.

I recommend buying them when the sets go on sale; it happens often. Use Barkeepers Friend to keep them clean; it works perfectly.

DUTCH OVEN

7 to 8 quart is a good size

This is a must have. Use it on your stovetop and in your oven. I bought my Le Creuset on sale and have had it for years. There are a lot of good quality brands available. Get the best you can afford; they will last a long time.

CAST-IRON GRILL PAN

I love this pan! Instead of using it on my stovetop, I place it in the oven. It makes cooking much easier and grilling inside is far less messy because the mess is contained in your oven. Season your grill pan the same way you seasoned your cast-iron fry pan.

SHEET PANS

18" x 13" is called a half-sheet pan

A heavy-duty sheet pan is a must. You want good quality pans that will not warp when your oven gets hot.

ROASTING PANS

These pans are not only for roasting. You can use them for one-pan meals and large casseroles when you are making large batches.

CASSEROLE DISHES

9" x 13"

These oven-proof dishes can go from the oven to the table and are workhorses in the kitchen since they can be used in so many different ways.

KNIVES

Chef's knife 8"—chops, slices, and minces
Paring knife 3 ½"—paring, peeling, and chopping
Serrated knife—cutting bread
Set of steak knives
Knife sharpener

Having sharp knives is essential. It is actually less dangerous to have sharp knives than to try and cut when your knives are dull and they can slip. It is a good idea to find a knife sharpener in your area. Taking knives to be sharpened regularly will make cooking easier.

Inexpensive knives are no bargain. Buy the best you can afford. A few good knives are all you really need.

KITCHEN TOOLS

Box grater
Colander
Fat separator
Food processor
Glass food storage containers with lids
Ice cube trays—usable for ice and small portions of sauces and herbs
Ladle
Large meat fork
Mandolin
Micro plane
Nesting mixing bowls
Pasta fork
Rubber spatula
Salad spinner (can also be used as a bowl and a colander)
Slotted spoon
Spatula
Tongs
Vacuum sealer
Wooden spoons

MEASURING TOOLS

Instant-read thermometer
Measuring cups dry ingredients
Measuring cups wet ingredients
Measuring spoons

KITCHEN SUPPLIES

PRACTICAL TOOLS

Can opener
Corkscrew
Flexible cutting mats or/and a cutting board
Garlic press
Kitchen shears
Nonstick silicone baking mats
Pizza cutter
Vegetable peeler
Whisk
Wood citrus juicer (a wooden spoon can be used instead)
Kitchen twine

SMALL APPLIANCES

Blender
Coffee maker
Food processor
Hand mixer
Immersion blender
Kitchen scale
Pressure cooker
Stand mixer
Toaster oven

BAKING

Muffin pan, 6 to 12 cup
Pie pan, 9"
Rectangular cake pan, 9"
Rolling pin
Round cake can, 8" to 9"
Springform pan, 9"

PANTRY

You don't need everything on the list but it's nice to know it's there when you need it.

PANTRY ITEMS
Anchovy paste
Artichokes, canned
Beans-assorted cans: black, cannellini, red, kidney
Bouillon low-salt, chicken, beef, vegetable, and fish
Breadcrumbs
Chickpeas
Chips
Cookies, sugar, assorted
Crackers
Clam juice
Clams, baby canned
Coffee
Instant espresso coffee for flavor
Dried fruits
Gelatin
Graham crackers
Milk, powdered, condensed, and sweetened condensed milk
Nut butters—almond, peanut
Tea, assorted—black teas, green teas, herbal teas
Tomatoes, canned
Tomato paste
Tomato sauce
Tuna cans

PANTRY STAPLES

Aluminum foil
Coffee filters
Flour sack kitchen towels
Parchment paper
Plastic wrap
Resealable plastic bags
Garbage bags
Sponges
Scrub brushes

BAKING SUPPLIES

Baker's chocolate
Baking powder
Baking soda
Brown sugar, dark and light
Cocoa powder
Confectioner's sugar
Corn syrup
Cornstarch
Dried yeast
Flour
Nuts, walnuts, pecans
Oatmeal
Sugar
Vanilla extract, real not imitation

HERBS AND SPICES

Allspice
Basil
Bay leaf
Cayenne pepper
Chili sauce
Chives
Cinnamon
Cloves
Cumin
Curry powder
Dill
Fennel
Garlic powder
Ginger powder
Nutmeg
Onion powder
Oregano
Paprika
Parsley
Pepper corns, black
Pepper, assorted
Pepper, white
Red pepper flakes
Rosemary
Sage
Salt finishing
Salt kosher
Thyme

CONDIMENTS

Capers
Honey
Hot sauce
Hummus
Jams & preserves
Ketchup
Chili sauce
Mayonnaise
Mustard, Dijon
Olives, assorted
Pickles
Salad dressing
Salsa
Soy sauce
Tabasco
Teriyaki sauce
Worcestershire sauce

OILS & VINEGARS *

Cooking spray
High-heat cooking oil
Extra-virgin olive oil
Flavored oils
Sesame oil
Wine vinegar, red, white
Cider vinegar
Distilled white vinegar
Rice vinegar

* about vinegars and oils (page 42)

PANTRY

GRAINS, RICE, PASTA

Assorted pasta
Buckwheat
Bulgar wheat
Couscous
Lentils
Pearl barley
Quinoa
Rice, white, brown, wild
Split peas

VEGETABLES

Garlic
Lemons & Limes
Leeks
Onions
Potatoes, white & sweet
Shallots
Scallions

FROZEN FOODS

Bread
Chicken
Ground turkey
Ice cream
Pound cake
Scallops
Shrimp

ALCOHOL

Beer
Brandy
Cream sherry
Marsala wine
Rum
Wine, red & white

ADDITIONS

MEASUREMENTS & CHARTS

At your fingertips
when you need them

EQUIVALENTS			
TEASPOONS =	TABLESPOONS =	CUPS =	GRAMS
3 teaspoons	1 tablespoon		14.3 grams
2 tablespoons	⅛ cup		28.3 grams
4 tablespoons	¼ cup		56.7 grams
5 ⅓ tablespoons	⅓ cup		75.6 grams
8 tablespoons	½ cup		113.4 grams
12 tablespoons	¾ cup		180 grams
16 tablespoons	1 cup		340 grams
32 tablespoons	2 cups		480 grams

LIQUID MEASUREMENTS				
GALLONS	QUARTS	PINTS	CUPS	FLUID OUNCES
1 gallon	4 quarts	8 pints	16 cups	128 fluid ounces
½ gallon	2 quarts	4 pints	8 cups	64 fluid ounces
¼ gallon	1 quart	2 pints	4 cups	32 fluid ounces
	½ quart	1 pint	2 cups	16 fluid ounces
	¼ quart	½ pint	1 cups	8 fluid ounces

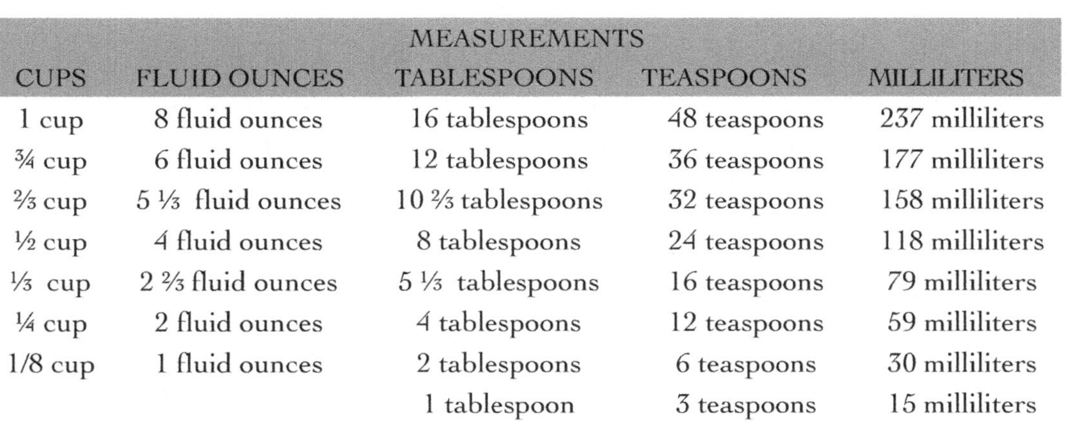

MEASUREMENTS				
CUPS	FLUID OUNCES	TABLESPOONS	TEASPOONS	MILLILITERS
1 cup	8 fluid ounces	16 tablespoons	48 teaspoons	237 milliliters
¾ cup	6 fluid ounces	12 tablespoons	36 teaspoons	177 milliliters
⅔ cup	5 ⅓ fluid ounces	10 ⅔ tablespoons	32 teaspoons	158 milliliters
½ cup	4 fluid ounces	8 tablespoons	24 teaspoons	118 milliliters
⅓ cup	2 ⅔ fluid ounces	5 ⅓ tablespoons	16 teaspoons	79 milliliters
¼ cup	2 fluid ounces	4 tablespoons	12 teaspoons	59 milliliters
1/8 cup	1 fluid ounces	2 tablespoons	6 teaspoons	30 milliliters
		1 tablespoon	3 teaspoons	15 milliliters

WEIGHT		
POUND	OUNCES	GRAMS
	1 ounce	28 grams
1 pound	16 ounces	454 grams

CONVERT FAHRENHEIT INTO CELSIUS
Subtract 32
Multiply by 5
Divide by 9

CHARTS

OVEN TEMPERATURES EQUIVALENTS				
HEAT	FAHRENHEIT	CELSIUS	THERMOSTAT FRANCE	GAS MARK UK
Cool	250°	120C	TH 4	1/2
Very moderate	300°	150C	TH 5	2
	325°			3
Moderate	355°	180C	TH 6	4
	375°			5
Moderate hot	410°	210C	TH 7	6
	425°			7
	465°	240C	TH 8	8
Very hot	475°			9
	520°	520C	TH 9	10

THE FINGER TEST TO DETERMINE WHEN YOUR STEAK IS DONE	
DONENESS	OPEN YOUR HAND, PALM UP, AND RELAX IT.
Raw	With your other hand, feel the fleshy part just below your lowest thumb joint. This is what raw meat feels like.
Rare	Touch the tip of your index finger to the tip of your thumb. Feel the muscle again. This is how rare meat feels.
Medium rare	Now touch your thumb and middle finger together. That is what medium rare feels like.
Medium	Touch your ring finger to your thumb to feel medium meat.
Well done	Touching your pinky to your thumb is well-done.

CHARTS

Dinner in Paris

Ease in the Kitchen

I rented a room in Paris at the apartment of an American acquaintance. The apartment was also rented to a young French woman and her baby. After a full day of work and taking care of her son, Valerie asked if I would join her for dinner. She went into the kitchen to start cooking dinner. "May I help?" I asked. "Non," she said with a smile. "It is nothing."

I watched from the doorway as she put a pot of water to boil and then placed some mushrooms, a little garlic, and some fresh herbs in a large frying pan to brown. Wasting no time, she cleaned the lettuce, made a simple vinaigrette, and sliced the bread. She took out a plate and arranged an assortment of crudités.

Turning her attention back to the mushrooms, she stirred the mixture and lowered the heat. She took a box from the cabinet, placed some fettuccine in the pot of boiling water, and proceeded to open the package of meat she had picked up at the butcher.

The pans on the small stovetop were adjusted to fit one more skillet. The flame on high, a little olive oil added, and the escalopes de veau (veal) were searing in the pan. She took the cheese from above the refrigerator, touched the center, unwrapped it, and let the odor fill her nostrils. Smiling, she said, "It should be perfect."

Once again, she turned her attention to the stove, flipped the veal over, drained the fettuccine, and added it to the pan of mushrooms. Then some crème fraiche, a little salt, and ground fresh pepper. Making room in the large skillet, she transferred the veal to the side, lowered the heat, and covered the pan to finish cooking.

Picking up the platter of crudités and basket of bread, she announced, "C'est prêt." Dinner was ready. We ate and talked in a slow, relaxed manner that could only happen when there is nowhere else to be. After finishing with the cheese and salad, instead of feeling full, I felt satisfied.

"Some dessert and café?" Valerie asked, as she placed two slices of fruit tart on the table. She laughed when she saw my expression. "Non, non, I picked it up

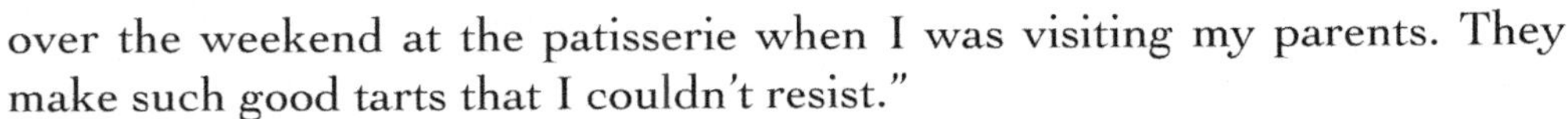

over the weekend at the patisserie when I was visiting my parents. They make such good tarts that I couldn't resist."

Dinner was delicious, remarkably elegant in its simplicity. The ease Valerie had in the kitchen amazed me.

"Where did you learn to cook?" I asked.

"At home," she replied, a little surprised by the question. She had grown up eating well and never considered cooking to be difficult. Quite the contrary, it was natural.

Taking the time to cook and savor the meal are at the core of what makes the French lifestyle so enjoyable. Whenever I think of Valerie and her ease in the kitchen, I'm inspired and reminded that the ritual of cooking and eating feeds not only the body, but also the soul.

"One cannot think well, love well, sleep well, if one has not dined well."

—Virginia Woolf

3.

ABOUT THE BASICS

BASICS

TECHNIQUES

Before you start—don't you want to know what it all means?

TRUST ME IT HELPS!

"Knowledge is power." —Sir Francis Bacon

BAKING—cooking in a lower temperature oven, 350°, usually used for food that develops structure while cooking such as cakes, bread, casseroles.

BRAISING—for large pieces of meat. The meat is browned in oil, then cooked with some liquid in a tightly covered pot in the oven or on your stovetop. This type of slow cooking helps tougher meats become tender and enables flavors to develop in the meat.

BRINING—used to add moisture to pork, chicken, and turkey. It is done by soaking the meat in a basic water/salt mixture. Though it helps pork, chicken, and turkey, it isn't used for beef, veal, or fish.

BROILING—the heat comes from above. It is usually done at the end of the cooking process to add color or to char the top of your dish.

DE-GLAZING—once you have seared your meat and browned your vegetables, adding a small amount of liquid to the pan, such as water, broth, or wine, then using a wooden spoon to dislodge all the bits of food that have caramelized and stuck to the bottom of the pan. Those bits are full of flavor and it is important that you reincorporate them into the sauce.

FRYING—food is cooked by immersing it in oil that is slowly heated to 350°. This method creates a crispy crust on the outside while keeping the center tender and moist.

GRILLING—cooking with direct heat from an open flame below the food.

MASHED—cooking and puréeing vegetables or a combination of them, combined with either broth or cream to make a creamy and flavorful purée.

ROASTING—done in the oven with dry high heat, generally 400°. The temperature browns the meat and vegetables, creating a flavorful crust.

SAUCES—are what turn food into something special. They add flavor, moisture, color, and texture to food. The French consider sauces to be the workhorse of cooking. Once you know how to make the basic sauces, your world will open up so you can be as inventive as you want.

SAUTÉING—using a sauté pan and a small amount of oil, the food is browned on one side for 2 to 3 minutes, then when it releases, turned over to brown the other side.

SEARING—an important step used when preparing food to cook in one of the above methods. You are browning the meat to caramelize the surface and create a crust that adds to the flavor of the meat—not a step that can be omitted.

SOUP—similar to a stew but made with more liquid. Soups have ingredients but are mostly liquid. Broths are full of flavor but the ingredients have been removed, leaving only the liquid.

STEWING—The meat is cut into pieces and cooked submerged in liquid until the meat is fork tender.

STIR FRYING—slice food diagonally to expose a lot of surface. Cooked very quickly over high heat with a small amount of oil, continually stirring until tender.

THICKENERS—the ingredients that make a liquid into a sauce. Liquids will slide off your food, but once thickened, the liquid starts to solidify and will stick to your food.

Going to the Marché with Mémé

Discovering the Wonder of Food

Following my grandmother on her errands on Marché day was always a treat. I was about eight years old and I tagged along watching as she strolled and chatted with all the familiar vendors. "What do you have today?" she would ask, and then tell them what she was looking for. She never purchased an item just because she had planned to use it. Instead she listened to their suggestions and then decided what she was going to buy—in the end, what she served was always a collaboration.

If there was something special, a fish that was unusual and caught in the morning or vegetables that were at their best, that is what we ate.

Shopping was an exploration into the land and the people who brought us the food. Buying their ingredients was to experience and share a part of them. For me, that was sheer joy.

But when it came to visiting Monsieur Casu le fromager, the cheese man, I was always a little bewildered. After our greetings, Mémé (my grandmother) would tell him what she wanted.

"Mais oui bien sur, Madame Maréchal," he would reply as he pulled out cheeses for us to taste.

Mémé would select four or five different categories—typically a blue cheese, one made from goat's milk, one from cow's milk, as well as a soft cheese and a hard cheese. Then she and Monsieur Casu would set about choosing the flavors and types that were just right within those categories.

Once that was done, he would look at her and say, "When are you going to serve them?"

"Ça sera pour le déjeuner demain," for lunch tomorrow, she replied.

"What time, à quelle heure exactement?" he asked.

She would give him the time, "Aux allentour de quartorze heur," around 2 p.m., she replied.

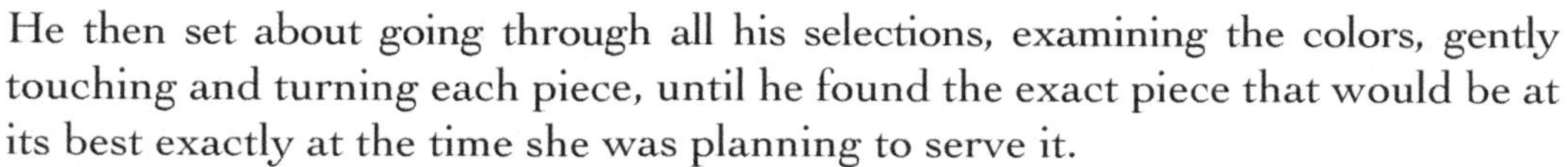

He then set about going through all his selections, examining the colors, gently touching and turning each piece, until he found the exact piece that would be at its best exactly at the time she was planning to serve it.

She would walk out delighted, but I was baffled. "How could he possibly know, comment peut-il savoir?" I asked.

She would look at me lovingly and explain, "Il connait son métier." That is his job and he is good at it.

But selecting the food was only half the adventure. The other half occurred when we sat down to eat. Every bite was anticipated and savored as everyone acknowledged the perfection of the ingredients that made up the meal.

What gives me the greatest joy is that now when I'm in France, I am still asked the same question. "What time are you planning to eat this?"

Thanks to farmers markets and the slow food movements, we can easily find food to nourish our bodies and souls that has been grown and nurtured by people who are passionate about what they do and gift us with the result of their love—and it is a gift.

ABOUT FLAVORS

You can't really be a good cook without knowing this!

THE IMPORTANT COMPONENTS THAT FLAVOR FOODS

BROTH is used to flavor foods. It is a liquid made by cooking assorted vegetables, meats, and bones in water to extract the flavors. Vegetables alone can be used to create a vegetable broth, or fish and vegetables to produce a fish broth.

THE FIVE TASTES:

SALTINESS—briny, saline, brackish
If dish is too salty, add an acid or sweetness.

SOURNESS—acidity
If the dish is too sour, add fats or sugars to counteract.

SWEETNESS—sugar
If the dish is too sweet, add acid. (Do not add salt; it will only highlight the sweetness.)

BITTERNESS—sharp, pungent, tart
If the dish is too bitter, add sweet, citrus, or vinegar.

UMAMI—savory, meaty
If the dish has too much umami, add sour or sweet to brighten the flavor.

HOW TO BALANCE FLAVORS WHEN THEY AREN'T QUITE RIGHT

RICH—you can add sweet or sour to cut the richness of the dish. (Fresh limes, lemon juice, a little vinegar.)

BLAND—salt can add flavor, bouillon will add a burst of flavor, cheese or strong herbs and seasonings, soy sauce, spicy pepper sauce.

SPICY—sour or sweet will help to tone down overly spicy foods. Adding a spoonful of plain yogurt and a little citrus also will help lessen the spice.

SALTY—sweet or sour will help but may not be enough. If possible, try diluting with water. When salting your dish, do so in intervals and taste as you go. Any dish that evaporates as it cooks will cause the flavors to intensify (especially the flavor of salt).

SOUR—sweet, salty, or bitter will help take the flavor away from sour.

BITTER—salty, sweet, or sour will help reduce the bitter flavor.

SWEET—sour, salty, or bitter will tone down the sweetness by adding other flavors to distract from the sweetness.

OTHER IMPORTANT COMPONENTS

The texture of the food (crunchy, soft, or hard) as well as the food's temperature (hot, room temperature, or cold) add to how we perceive the food's flavor and are important to consider when cooking.

THREE FLAVOR ENHANCERS I WON'T COOK WITHOUT

When I need "something" to balance out the flavor of what I am cooking there are three items I go to: soy sauce, anchovies, or bouillon.

- Soy sauce adds a bit of saltiness and savoriness, known as umami, without adding the traditional flavor of Chinese food. It is the perfect addition to tomato sauce that still has a bit of sourness. I find that it works far better than the traditional addition of sugar. When I'm cooking a wine-based stew for hours, a tablespoon or two of soy sauce at the end rounds out the flavor to give it a complexity of flavor without overpowering it. As far as I'm concerned, it is my magic sauce.
- Anchovies are also magical. Add them to increase the robustness and depth to what you are cooking. Don't panic if you are not an anchovy fan; it doesn't add any fishiness to your dish. Instead, what you will taste is great flavor. I always have a tube of anchovy paste in my refrigerator.
- My other must-have is bouillon. It is concentrated flavor that is a must-have when cooking. In the past, broths were made using quality ingredients that were left to *mijoter*, simmer on the back of the stove for hours. The flavors would reduce and concentrate into an intensely powerful essence that was used to create sauces, stews, soups, or anything to which you wanted to add that burst of flavor.

Nowadays, we generally don't have all day to create strongly flavored stocks. Using bouillon is a great shortcut to adding that intensity to the foods we cook.

The downside with bouillon is that it can be very salty. There are three ways to counteract that:

1. Add the bouillon at the end when adjusting the flavor.
2. Don't add a lot of salt as you're cooking. Add it only at the end if needed.
3. Buy low-sodium bouillon. Try different brands to find the one you like best.

ABOUT FLAVORS

Vinegars

Vinegar originating from the French
vin (wine) aigre (sour)

The definition of vinegar, according to Merriam Webster, is "a sour liquid obtained by fermentation of dilute alcoholic liquids and used as a condiment or preservative."

The power that vinegar has is its ability to boost and brighten flavors. It enhances foods that are bland and cuts the heaviness of overly rich foods by creating flavor contrasts.

TYPES OF VINEGARS:

APPLE CIDER made from apple cider. It has a fruity tart flavor that is good in marinades and salads and adds a little acid to your foods.

BALSAMIC VINEGAR originated in Modena, Italy. It is usually made from Trebbiano grapes that are pressed, cooked, and reduced to age in barrels for months or many years, resulting in a distinctive syrupy thick blend. Though Modena balsamic vinegar is expensive, there are others that are more affordable.

MALT VINEGAR is popular in England, made from barley kernels that are brewed and aged to create a unique malt flavor. According to the English, it isn't fish and chips without malt vinegar. It also adds a great flavor to pickled vegetables.

RICE VINEGAR comes from Japan and is a foundational flavor that gives that distinctive tang to pickled vegetables, a light salad, and sauces for fish and meats.

WHITE VINEGAR is made from acetic acid and water. It creates a strong crisp flavor. Its strength means you need to be careful using it. On the other hand, it is perfect for pickling.

WINE VINEGAR is made from either the red or white grapes. The better the quality of the wine that is used, the more subtle and interesting the resulting vinegar flavor will be. Like Balsamic, wine vinegar is aged in wooden casks for years.

SHERRY VINEGAR comes from Spain. Sherry is a wine that has been fortified using alcohol such as brandy that gives it a distinctive and complex flavor with a slight sweet taste. Used in vinaigrettes, it adds a subtle flavor. It is also good used as the acid added to sauces or marinades.

CHAMPAGNE VINEGAR is made from fermented champagne and is sweeter and lighter than other vinegars. It works well added to vinaigrettes and as a finishing touch to sauces.

If you find your dish is too vinegary, you can add a pinch of baking soda to neutralize some of the vinegar. Stir and taste to see if you need to add another pinch of baking soda.

Oils

Is the oil you are using suitable for the task?

IS THE OIL YOU ARE USING SUITABLE FOR THE TASK?

Everyone touts the benefits of cold-pressed extra virgin olive oil and how it is the best oil available. They also warn not to use it to cook food at high temperatures. Okay, but what oils are good at high heat and why? I learned that using the wrong oil or the right oil the wrong way can be harmful to our health.

WHEN USING COOKING OILS, THERE ARE THE THREE QUESTIONS YOU NEED TO ANSWER:

1. Is the oil you are using unrefined or refined? If it is refined, how is it processed?
2. What is the smoke point of the oil you are cooking with?
3. Does the oil you are using have flavor?

HOW OILS ARE PROCESSED AND WHY IT MATTERS:

UNREFINED OILS, also known as cold-pressed, raw, or virgin, are oils that are extracted and bottled without processing. Extra-virgin olive oil is considered to be the highest quality oil available. Since it isn't processed, it retains its flavor and all its health benefits.

REFINED OILS are processed using chemicals and high heat. The result is an oil that has a longer shelf life and a milder flavor. That may be good for mass -market sales but that way of processing results in oils that are not healthy for our bodies.

NATURALLY REFINED OR EXPELLER PRESSED are oils that are processed without using heat or chemicals. Instead, the oil is extracted by using pressure to squeeze the oil from the seeds.

WHY YOU NEED TO KNOW YOUR OIL'S SMOKE POINT:

The smoke point is the temperature at which oil starts to burn and smoke. This is important because burn or smoke point is when the oil gets a bitter taste, the fumes become harmful, and the oil starts to break down, becoming harmful to our bodies.

- **UNREFINED OILS** have a low smoke point so they are best used for low to medium heat and as a finishing oil in sauces and salad dressings.

- **REFINED OILS** have a higher smoke point so, in theory, they are good oils
- for high heat, except that the heat and chemicals used for processing
- alters the oil so it isn't healthy to use.

- **NATURALLY REFINED OIL** is what we want. It has the higher smoke point required but hasn't been tainted during the process, making it safe for us to use.

When you purchase oil for high-temperature cooking, make certain it says "expeller pressed" or "naturally refined."

SMOKING POINTS OF HIGH HEAT OILS:

Avocado oil 520°
Safflower oil 450°
Peanut oil 450°
Sunflower oil 440°
Grapeseed oil 400°

FLAVOR MATTERS

Consider the flavor of the oil you are using and how it will interact with your food. You don't want to overpower your ingredients, but rather use the flavor of the oil to either complement, contrast, or add no flavor at all.

NEUTRAL OILS

Avocado oil
Mild extra-virgin olive oils
Peanut oil
Safflower oil
Sunflower oil

OILS WITH STRONG FLAVORS

Extra-virgin olive oil
Hazelnut
Hemp oil
Pistachio
Toasted sesame oil
Walnut

FINISHING OILS are used to finish a dish not for cooking it:
Since strongly flavored oils can be expensive, it's a good option to use them as finishing oils, letting them stand out that way. A good tip: if you want to use them to make a vinaigrette, you can use a mild extra-virgin olive oil as your main oil and

drizzle the salad with the finishing oil to get the taste you're after.

SOME IDEAS FOR USING FINISHING OILS:

- A drizzle of walnut oil used to finish a tomato soup highlights both flavors in an unexpectedly subtle way.
- Sprinkling a strong-flavored cold-pressed olive oil on croutons and serving them on top of a classic vegetarian vegetable soup is a great way to brighten the flavor.
- Try adding toasted sesame oil to scrambled eggs or drizzle it on top of a tomato salad to surprise your taste buds.

IN CONCLUSION:

1. If you are using a refined oil, only use oils that are labeled "naturally refined" or "expeller pressed." These are the oils that have not been altered by heat or chemicals and won't be harmful to your health.
2. Know the smoke point of the oil you are using and don't use it beyond that point. The Heart Association advises that if you let your oil smoke, you should get rid of it and start again.
3. Use oils that have low smoke points as finishing oils that are not heated.
4. If your oil smells bad, it has oxidized and become rancid; you need to discard it.
5. In general, oils should be kept in a cool, dark place.
6. Buy small quantities of the oils that you do not use often. It's better to run out than to have to replace them because they've gone bad.

Herbs & Spices

Want to change your flavors?
This is where you start.

HERBS AND SPICES ADD FLAVOR, AROMA, COLOR, AND INTEREST TO FOOD.

Herbs, such as basil, thyme, and mint, come from the green leafy part of the plant. Spices, such as cinnamon, ginger, and mustard seeds, come from the rest of the plant: seeds, roots, bark, stem, and the bulb.

MY RECOMMENDATION:
Every time you use a spice or herb, you should spend time smelling and tasting that spice. Your goal is to become so familiar with your spices that you understand how they are going to affect the food you are about to add them to.

Properly storing herbs is important to preserving their flavor. Fresh herbs can be placed in a glass of water either on your sunny windowsill or in the refrigerator. Do not submerge the leaves; only the stems should be in water. I like rinsing the herbs and wrapping them tightly in a paper towel and then in plastic wrap and refrigerating them. They last five to seven days.

Spices also have a limited lifespan, so it is better not to buy large quantities, especially of the ones you don't use often; you can generally find small quantities of all spices.

Dried spices lose their flavor over time. Do not store them in direct sunlight or near a heat source like your stove. Your spices will lose their essential oils and their potency.

It's the combination of certain herbs and spices that determines the flavor palate of ethnic foods such as Italian, Chinese, Spanish, and so forth.

HERB MIXES TO FLAVOR FOODS FROM DIFFERENT CULTURES

THE CHART BELOW DEFINES THE FLAVORS OF DIFFERENT CULTURES.

CARIBBEAN	CHINESE	FRENCH	GREEK	INDIAN
Chili	5 Spice Powder	Bay leaf	Basil	Cardamom
Cilantro	Black pepper	Chervil	Bay leaf	Cayenne
Cinnamon	Chili	Chives	Cinnamon	Cinnamon
Cloves	Cinnamon	Fennel	Cloves	Coriander
Curry	Cloves	Garlic	Dill	Cumin seeds
Dill	Fennel seeds	Marjoram	Fennel	Ginger
Garlic	Garlic	Nutmeg	Garlic	Mustard seeds
Ginger	Ginger	Parsley	Mint	Turmeric
Nutmeg	Green onion	Rosemary	Nutmeg	
Oregano	Sesame seeds	Saffron	Oregano	
Parsley	Sichuan pepper	Sorrel	Parsley	
Tamarind	Star anis	Tarragon	Thyme	
Thyme	White pepper	Thyme		

ITALIAN	MEXICAN	MIDDLE EASTERN	SPANISH	THAI
Basil	Chili	Cinnamon	Bay leaf	Basil
Fennel	Cilantro	Cloves	Cayenne pepper	Chili
Garlic	Cinnamon	Coriander	Fennel	Cilantro
Oregano	Coriander	Cumin	Garlic	Coriander
Parsley	Cumin	Dill	Oregano	Cumin
Rosemary	Garlic	Garlic	Paprika	Curry
Saffron	Oregano	Ginger	Parsley	Garlic
Sage	Saffron	Mint	Rosemary	Ginger
Thyme		Nutmeg	Saffron	Mint
		Oregano		Turmeric
		Parsley		
		Poppy seeds		
		Sesame		

Recipes often call for a mix of herbs. While you can buy these mixtures in most grocery stores. I find it best and less expensive to make them. You can store them for 2 to 3 months or make them when called for in a recipe.

THREE OF THE MOST POPULAR ONES ARE:

HERBES DE PROVENCE

Use dried herbs.
Grind the rosemary and fennel; this breaks them up to release their flavor;

2 tablespoons thyme
2 tablespoons marjoram
2 tablespoons summer savory
2 tablespoons rosemary
1 tablespoon tarragon
1 tablespoon basil
1 tablespoon fennel seeds

BOUQUET GARNI

Tie herbs using kitchen twine, put in pan, cook, remove when done.

3 sprigs parsley
1 sprig thyme
1 bay leaf

FINES HERBES

Use fresh herbs, finely chopped. To keep the fresh flavor, add the herbs at the end of cooking. Use in sauces, omelets, soups, vinaigrette, roast chicken, etc.

1 tablespoon parsley
1 tablespoon chives
1 tablespoon chervil
1 tablespoon tarragon

ADDING A LITTLE HEAT

There are spices you can add to your dishes that will give them heat that adds just the right spice. Play around with the following list and see what you like best. It all depends on your taste buds and how spicy you like your food.

Cayenne pepper
Cracked black pepper
Frank's red hot sauce
Jalapeño peppers
Sraracha sauce
Tobasco sauce

GARLIC PASTE

Garlic paste is a great way to add flavor to any meat or fish you are cooking. Use the proportion of garlic to salt as a guide depending on the quantity you need. Once you have a paste spread it on your food.

3 large cloves of garlic
1 teaspoon of salt
1 teaspoon ground pepper
1 teaspoon olive oil

On a cutting board smash the garlic with the flat side of a knife.
Remove the papery skin.
Roughly chop the garlic.
Add 1 teaspoon of kosher salt. Using the abrasivness of the salt and the flat side of your knife, crush the garlic into a paste.
Combine with the olive oil to make the paste.

1 teaspoon of fresh herbs
½ teaspoon of dried herbs

If you want to add herbs:
Place the garlic paste into a bowl.
Add finely chopped herbs.
Combine, adding 1 tablespoon of olive oil.
Continue mixing until they become emulsified into the paste.

Preserving Herbs

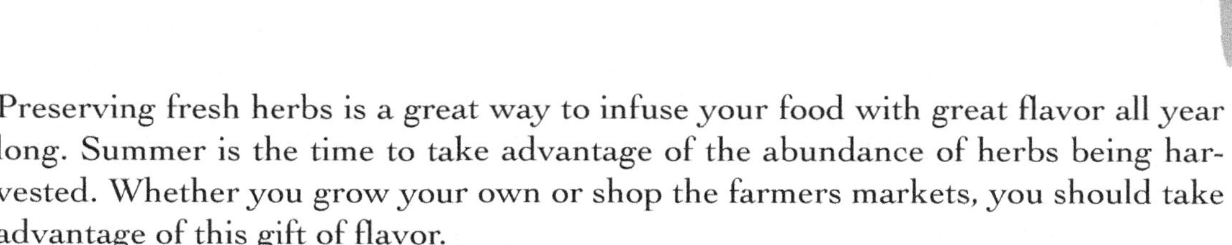

Preserving fresh herbs is a great way to infuse your food with great flavor all year long. Summer is the time to take advantage of the abundance of herbs being harvested. Whether you grow your own or shop the farmers markets, you should take advantage of this gift of flavor.

It's easy to do, doesn't take a lot of time, and will give you pleasure all year long—your taste buds will be delighted!

Having the herbs you need at your fingertips makes cooking much easier.

DRYING HERBS

The best herbs to dry: marjoram, oregano, rosemary, sage, and thyme.
Dried herbs are three to four times stronger than fresh herbs. They will last longer if stored in a dark dry spot.

- Group the same type herbs together and tie stems together. Hang them upside down to dry. Once they're completely dry, remove the leaves from the stems and store in a glass air-tight container. Make certain to label them with their names and dates.

- Herbs can also be dried in your microwave on a paper towel, although this method is not as effective at preserving their full flavor. Spread the herbs out so they do not overlap and cover with a paper towel. Microwave for about two minutes, checking after one minute to see how the herbs are doing. Microwave time will depend on the density of the herbs. Store in glass container, as above, or place in resealable bags, removing as much air as possible before closing and labeling.

- Dehydrators work well. You need to follow the directions that come with the machine and store as above.

HERB PASTES

• Put the herb of your choice in the bowl of a food processor and start processing while adding enough olive oil to make a paste. Spoon the paste into a glass jar and refrigerate; it will keep for at least three months. Alternatively, spoon the paste into an ice cube tray and freeze. Once frozen, put them into a resealable freezer bag. They will keep frozen for 10 to 12 months.

• Be creative and combine your own herbs to make your own blends. Since everything looks the same when it is frozen, make certain to label and date all your different bags.

FROZEN HERBS

Once frozen, the herbs will last 10 to 12 months—just in time for next summer.

• Chop the herbs so they are ready to use. Fill an ice cube tray with the chopped spices and top off each cube with either water or olive oil. Either one works. Once they are frozen, remove them from the tray and place in a resealable bag that you've labeled. When you are ready to use a cube, just remove it from the bag and drop it into what you are cooking.

• Another way to freeze the herbs is to lay the fresh herbs on a tray or plate and place them in the freezer. Once they are completely frozen, place them in a resealable plastic bag and roll them up, removing as much air as possible. Label with types of herbs, date, and seal the bag closed.

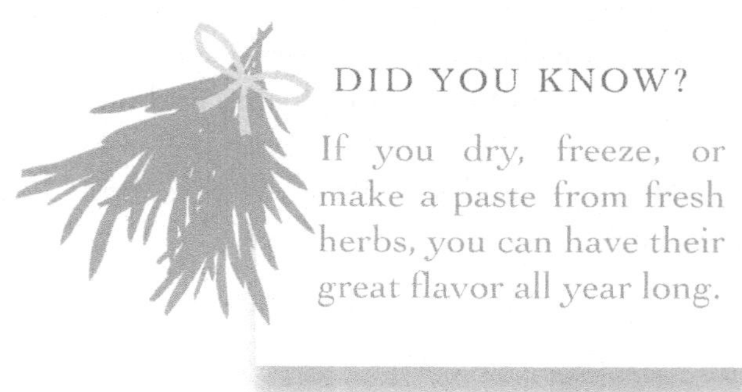

Salt

The most important ingredient.

Salt wakes food up and lets its flavors shine. Without salt, food would be bland and uninteresting.

Salt is a mineral, sodium chloride (NaCI), and is not only essential for life (our bodies need it to function) but it is also one of the five basic tastes our palate identifies. Salt brings out food's natural flavors, so it is vital to cooking.

There are many different types of salts. Their distinctive tastes, textures, and sizes are what determines how we perceive their various flavors.

TABLE SALT—the traditional all-purpose salt available everywhere. It is a refined salt with fine grains. Because of this, it tastes saltier than other coarser salts.

SEA SALT—the salt retrieved by letting sea water evaporate and harvesting the remaining salt. Generally the salt is left as is and not processed, giving it more flavor and minerals than table salt.

KOSHER SALT—the main difference between kosher and other salts is that its flakes are coarse and large. It is less salty than other salts but that may be because of its size so we put less on. It is the salt preferred by chefs reportedly because it is easy to pinch and spread over food. It is the salt I use when I cook.

FINISHING SALTS—tend to be the more exotic salts that come from different parts of the world. The flakes tend to be larger, coarser, different colors, and different flavors. Because of their uniqueness they tend to be used at the end of the cooking process just before the food is served. Their crunchiness adds bursts of flavor as you eat. Salt adds great contrast to sweet dishes. Adding a pinch of finishing salts to fruits like watermelon makes the fruit taste sweeter. The addition of a finishing salt to chocolate, caramel, and ice creams makes them sublime.

HERE ARE A FEW OF THE FINISHING SALTS AVAILABLE.

(These are the ones I found in my pantry.)

- Sel Gris—France
- Fleur de sel—France
- Maldon—England
- Himalayan pink salt—Pakistan
- Hawaiian black salt—Hawaii
- Gros sel de Guérande—France
- Birch smoked salt—Iceland

THE SALT I USE AND RECOMMEND FOR ALL RECIPES IS KOSHER SALT. It gives you better control of how much salt you add and that is important. Use finishing salts but only once the dish is finished—your dish will benefit from that addition.

Pepper

Pepper was once like gold. Grind it yourself and savor its flavor.

Pepper's strong, spicy flavor is a potent addition to recipes. It can be used in all dishes, including sweet desserts, because of the contrast it offers. Though pepper is spicy, it isn't a spice. It's actually a fruit. Peppercorns have been included in our cooking throughout history and were one of the spices Christopher Columbus was searching for when he discovered the new world. At that time pepper was as valuable as gold.

Freshly grinding your pepper when you need it is the best way to get the fullness of the flavor it has to offer. Pre-ground pepper is practical but because it has been exposed to air, it loses a lot of its intensity.

DIFFERENT TYPES OF PEPPER:

BLACK PEPPER—from the fully-grown dried fruit of the pepper vine. Black pepper is the most mature and has the strongest flavor of all pepper. It adds spice and vibrance to food.

GREEN PEPPERCORNS—the immature berries that are picked and are either freeze-dried or brined. The flavor is not as severe as black pepper. Green peppercorns are used in pepper sauces.

WHITE PEPPERCORNS—start out as black but the outside skin is removed, giving it a milder more subtle taste. Because it is white, it is used in white sauces or in dishes that are white like mashed potatoes.

PINK PEPPERCORNS—not the same as black peppercorns. They come from the Peruvian pepper tree that grows in warm dry weather. They are related to the cashew nuts, meaning you have to be careful if you have nut allergies. Their unique color and mild, fruity flavor makes them one of my favorites.

By the way, pepper really does make you sneeze. It is the piperine that is found in the pepper that irritates your nose and make you sneeze.

Dairy

What would we do without dairy?

MILK comes from mammals and is a nutritious form of food for infants. It is high in calcium and vitamins D and B and potassium and is important for the prevention of osteoporosis. When it is used in baking, it adds moisture and flavor. It can be used to thin or thicken sauces.

POWDERED MILK is dehydrated, pasteurized milk. It doesn't taste as rich as regular milk but it can be used in all the ways milk can. Keeping a box of powdered milk is always a good idea so you have it when you need it.

I recently discovered that milk can be frozen for three to six months. You need to leave space in the container—about three inches for the milk to expand as it freezes. This allows you to buy milk in larger quantities than you need and freeze it until you need it. It's a great way to increase milk's shelf life and helps you take advantage of lower prices. Remember to always label and date your container. Thaw milk by either placing in the refrigerator or letting the container soak in a bath of cold water. Be sure to shake the milk well before serving so the milk fat has a chance to recombine with the liquid. It is possible that thawed milk will have a slightly different texture but be assured it is perfectly safe to consume.

EVAPORATED MILK comes in a can and is milk with about half the water removed. One of its benefits is that it has a long shelf life. It is often used as a substitute for milk in cooking because of its creaminess. It can also be used as milk by adding back the water.

SWEETENED CONDENSED MILK is a mixture of whole milk and sugar and comes in a can. Growing up in France, this milk was used to sweeten coffee. Now it is mostly used in baking and can be stored in your pantry unopened without concern of it going sour as regular milk does.

BUTTERMILK has a thicker texture and a more acidic taste than regular milk. Yogurt can be used as a replacement for buttermilk in a recipe. It is often used in baking, soups, salad dressings, and sauces.

DID YOU KNOW?

Milk can be frozen. Make sure to shake it well when you thaw it.

BUTTER is milk or cream churned, separating the fats from the liquid. Butter is made up of 80% butterfat and is semi-solid. Butter is used to sear food and combines with other ingredients for baking. Added to sauces, soups, and stews, butter adds texture and flavor. Cooked on its own, letting it brown, it becomes a sauce, used on fish, pasta, or vegetables. Butter can also be frozen and stored for when you need it. Place it in the refrigerator overnight, and it should be ready for use the next day.

HEAVY CREAM is a good addition to sauces or fillings. If whipped, through the addition of air bubbles it becomes whipped cream. Added to desserts or baked goods, it lightens their density. Heavy cream, like milk, can be frozen.

HALF AND HALF is a combination of milk and light cream. It cannot be whipped but it adds flavor and texture to dishes without adding the fat that heavy cream contains.

YOGURT can replace heavy cream or mayonnaise. Use in salad dressings to make them creamy. Use it in soups instead of cream to make soup lighter. Mix it with fruits to be eaten as is or to create smoothies or frozen yogurt desserts. Yogurt is also delicious used as the base for dips.

Yogurt can be frozen but the texture will be different when thawed so it is best to use it for cooking, added to soups or for baking or maybe in smoothies.

CHEESE is made from different types of milk to produce hundreds of diverse flavors. Cheese adds richness, texture, and flavor to foods. Slicing a piece of cheese to be eaten on a chunk of baguette is an experience that is an essential part of the French diet.

"How can you govern a country which has 246 varieties of cheese?"

—Charles de Gaulle

COTTAGE CHEESE is delicious on its own. It is a good substitute for heavy cream in soups that are emulsified. Use it as a substitute for ricotta cheese in lasagna. Cottage cheese can be frozen but the consistency changes dramatically so unless you use it in soups where it will be completely combined or in baked products, it's probably better not to bother.

SOUR CREAM has a slight sour taste that is great to combine with dips, sauces, and desserts.

CREAM CHEESE, similar in consistency to butter, can be used on bread. Mix cream cheese in desserts like cheesecakes or mousses.

CRÈME FRAICHE is thicker than heavy cream and is slightly more acidic. It is a good addition to sauces, both savory and sweet, or try it on fresh fruits.

ARE EGGS DAIRY?

EGGS are not dairy though they are often grouped together. Dairy comes from mammals while eggs come from birds. Eggs are nutritious, they contain protein and vitamins, and are low in calories. Eggs can be eaten alone or combined with other ingredients. They add structure and stability for baking. They are used in custard or glazes. Yolks are used to thicken sauces. Egg whites can be whipped, adding air to them, creating stiff peaks that can be added to sauces, cakes, soufflés, or sweetened and baked to make meringues, light crispy cookies that are delicious at the end of a meal.

ABOUT THICKENERS

When I learned the power of thickening, I started feeling like a cook.

THE IMPORTANCE OF THICKENING AGENTS

Thickeners add body, texture, and viscosity to your cooking liquid. Without thickeners the liquid would just run off the food. Thickeners give liquids the stickiness needed for sauce to adhere to the food.

There are also thickeners like gelatins that are used to add solidity to liquids, such as aspics, desserts like Jell-o, trifles, and candy.

BEURRE MANIÉ—the combination of butter and flour kneaded together (butter coats the flour). Mix equal amounts of room temperature butter with flour in order for the flour to be evenly distributed throughout the sauce, without creating lumps. Once they are combined, roll them into balls (about the size of a cherry) and refrigerate until you are ready to use them. To thicken your sauce break up the dough ball into your dish. While it melts mix it into the sauce and let it thicken. Add more if needed.

CORNSTARCH—Cornstarch slurry will quickly thicken sauces. Combine equal parts cornstarch and cold water. Important: sprinkle the cornstarch over the water without stirring. Once the cornstarch is totally absorbed, stir it to combine with the water; this will prevent any lumps. Add the mixture to the food you want to thicken. Stir it in and let it thicken with the heat. This is the thickener used in Chinese cooking and some fruit pies such as blueberry.

DAIRY PRODUCTS—Heavy cream, sour cream, crème fraiche, and yogurt are all good ways to thicken soups and sauces. Heat the sauce but do not let it boil or it may separate.

EGG YOLKS—Egg yolks are traditionally used to thicken sauces. Start by mixing an egg yolk with a little cream to create a uniform mixture. Bring the sauce you want to thicken to a fast simmer. Gradually add a little of the hot sauce to the egg yolk to temper the sauce. (Tempering means to slowly warm the egg mixture by adding in a little of the hot liquid to prevent the eggs from cooking when added to the hot liquid.) Once tempered, combine the liquids and continue stirring over medium heat as the sauce thickens.

FLOUR SLURRY—Combine 4 tablespoons of flour with 1 cup of water or broth in a covered jar. Shake well to combine. Add the flour slurry to the sauce by slowly mixing it in and letting the sauce thicken over heat. Add more if necessary.

MASHED VEGETABLES—Mashed vegetables are great thickeners, especially if you are trying to avoid carbohydrates and are interested in lightening up your recipe. Tomato paste is a good thickener if you are adding it to a sauce that includes tomatoes. Other vegetables will give you the same results. I add zucchini to tomato sauces; it thickens and mellows the flavor beautifully. When you emulsify the sauce, you can't taste the zucchini. Potatoes and cauliflower are also great ways to thicken soups.

REDUCTION—Evaporation is another way of thickening sauces and liquids. The advantage of reduction is that as it thickens, it intensifies and concentrates the flavors. Heat the liquid to be be reduced over medium heat until the volume is reduced by half or more.

ROUX—A roux is a traditional method of thickening a sauce and is usually the first step to making a sauce. Start with equal parts butter and flour. Melt the butter in a saucepan and add the flour. Stir until the flour and the butter are incorporated into a paste. Continue to cook the roux for a few minutes to remove the taste of the flour. Slowly add the liquid while stirring to make sure the liquid combines with the flour mixture while the heat thickens the sauce.

There are four different types of roux: white, blond, brown, and dark brown. The length of time you cook the butter and the flour mixture will change the color of the roux. To get a dark brown roux can take up to 45 minutes of cooking and stirring. The darker the roux, the stronger the flavor. Traditionally the darker colors are used in Cajun and Creole dishes.

MORE THICKENERS:

Arrowroot—is made from a root and helps thicken food.
Agar-agar—is made from seaweed and acts like gelatin when added to liquids. If you are vegan, this is the ingredient to use.
Gelatin—is a protein that comes from animals and is used to solidify liquids.
Pectin—is derived from fruits and is often used to thicken jams.

SEASONAL EATING

The benefits of eating food that is grown where it is going to be eaten is that it is allowed to ripen to its peak before being harvested, resulting in food that not only tastes better but is nutritionally rich. Eating locally also supports your community farmers.

By contrast, food that needs to be transported needs to be picked unripe to increase its shelf life. This process causes food to lose both flavor and nutrition. The process of transporting food increases the carbon dioxide emissions into the atmosphere, causing higher levels of air pollution.

AN ASSORTMENT OF SEASONAL PRODUCE			
SPRING	SUMMER	FALL	WINTER
Asparagus	Berries	Apples	Beets
Avocado	Broccoli	Cabbage	Brussels sprouts
Cherries	Cucumbers	Cranberries	Carrots
Greens	Herbs	Garlic	Cauliflower
Radish	Peaches	Grapes	Leeks
Rhubarb	Plums	Onions	Potatoes
Strawberries	Summer squash	Pears	Winter squash
	Tomatoes	Pumpkin	
	Watermelon		

FREEZING

Shop your freezer before you go to the store.

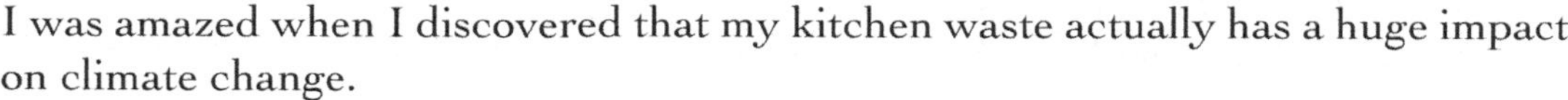

I was amazed when I discovered that my kitchen waste actually has a huge impact on climate change.

"Wasting food has irreversible environmental consequences: it wastes the water and energy it took to produce it, and generates greenhouse gases—7 percent of the world's emissions—like methane, carbon dioxide and chlorofluorocarbons, which contribute to global warming. Food that sits decaying in landfills also produces nitrogen pollution, which causes algae blooms and dead zones. According to the World Wildlife Federation, the production of wasted food in the United States is equivalent to the greenhouse emissions of 37 million cars." (Food Waste in America 2021: Statistics & Facts, RTS.com.)

Americans waste 30 to 40% of their food supply; that equals 219 pounds of food per person each year.

The good news is there is something we can do: freezing food is one of the quickest ways we have to preserve food, and preserving food, instead of discarding it, is what we need to do.

ACTUALLY, THERE ARE MANY BENEFITS TO FREEZING FOODS:

- It extends the shelf life of food. Freezing food at its peak keeps it in that state until you are ready to use it.
- When you cook, make more than you need and freeze the extra in individual portions for when you do not have time to cook.
- Save money by buying food on sale. Freeze it to cook it at your convenience.
- When you buy more than you need, don't let it go bad; freeze it instead.
- Freeze small amounts of leftovers that you can add to soups or stews to add flavor.

Most of us have the experience of losing food in the freezer, that deep, dark place where food goes in and unknown blobs come out. Definitely not appetizing. If that is your experience, the best thing to do is to clear it out. I know discarding food is not optimal, but if you aren't going to eat it, you need the space and a few rules about how to fill your freezer.

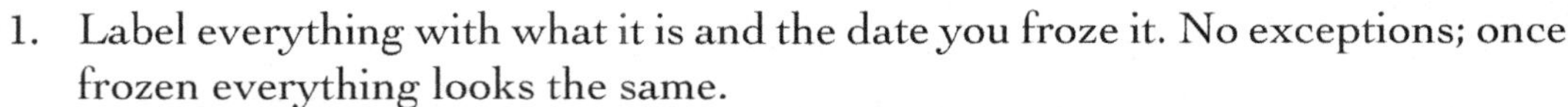

1. Label everything with what it is and the date you froze it. No exceptions; once frozen everything looks the same.
2. Cool food completely before freezing.
3. Wrap everything tightly to protect it from air.
4. Remove as much air as you possibly can before freezing.
5. Freeze in small portions that you will use.
6. Allow room for foods to expand during the freezing process.
7. To keep food separate once frozen, place parchment on a cookie sheet, lay out the items to freeze so they don't touch. Let them freeze and then place in a resealable bag.
8. The fresher the food you freeze is, the better it will be when you thaw it.

A vacuum sealer is a great tool for freezing food. It prevents freezer burn by removing the extra air and enveloping the food with a protective coating allowing you to preserve food longer.

SHOP YOUR FREEZER. Freezing only works if you use the food you freeze. Instead of heading to the store, go to your freezer to see what's for dinner and only head to the store to supplement what you already have.

It has taken a while but I'm starting to look at the food in my refrigerator differently. I think about what I need to do to insure I do not let the food go to waste. It's a start.

THAWING FROZEN FOOD

It is best to thaw your food in the refrigerator. If it's large and dense you may need to let it thaw overnight. You can also soak it in a bowl of cold water.

Usually the best way to reheat your food is the same way it was cooked. If you are using the oven, preheat it to 350° and cover the food you are cooking so it heats up slowly.

Some foods may need to be reconstituted, like potatoes and gravy. As they are heated they have a tendency to separate. The best way to reconstitute them is to continually whisk them until they come back together.

" The kitchen is the heart of every home, for the most part. It evokes memories of your family history."

—Debi Mazar

COOKING TERMS

What you need to know

AL DENTE—When pasta, rice, or vegetables are cooked with a little bit of firmness left in the center, also known as bite.

AU GRATIN—French term meaning a dish finished by topping with cheese or breadcrumbs and then browned in a hot oven to create a brown crust.

BAINE-MARIE—is a hot water bath used to cook delicate foods such as custards and foods that need to have an even gentle heat that surrounds the dish in the oven.

BEURRE MANIÉ—a thickener made by mixing equal amounts of softened butter with flour and rolling into small balls. Since the butter coats the flour it prevents it from creating lumps.

BLANCH—A way to cook green vegetables and nuts by dipping into boiling water for a minute or two and then removing and immersing in ice water to stop the cooking. This needs to be done when you are planning to freeze vegetables.

BLEND—Combining two or more ingredients so they are well mixed and smooth.

BOIL—Water brought to a high temperature so there are rolling bubbles that cover the surface.

BOUQUET GARNI—A mixture of herbs parsley, thyme, and bay leaf that are tied together with a string and placed in the stew or soup as it cooks. At the end of cooking, the herb packet is pulled out and discarded. If you use pepper corns or loose herbs, you'll need to place the herbs in a bag, such as a square of cheese cloth tied closed with string. Coffee filters will work like cheese cloth.

BRAISE—Cooking protein or vegetables so they brown on both sides and then adding liquid to the pan (only halfway up the side) and, continue cooking slowly until the food is tender and cooked through.

BUTTERFLY—Slicing food, usually meat or fish, through the center, leaving it connected on one end, so it opens up.

CARAMELIZE—Heating food to turn the sugars into a brown caramel that adds flavor to the food.

CHIFFONADE—A way of cutting that produces thin slices. Leaves such as basil leaves are stacked on top of each other, rolled together, and then the roll sliced thinly to create long thin strips.

CLARIFY—To separate solids from the liquid in order to create a clear liquid.

CREAM—Combining fat, butter, and sugar with a mixer or whisk at moderate speed until they are totally combined and become light and fluffy.

CURDLE—When milk separates into lumps and curds. An egg sauce can curdle when overheated.

DEEP FRY—Submerging food in hot oil to cook.

DE-GLAZING—Adding liquid to a hot pan after cooking to separate all the crispy pieces stuck at the bottom of the pan. Those bits are what give sauces their flavor.

DEGREASE—To remove the fat that accumulates on the top of stews, stocks, or sauces. When fat cools, it solidifies and can be easily removed.

DICE—Cutting ingredients into even-sized small cubes.

DISSOLVE—Turning a solid into a liquid. Such as sugar into hot liquid.

DREDGE—Coating moist food with dry ingredients such as flour or breadcrumbs, before cooking.

DRIZZLE—Coating lightly with a liquid to add it to your dish.

EMULSIFY—Combining two liquids that do not normally combine such as oil and vinegar so they stay combined.

FLAKE—To lightly break apart food to combine with other ingredients.

FLAMBÉ—Adding alcohol to a hot dish and then lighting it on fire to burn off the alcohol, leaving just the flavor.

FLUFF—Using a fork to separate cooked grains before serving.

FOLD—Using a rubber spatula to combine delicate, air-filled ingredients such as whipped cream with a denser ingredient like chocolate by cutting through the center and turning the combination of ingredients over on itself to gently combine.

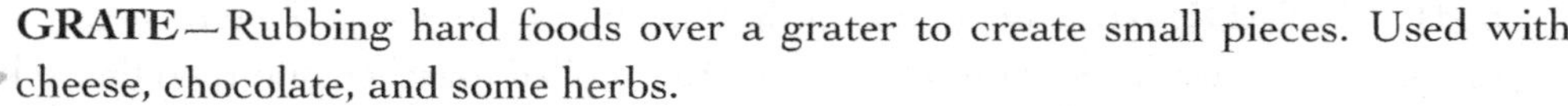

GRATE—Rubbing hard foods over a grater to create small pieces. Used with cheese, chocolate, and some herbs.

GRATIN—A dish with the top covered with either breadcrumbs or cheese allowed to brown in the oven creating a crispy crust.

GRILL—To cook on a grill with coals or gas heat at high temperatures. You can also grill in your oven under the broiler.

JULIENNE—To cut food, usually vegetables, into match-stick size pieces.

KNEAD—To work dough with the palm of your hands until it becomes elastic and smooth, usually used when baking.

LUKEWARM—Temperature equal to about body temperature.

MACERATE—Soaking, usually fruits, in sugar or a flavored liquid, sometimes liquor to imbue them with flavor.

MAILLARD REACTION—Discovered by a French scientist Louis Camille Maillard in 1912, it is a complicated chemical reaction usually produced by heat interacting with amino acids and sugars to create brown foods and lots of flavor.

MARINATE—Adding flavor to food by soaking in aromatics (marinade) for some time to add flavor and to tenderize. This can also be done by coating the ingredients with a dry mix.

MINCE—To cut ingredients very small.

MISE EN PLACE—Means "everything in its place" in French. Preparing and organizing all the ingredients you are going to use before you actually start to cook.

PAILLARD—A boneless piece of meat that is butterflied and pounded flat to tenderize.

PAN FRY—Cooking food in a pan over medium-high heat. Using oil, brown the food completely on one side before turning over to finish cooking it.

PARBOIL—Partially cooking food in boiling water before removing it.

PIT—To remove the stone or pits inside fruits.

PEEL—To remove the outer layer of vegetables or fruits.

PICKLE—Preserving food in a salted, vinegar brine.

POACH—To cook food slowly covered in a hot liquid that is just under boiling. This can be done with water, broth, wine, or a combination.

PURÉE—To transform cooked foods, usually vegetables, into a mash. This can be done using a sieve, food mill, or food processor.

REDUCE—Heating a liquid, and letting it evaporate as it cooks, condensing its flavor.

RENDER—To cook fat that is solid and melting it into a liquid, so it can be discarded or used for another use, such as bacon.

ROAST—Cooking food in the oven using hot dry heat.

ROUGH CHOP—Chopping ingredients roughly to about the same size but not necessarily small.

ROUX—A flour and fat mixture that is cooked to create a paste. A liquid is added to create a thickened sauce.

SAUTÉ—To cook small amounts of food in a little fat over high heat.

SCALD—To heat a liquid to just under boiling. Small bubbles appear around the edges of the pan before the liquid starts to boil.

SCORE—Cutting narrow slices on the thick layer of fat, to help release it, or on the skin of fish to prevent it from curling.

SEAR—Cooking with high temperature to brown the surface of the ingredient. This caramelizes the food, adding flavor.

SHRED—To tear food into small but long pieces. Shredding chicken to add to soup.

SIEVE—A utensil used to separate the liquid from the solid pieces of food.

SIFT—To combine different dry ingredients so they are integrated.

SIMMER—To cook liquids just under the boiling point. Generally cooking between medium and low heat.

SKIM—To remove the impurities that rise to the surface of cooking liquids by spooning them off the top.

SOUP—A liquid food usually containing solids, protein, vegetables, or grains.

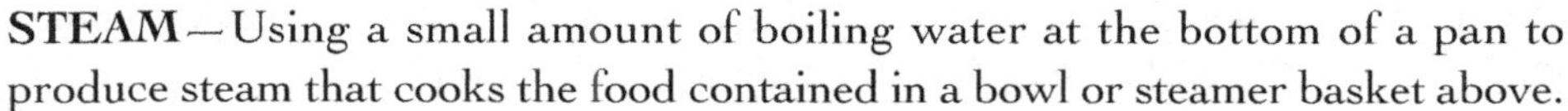

STEAM—Using a small amount of boiling water at the bottom of a pan to produce steam that cooks the food contained in a bowl or steamer basket above.

STEW—To cook food in a liquid over medium heat either on the stove or in the oven until it is very tender.

TEMPER—To bring two liquids that you want to combine to a similar temperature before combining. This is usually done with egg yolks that are added to a sauce you want to thicken.

TOAST—To brown the outside of food to create a texture and flavor.

TOSS—To delicately combine foods such as salads to coat with dressing.

TRUSS—Using kitchen twine or skewers to tie up poultry so it holds its shape as it cooks.

WHIP—Beating ingredients together to combine and add air to them in order to lighten and create a smooth mixture.

WHISK—A tool used to blend and incorporate air into the batter. This process is called to whisk.

ZEST—to remove the outside of citrus—just the colorful part that has all the flavor and not the white pith which is just below, as it is bitter. Use a micro plane, grater, peeler, or knife. This must be done before you juice the citrus.

"Know the rules well,
so you can break
them effectively."

—Dalai Lama

4.

WHERE TO START

WHERE TO START

FIRST THINGS FIRST

These 5 steps will make cooking a lot easier!

1. **READ THE ENTIRE RECIPE THROUGH BEFORE YOU START**

You need to know you have all the required ingredients, understand the directions, and are clear about the meaning of every term used before you start.

You don't want to discover that you've run out of an essential ingredient in the middle of putting everything together. Who wants to have to run to the store midway through the cooking process? Or realize that the recipe calls for marinating overnight and you were planning to serve it for dinner? Even worse, what if you're making dessert for guests when you notice that at the bottom of the recipe it says you need to refrigerate the dessert for at least 6 hours to ensure that it sets before serving and your guests are arriving in an hour?

You don't need that kind of stress! To be honest, I often read and re-read the recipe to make certain I understand what I need to do.

2. **MISE EN PLACE IS A FRENCH TERM THAT MEANS EVERYTHING IN ITS PLACE**

This step is so important that it transformed my life in the kitchen!
What it means is that you need to set out and prep everything you are going to use before you start to cook. This is a step that every chef does and you need to do it too.

3. **CLEAN YOUR KITCHEN BEFORE YOU START COOKING**

Empty your dishwasher and clean your sink before you start. I know it sounds crazy but having that space available to put used bowls, utensils, pots and pans as you prep and cook means that when you are done you are not left with a huge mess. A big mess can make you not want to cook at all.

4. KEEP YOUR KITCHEN CLEAN AS YOU COOK

Take out a large bowl to use as a garbage bowl. This allows you to keep your work area clean as you work. It is quicker to have a bowl for discarded scraps than to walk over to your garbage. It also ensures that your work area is clear and clean.

5. R.P.A. - READ, PREPARE, ADJUST

On the top of each recipe are the words "read, prepare, adjust" to remind you to first read the recipe, then prepare all your ingredients (mise en place), and finally adjust the flavors to your tastes. These are essential steps to cooking good food.

PLEASE DON'T SKIP THESE 5 STEPS!

They actually make cooking easier!

DISH TOWELS

According to chefs, this is an essential kitchen tool.

Dish towels used as a side towel are always tucked into a chef's waist, there to be used whenever needed. They replace paper towels. Help the planet and save money; stop using paper towels!

I recommend white dish towels inspired by the flour sacks that were used to store flour and grains at the turn of the twentieth century. They are inexpensive, made of 100% thin cotton and have a loose weave that makes them very absorbent.

HERE IS HOW I USE THEM AND SOME SUGGESTIONS FOR YOU.

CLEANING UP—I always use a dish towel to clean up as I cook. Because I can wash them, I never need to worry how I use them. A quick machine wash and they are ready to go again.

BOWLS—To prevent bowls from sliding when I'm mixing ingredients, I moisten a dish towel, twist it into a circle and nestle the bowl into the center to prevent it from moving.

VEGETABLES—After rinsing vegetables I place them in the center of a dish towel and pick up the sides, squeezing gently to remove moisture.

CHEESE CLOTH—I needed some cheese cloth to strain a custard. Since I didn't have any, I used a dish towel and it worked perfectly.

POTHOLDERS—When I have a dish towel at my fingertips I don't need to waste time and space looking for potholders.

CUTTING BOARD—I use a folded damp dish towel under the cutting board board to prevent it from sliding while I'm chopping.

SALAD SPINNER—Wash your salad, shake it off, and place it in the center of dish towel. Pull up the corners and, without squeezing, shake the salad over your sink. You can also gently pat it dry.

TIGHT-FITTING LID—If you're cooking grains and need a tight-fitting lid for the pan, lay the towel out and place the lid on top, pull the ends of towel around the lid and knot them, or tie with a string so they don't catch fire.

SANDWICHES—Traditionally tea sandwiches are kept fresh by placing a damp dish towel on top. It works perfectly for any type of sandwich. Placing a piece of wax paper between the sandwich and the towel will prevent them from getting soggy.

BREAD—Keep it warm by wrapping it in a dish towel in a basket.

TRIVET—A folded dish towel under a hot dish or pot prevents it from damaging your table.

INSTEAD OF PAPER TOWELS—Use them anywhere you would use paper towels; not only are you helping the planet but since you can drop them in the washer, you're saving money.

Oh and I almost forgot—dry your dishes and glasses with the flour sack dish towel; they are lint free.

APRONS

Are good for you.

WHY WEAR APRONS?

Food splashes, grease splatters and stains happen. Aprons are important! Unfortunately, I don't like wearing them. Instead, I wear spots all over my tops—not smart.

I have a drawer full of aprons. Most of them I got as gifts with great images or sayings on them. They're fun, but no more. The problem is that they're stiff and don't fit well—hence I don't wear aprons.

That is, until I found a simple chef's apron that is soft and flexible, adjusts to fit, and has pockets. It's easy to clean and, most important, it keeps me clean. Available at french-secrets.com/pages/book

I now wear them all the time.

In case you do get grease spots, this should help remove them.

1. Determine if your clothing can be washed.
2. Treat the spots before washing and drying. (Drying sets the spot.)
3. Dab some clear liquid dish soap on the grease and gently rub in.
4. Let set for 2 or 3 hours before washing.
5. After washing, check that the spots are gone before drying. (If the spots are still visible, repeat the process.)

APRONS SAVE
YOUR CLOTHES

Get the right one and
you'll wear it all the time

"Cooking is one failure after another, and that's how you finally learn."

—Julia Child

5.

THE ESSENTIALS

To good cooking

A Passion Passed Down Through Food

This Is Why I Learned to Cook.

Celine was a name that was synonymous with good food in my home. She was my grandmother's cook. All my life my mother told me stories about watching Celine in the kitchen. Her secret, she would say in a hushed tone, was her sauces; "Sauces," she emphasized, are the secret to being a great cook.

Celine didn't just make sauces; she turned food into something you looked forward to. She understood that the meal really started with the aroma of the food simmering on the stove. She'd plan the *repas* so it would build to a crescendo and conclude with the perfect sweet. But the meal only really ended when the coffee was served. We'd relax and let the banter and laughter continue as we sat, enchanted by the pleasures we'd just consumed.

Celine knew that if the food was good, the conversation would follow. She knew she was not just creating food to nourish us. She was participating in creating a way of life.

Celine's job was to cook, but her legacy was passion. She focused on food with the understanding that it would bring people together. She knew how important that was and loved the fact that she affected our lives with the food we ate and the relationships that were nurtured.

How could you not be thankful for that kind of love?

SAUCES

This is where the magic begins.

ABOUT SAUCES

Sauces are so important because a good sauce can turn ordinary meals into spectacular ones!

THAT'S POWER!

"An ounce of sauce covers a multitude of sins."
—Anthony Bourdain

"Sauces comprise the honor and glory of French cookery."
—Curnonsky

"It is the sauce that distinguishes a good chef."
—Fernand Point

Since sauces are critical to cooking, I've devoted a large section to explaining their origins and how they are made.

MY RECOMMENDATION:

The best thing you can do is spend some time making each sauce. You'll learn how they are made and discover that they are not as difficult or intimidating as you might have thought. Once you understand their flavors, you'll be free to use them as you wish. This will enhance your power to create great meals.

A LITTLE HISTORY:

"French chef Marie Antoine-Carême was the first to organize all the French sauces into groups that were based on four foundational sauces. Later, French chef Auguste Escoffier added one more sauce so that there were now five mother sauces, which he codified in recipe form in *Le Guide Culinaire* in 1903."

THE FIVE MOTHER SAUCES ARE:

Béchamel
Velouté
Espagnole
Tomate
Hollandaise

By adding simple ingredients to a mother sauce, it becomes what is known as a derivative or daughter sauce.

There are so many derivative sauces that flow charts have been created to display them. For example, bechamel is a mother sauce made from a roux (cooked flour and butter) with the addition of milk. The daughter sauce is mornay sauce and that is made from the bechamel sauce with the addition of cheese.

I have to acknowledge that some of these sauces used to be complicated and it took a lot of practice to master the technique. The good news is that with technology, an immersion blender, or a kitchen blender, these sauces have become easy.

As you start, sauces can seem daunting but in reality they are not hard. I can repeat that over and over but the only way you'll discover that for yourself is to actually make the sauces.

Do you want to see more techniques? Watch videos, read more explanations, and ask questions. Get access to the online book extras. Sign up at: french-secrets.com/pages/book

DID YOU KNOW?

If you want to be a good cook, it's all about the sauces!

MOTHER & DAUGHTER
SAUCES

MOTHER SAUCES MAIN INGREDIENTS	DAUGHTER SAUCES DERIVATIVE SAUCES
Bechamel Milk and a roux	**Crème sauce**—Cream, lemon **Mornay sauce**—Gruyere, cream, butter **Soubise sauce**—Diced onion, simmered, and strained **Nantua sauce**—Cream, butter, paprika, diced shellfish **Cheddar cheese sauce**—Cheese, Worcestershire, Dijon mustard **Mustard sauce**—Dijon mustard, white pepper
Tomato Sauce or Sauce Tomate in French, Tomato, stock,and a roux	**Creole sauce**—Onion, celery, garlic, pepper, thyme, cayenne **Spanish sauce**—Creole sauce, mushrooms, olives **Milanese sauce**—Mushroom, butter, ham **Provençale sauce**—Onion, capers, black olives, herbes de Provence **Bolognese sauce**—Meat, onion, carrots, celery
Velouté Stock and a roux	**Supreme sauce**—Chicken stock, mushrooms, cream **Normandy sauce**—Fish velouté, mushrooms, yolks, heavy cream **Bercy sauce**—Fish velouté, white wine, lemon, parsley, shallots **Allemande sauce**—veal stock, egg yolk, cream, lemon **Aurora sauce**—Allemande, tomato paste, butter **Poulette sauce**—Allemande, mushrooms, parsley, lemon **Ravigote sauce**—Veloute sauce, Dijon mustard

MOTHER SAUCES MAIN INGREDIENTS	DAUGHTER SAUCES DERIVATIVE SAUCES
Espagnole Brown stock, tomato, and a brown roux	**Marchand de vin sauce**—Red wine reduction **Bordelaise sauce**—Red wine, shallots, bay leaf, thyme, butter **Robert sauce**—Onion, Dijon mustard, butter, sugar **Charcutière sauce**—Onions, white wine, dry mustard, sugar, lemon **Lyonnaise sauce**—Onions, butter, white vinegar **Chasseur sauce**—Mushrooms, shallots, white wine, tomatoes **Madeira sauce**—Flour Madeira wine, onion, mushrooms
Hollandaise Clarified butter, lemon juice, and an egg yolk	**Béarnaise sauce**—Shallots, tarragon, white vinegar, butter **Foyot sauce**—Béarnaise, egg yolks, butter **Choron sauce**—Béarnaise, egg yolks, tomato paste, cream, chervil **Maltaise sauce**—Orange juice, orange zest **Mousseline sauce**—Whipped cream

BECHAMEL OR WHITE SAUCE

Béchamel is also known as a white sauce. It is typically used in scalloped potatoes, white lasagna, mac and cheese, and gratins. It is the base sauce for a number of derivative sauces, such as Mornay, Soubise, and Mustard sauce.

The proportion of this recipe will give you a medium-thick sauce that is most often used. But if you need it thinner, add more milk, or less to get a thicker sauce.

Makes: 1 cup
Prep time: 10 minutes
Total time: 10 minutes

If you need more sauce you can double or triple the ingredients below, maintaining the proportions. The amount of milk can vary depending on how thick you want the final sauce to be.

Ingredients
2 tablespoons butter
2 tablespoons white flour
1 cup milk
Salt and white pepper to taste
Pinch of nutmeg—optional

Directions

1. Make a roux in a heavy bottom saucepan, melt butter until it becomes frothy. Add flour, stirring with a wooden spoon, or whisk until it forms a paste.
2. Continue to stir and cook for 2 minutes without letting roux darken.
3. While you whisk, slowly add milk letting it combine before adding more.
4. Once all milk is added and sauce is smooth, continue to cook on low for a few minutes to let sauce thicken.
5. Continue to stir until bechamel is smooth and thick.

SIDEBAR

VARIATIONS

Once you have made the bechamel sauce Try these seconday sauces.

Mornay sauce—add gruyere and or parmesan
Mustard sauce—add 1 teaspoon of dry mustard to the flour when making roux.
Soubise sauce—add thinly sliced onions cooked in water, drain, and add to the béchamel. Pass the sauce through a sieve.

STORAGE

Refrigerate: 5 to 6 days
Freeze: 3 to 4 months
Reheat slowly, whisking if it starts to separate.

Roux (page 60)

VELOUTÉ SAUCE

A simple sauce that can be used as is or as the base for many other sauces, known as derivative or daughter sauces.

Makes: 2 cups
Prep time: 20 minutes
Total time: 50 minutes

Ingredients
3 tablespoons butter
3 tablespoons flour
2 cups chicken, veal, or fish stock depending of what you will use it with.

Directions
1. Heat the 2 cups of broth; reduce heat to keep warm.
2. In a separate skillet over medium heat, make a roux, melt butter without letting it brown.
3. Add flour and blend with wooden spoon until it becomes a paste and cook for a minute or two without letting it brown.
4. Pour in half the stock, whisking continuously until sauce thickens. Make certain to whisk out any lumps.
5. Add in rest of the stock; continue whisking and bring to a boil.
6. Reduce heat to a simmer and continue cooking, for 30 minutes. Continue to stir as sauce evaporates and concentrates.
7. Remove any skin that appears on surface.
8. Optional—to produce a smooth sauce, pour sauce through a sieve.
9. Season with salt and white pepper to taste.
10. Use immediately.

SIDEBAR

SERVE WITH:

Poultry and seafood

VARIATIONS

Make a velouté sauce and try these variations. Add white wine, lemon juice, and mustard. Or mushrooms, parsley, and lemon juice. Perhaps white wine, shallots, lemon juice, and parsley. Whatever you choose, the results will be good.

STORAGE:

Refrigerate: up to 5 days.
Freeze: 3 to 4 months

Roux (page 60)

TOMATE SAUCE
TOMATO SAUCE

Slightly different from classic Italian tomato sauce in that it starts with a roux.

Makes: 6 cups
Prep time: 30 minutes
Total time: 2 hours
Preheat oven to 350°

Ingredients
½ cup chopped salt pork
½ cup diced carrots
½ cup diced onion
1 bay leaf
1 sprig thyme
6 tablespoons butter
4 tablespoons flour
6 cups tomatoes, seeded and mashed (about 20 medium tomatoes)
1 cup vegetable or chicken stock
6 cloves crushed garlic
Salt and pepper to taste
Pinch of sugar—(I prefer using 2 tablespoons of soy sauce)

Directions
1. Cook salt pork until fat has melted.
2. Add carrots, onion, bay leaf, and thyme. Stir until vegetables begin to soften. Set aside.
3. In a large ovenproof pot make a roux, melt 4 tablespoons butter, add 4 tablespoons of flour and mix until you create a paste.
4. Add crushed tomatoes and stock. Stir to let sauce thicken and bring to a boil, add garlic and ingredients you set aside.
5. Place in 350° oven and cook covered for 90 minutes.
6. Pass through a sieve and discard chunks left behind.
7. Taste and add either sugar or soy sauce to balance flavors and reduce acidity.
8. Add some butter to the top to prevent a skin from forming. Serve.

SIDEBAR
VARIATIONS

Try these secondary sauces:

Bolognese sauce —ground beef, red wine, and oregano (page 112)

Neapolitan—garlic, anchovy, and capers

Spanish—hot pepper sauce, mushrooms, black and green olives

STORAGE

Refrigerate: 7 days
Freeze: 4 to 6 months

NOTES
This is a great sauce to have ready in the freezer for when you want to cook with a lot of flavor without spending tons of time.

About Soy Sauce (page 41)
Roux (page 60)

ESPAGNOLE SAUCE

This is a basic brown sauce that is full of flavor. It is the perfect base for other daughter sauces. Add cream, mushrooms, cognac, or sherry. Starting with great flavor is the key to making delicious food.

This is not a quick sauce to make but the flavor is worth the effort.
Makes: 3 cups
Prep time: 50 minutes
Total time: 1 hour 50 minutes

Ingredients
½ cup diced carrots
½ cup diced onion
½ cup diced celery
¼ cup olive oil
½ stick butter
¼ cup flour
4 cups cold beef broth
¼ cup tomato purée
2 cloves garlic
1 bouquet garni (bay leaf, thyme sprig, and parsley tied together with kitchen twine.)

Directions
1. Cook onion, carrots, and celery in olive oil and butter until golden.
2. Add all flour. Cook, stirring. Turn heat to low and continue cooking and stirring until the mixture has turned golden brown—about 10 minutes. (Do not let it burn!)
3. Slowly add cold stock, whisking to prevent lumps.
4. Add tomato purée, garlic, and bouquet garni.
5. Simmer for 1 hour, continue stirring from time to time. Cook until sauce has reduced by half.
6. Allow sauce to cool and then refrigerate.
7. Remove bouquet garni and any fat or skin that forms on top.
8. Pour through a sieve and discard the solids.

SIDEBAR

STORAGE:

Refrigerate: 5 days
Freeze: 3 to 6 months

Once made, pour it into individual containers, labeled and dated, and freeze. Having this sauce in the freezer means it's there when you need great flavor.

NOTES:

This is such a rich, full-flavor sauce that it is worth making a lot and freezing it to use in different ways.

bouquet garni (page 49)

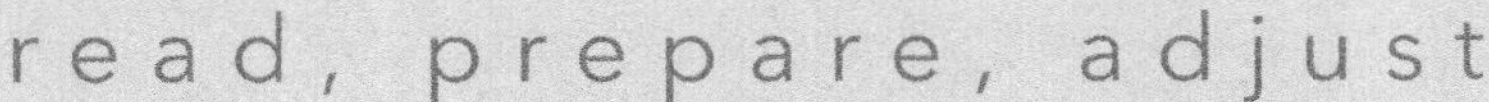

QUICK HOLLANDAISE

SIDEBAR

STORAGE:

Hollandaise cannot be reheated. You need to eat it when you make it.

NOTES:

If you are not serving the sauce immediately, place it in an insulated container to keep it warm up to an hour.

Use a kitchen blender if you don't have an immersion blender.

"Traditional hollandaise is notoriously difficult to make. Cook the eggs too much, and you get scrambled eggs. Don't cook them enough, and your sauce won't thicken. Allow your sauce to cool as you make it, and your butterfat will crystallize, breaking your sauce."
—Serious Eats

Not anymore. With the invention of blenders, especially immersion blenders, creating a hollandaise sauce is easy!

Serves: 4 to 6
Prep time: 1 minute
Total time: 3 minutes

Ingredients
3 egg yolks
1 tablespoon water
1 tablespoon lemon juice
¼ teaspoon salt; omit salt if you use salted butter.
White pepper
Pinch cayenne pepper

Directions
1. Melt butter and place it in a measuring cup.
2. Pour all ingredients (the egg yolks, water, lemon juice) except melted butter into container, or a tall glass that is slightly larger than immersion blender.
3. Place head of blender on the bottom of the container and start blending.
4. Immediately start pouring the butter into the container. It will start emulsifying. Continue for approximately 30 to 45 seconds, until all the butter is added and sauce is completely emulsified. You can raise and lower the head of the blender as you add the butter.
5. The hollandaise will be thick and creamy.
6. Taste and season with salt and pepper if needed. Add a pinch of cayenne if you want to add a little spice.
7. Serve immediately.

MAYONNAISE
HOMEMADE

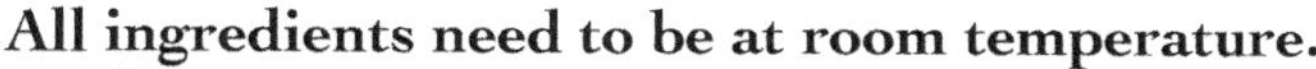

You need to use an immersion blender for this recipe to work. The technique and results are so easy and delicious it's worth it. Use a tall jar slightly wider than the head of the blender or the one that came with your blender.

All ingredients need to be at room temperature.
Makes: 1 cup
Prep time: 5 minutes
Total time: 12 minutes

Ingredients
1 whole egg
½ teaspoon lemon juice (about ½ lemon) or 1 teaspoon white wine vinegar
¼ teaspoon Dijon mustard (add more to taste)
¼ teaspoon salt
1 cup light olive oil (Olive oil can be strong; for a more neutral taste, try grape seed or canola oil.)
1 medium garlic clove, optional—this adds lots of flavor; if you want a milder mayonnaise omit the garlic.

Directions
1. Put egg, lemon juice, Dijon mustard, and salt into tall container.
2. Wait a minute to let ingredients settle before adding oil.
3. Place immersion blender straight down to the bottom of the container so it touches the bottom. (Make certain that all of the non-oil ingredients cover the head of the stick.)
4. Turn immersion blender on high and keep it touching bottom until you see it start to emulsify, then pull stick blender up and down again to emulsify rest of the oil, making certain everything is combined. It will happen quickly.
5. Taste and add more salt if necessary.
6. Place the mayonnaise in a jar and refrigerate.

SIDEBAR

VARIATIONS:

Once the mayonnaise has emulsified, you can add finely chopped herbs, pesto, cilantro, lime, hot sauce, or ginger. Use a spoon to fold the additives in.

NOTES:

If you are used to the taste of store-bought mayonnaise. I urge you to try this. The taste is superb but be warned it is different from store-bought mayonnaise.

STORAGE:

Refrigerate: 3 to 4 days

HERB BUTTER
COMPOUND BUTTER

This butter is delicious served with grilled or baked fish as well as steaks. It is a great way to savor the taste of fresh herbs.

Try this recipe but don't hesitate to try different combinations of fresh herbs.

Serves: 6 to 8
Prep time: 10 minutes
Total time: 15 minutes

Ingredients
1 teaspoon roughly chopped fresh tarragon
1 teaspoon roughly chopped fresh thyme
1 teaspoon roughly chopped fresh dill
1 tablespoon roughly chopped fresh parsley
1 stick (8 tablespoons) sweet or salted butter, room temperature

Directions
1. Put all ingredients in a blender and blend until the butter is smooth and all the herbs are well blended into the butter.
2. Place the mixture into a bowl and serve at room temperature.
3. Put some herb butter on the hot fish fillet or the steaks and let it melt.

Make herb butter ahead of time so it is soft when you serve it. If you think it is too soft, put it into the refrigerator for 30 minutes.

SIDEBAR

ENTERTAIN:

This butter has such a fresh flavor that your guests will wonder what you did to infuse so much flavor to your butter.

STORAGE:

Refrigerate: 5 days
Freeze: 6 months

NOTES:

To make butter slices, spoon the butter onto a piece of wax paper, shape it into a log, and roll it up to make a roll of herb butter. Twist the ends to seal and refrigerate.

Once the butter is cold, unwrap and cut it with a sharp knife into slices you can serve.

VARIATIONS:

You can also make compound butters using just one herb such as basil or coriander.

Add 2 tablespoons of lemon juice to create a bright flavor.

SAUCE MEUNIÈRE

This basic sauce is a classic sauce for fish. Its simplicity and flavor make it perfect to use on other dishes. I also like serving it on boiled potatoes and steamed vegetables.

Serves: 4 to 6, makes ½ cup
Prep time: 2 minutes
Total time: 12 minutes

Ingredients
1 stick butter, unsalted
2 tablespoons lemon juice
2 tablespoons chopped parsley

Directions
1. Melt butter in heavy saucepan on medium heat.
2. Cook until the butter turns golden brown, 4 to 6 minutes. Do not let it burn.
3. Whisk in lemon juice and parsley.
4. Serve immediately.

SIDEBAR

SERVE WITH:
Fish, potatoes, vegetables, chicken, and any other dish you can think of.

DON'T FORGET

Sauces can transform good food into great food.

BEURRE NOISETTE
BURNT BUTTER

SIDEBAR

SERVE WITH:

Traditionally used on fish and vegetables but it is also great on meat.

ENTERTAIN:

The nutty flavor of burnt butter adds such a delicious flavor to food that it will make any dish stand out. Isn't that what you want when you entertain?

NOTES:

Do not use salted butter. It will be too salty.

VARIATIONS:

Add a touch of lemon to the burnt butter to give it the perfect touch of acidity.

Brown butters are simple; they are literally butter that is cooked until it turns a golden brown, giving it a nutty flavor that is
delicious on vegetables or fish. This is a must-try sauce.

Serves: 8
Prep time: 2 minutes
Total time: 8 minutes

Ingredients
1 stick sweet butter cut into pieces

Directions
1. Heat pan and add butter pieces, stirring as it melts.
2. Once it starts sizzling, lower the heat to simmer.
3. Stir as it starts to separate and begins to brown.
4. Once browned, take it off the heat and pour into a heat-proof measuring cup to stop it from cooking and getting burnt.
5. Pour it on what you are going to serve it with.

BUTTER SOY SAUCE

When I first came up with this combination, I was surprised by how good it was. Adding butter changes the flavor of the soy sauce to a sauce that is less harsh and a bit softer than soy sauce alone. The combination of these two ingredients is the perfect addition for steamed or sautéed vegetables—it's really worth trying.

Serves: 4
Total time: 5 minutes

Ingredients
5 tablespoons of butter
1 tablespoon of soy sauce

Directions
1. Melt 5 tablespoons of butter on low heat.
2. Once the butter is melted, take pan off heat and mix in soy sauce. Do not add the soy sauce until the butter is off the heat; you don't want it to burn. Blend well.
3. Pour over the vegetables and serve. I like to have extra in a pitcher to pass around.

DID YOU KNOW?

Soy sauce adds a touch of savory to food. That flavor is known as umami.

SIDEBAR

SERVE WITH:

Broccoli. spinach, carrots, string beans, for starters.

VINAIGRETTE

BASIC OIL AND VINEGAR DRESSING

SIDEBAR

Basic ratio—
1 portion vinegar
3 portions oil

Knowing the basic proportion for a basic vinaigrette is simple and important. Once you have that balance, it is easy to alter the flavor with the ingredients you use. I add mustard and sometimes change the flavor of the vinegar or the oil. Substituting vinegar for lemon juice creates a very light and fresh-tasting dressing.

Makes: 1 cup of dressing
Prep time: 8 minutes
Total time: 8 minutes

Ingredients
¼ cup red wine vinegar
1 tablespoon Dijon mustard
¾ cup extra virgin olive oil
2 tablespoons chopped herbs such as parsley, basil, and chives (optional)
Salt and pepper to taste

Directions

1. Combine the vinegar, mustard, herbs, and salt and pepper in a low bowl using a fork.
2. Slowly drizzle the oil into the bowl while you whisk it into the mustard mixture. Let it emulsify before adding more oil.
3. Continue until the oil is totally combined into the mustard.
4. If you notice that the oil is separating, stop adding and keep blending until it is completely emulsified again before adding more oil. Important: add in the oil slowly or the vinaigrette will separate.
5. The dressing will keep refrigerated but you need to bring it to room temperature before using and shake well.
6. Just before serving, toss the salad with a small amount of dressing to lightly coat the salad leaves.
7. Taste and add more vinaigrette if necessary. There is nothing good about too much dressing; the lettuce leaves will become soggy and limp. You want a fresh, crisp salad.

VINAIGRETTE continued

SIDEBAR

Balsamic vinaigrette
Using the basic proportions, substitute the vinegar for balsamic vinegar. Add 1 small clove of finely chopped garlic and ½ teaspoon of sugar. Shake well. Serve.

White wine vinaigrette
1 tablespoon Dijon mustard
2 to 3 tablespoons white wine vinegar
⅛ teaspoon salt ⅛ teaspoon ground pepper
½ cup good quality oil (olive oil)

As long as you keep the proportions of vinegar or acid (lemon) to oil, you can change how you flavor the dressing.

THERE ARE 4 DIFFERENT WAYS YOU CAN MAKE YOUR VINAIGRETTE:

1. By hand—as above
2. In a jar—Place all the ingredients plus ¼ cup oil into the container, seal and shake well until the mixture is emulsified. Continue adding the oil ¼ cup at a time making certain to shake until the mixture is emulsified.
3. Using an immersion blender—place all the ingredients into the tall container that came with the blender or something similar. Insert the blender to the bottom, start the motor and as the sauce starts to emulsify, raise the head of the blender until all the oil is blended.
4. The traditional way vinaigrette is made in France is directly in the bottom of the salad bowl before adding the greens. Often it is made with just 1 part vinegar, salt and pepper, and mix with a fork, slowly whisking in the 3 parts oil. Add the lettuce and toss the salad just before serving.

Without the mustard, the dressing will not emulsify but it will blend well enough to coat the lettuce.

PISTOU INSTEAD OF PESTO

The flavor of basil is strong, pungent, and fresh. Basil is a surprisingly versatile herb that can be used to add punch to both savory and sweet foods.

Pesto, is the traditional Italian sauce made with basil. It's made with basil leaves, garlic, olive oil, pignoli nuts (pine nuts), and Parmesan cheese—it's delicious. The French version omits the nuts and cheese. I prefer preserving basil this way; I find it last longer when stored in sealed container in the refrigerator.

Prep time: 15 minutes
Total time: 25 minutes

Ingredients
4 ½ cups basil leaves
8 cloves garlic
½ cup or more olive oil
Salt ½ teaspoon or more to taste

Directions
1. Using a food processor, place the garlic, ½ teaspoon of salt, and the basil into the bowl.
2. Pulse a few times to break up the basil and garlic.
3. Add ½ the oil through the feed tube. Continue pulsing the motor on and off until the mixture is emulsified. Add more oil as needed. If you want to thin the sauce, add more olive oil.
4. Store the pistou in a container with a tight lid and refrigerate.

SIDEBAR

VARIATIONS:

If you prefer the taste of the classic pesto, you can add the cheese and nuts to a small amount of pistou. When you're ready to use it, place everything back into the food processor to combine and serve.

SERVE WITH:

Whenever you want to add that wonderful flavor of summer to your dish, just add a spoonful of pistou. Use it as you would pesto—on pasta, pizza, bruschetta, vegetables, in dips, or in vegetable soup as they do in Provence to create soupe au pistou.
As with all robust flavors, how you use it is up to your imagination.

STORAGE:

Refrigerate: 1 month

Freeze: 4 to 6 months

LEMON DRESSING

Sometimes adding a lemon dressing to your salad is the perfect addition to your meal. Lemon is a great contrast to heavy foods and helps start the digestion process.

Makes: ¾ cup of dressing
Prep time: 8 minutes
Total time: 8 minutes

Ingredients
¼ cup lemon juice
1 teaspoon Dijon mustard
½ cup extra virgin olive oil
2 teaspoons chopped herbs such as parsley, dill, and chives (optional)
Salt and pepper to taste

Directions
1. Combine lemon juice, mustard, and salt and pepper; whisk together.
2. Drizzle the olive oil in while whisking.
3. Add the herbs and serve.

SIDEBAR

VARIATIONS

Changing the acid in the dressing is a great way to alter the flavor.

Read the section on vinegars on page 42 so you can experiment.

CUCUMBER DILL SAUCE

SIDEBAR

SERVE WITH:

This is a great tasting sauce that can be used on many different foods to add flavor. Try it as a condiment or on vegetables and brown rice or as a topping on steamed vegetables.

This is a perfect sauce to serve with fish—especially salmon. I also like using it as a condiment for sandwiches or as a dip served with vegetables.

Serves: 8 (make 1½ cups sauce)
Prep time: 10 minutes
Total time: 40 minutes

Ingredients

1 cucumber peeled, grated, using a towel squeeze to remove all excess liquid.
1 cup plain yogurt
2 teaspoons chopped fresh dill
2 cloves minced garlic
2 tablespoons lemon juice
Salt and pepper

Directions

1. Mix all ingredients.
2. Refrigerate at least 30 minutes or until ready to serve.

TZATZIKI

This is a light but very flavorful sauce that originated in Greece. A yogurt-based sauce made with cucumber, garlic, and herbs. It's used as a salad dressing or a sauce. Traditionally it's served as an appetizer with feta, olives, pita bread, or as a sauce on a gyro, falafel, with lamb or a Greek salad. Try it as a sauce with beef, fish, on salads, sandwiches and as a dip with assorted vegetables.

Makes: 2 ½ cups
Prep time: 15 minutes
Total time: 15 minutes

Ingredients
1 large cucumber, washed and grated with large opening of a box grater. No need to peel or seed.
1 clove garlic, crushed fine
2 tablespoons fresh dill, chopped fine
1½ cups full-fat Greek yogurt
1 tablespoon lemon juice
2 tablespoons olive oil

Directions
1. Squeeze the grated cucumber to remove as much liquid as possible before putting it into a bowl.
2. Add the remaining ingredients, yogurt, garlic, dill, lemon juice, and olive oil, and mix well.
3. Let sit 10 to 15 minutes before serving to allow the flavor to develop.

SIDEBAR

STORAGE:

Store in fridge in tightly covered jar 3 to 4 days.

SERVE WITH:
As with all flavorful sauces, they can and should be used in as many ways as you can think of. Try it in an omelet, or as a dash in soup like potato leak soup. I always like to make more than I need and experiment with the leftovers.

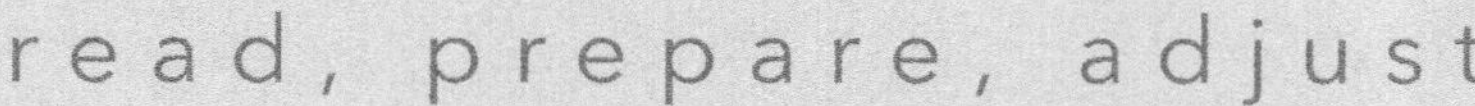

TAHINI DRESSING

Tahini, made from sesame seeds, originated in the area of the Eastern Mediterranean. It is a nice alternative salad dressing. Use also as a condiment, a dip for vegetables, or served on brown rice with vegetables.

Makes: 2 cups dressing
Prep time: 10 minutes
Total time: 10 minutes

Ingredients
1 cup tahini sesame seed paste—I prefer the paste made from light-colored seeds.
¾ cup lukewarm water, or more for consistency
3 cloves garlic
¼ cup fresh lemon juice, or more to taste
¼ teaspoon salt, or more to taste
2 teaspoons fresh parsley, minced (optional)

Directions
1. Combine the tahini paste, lukewarm water, garlic, lemon juice, and salt together in a food processor or blender until sauce is creamy and ivory-colored.
2. After a few minutes of blending, sauce will turn into a rich, smooth paste. If mixture is too thick, slowly add more water until it reaches the consistency you want. You may need quite a bit of water, depending on the thickness of your tahini paste, to achieve a consistency of heavy cream.
3. If using tahini to top off hummus or a meat dish, keep it thick and creamy. As a condiment for pita or falafel, a more liquid sauce is usually preferred. Taste often during the blending process; add more lemon juice or salt, if desired.

SIDEBAR

VARIATIONS:

Adding strong flavors such as roasted tomatoes, fresh or powdered ginger or curry powder can add a great twist to the original recipe.

Baked tomatoes (page 140)

BLUE CHEESE DRESSING

You can use this simple recipe on salad, as a dip with vegetables, or as a sauce on steamed vegetables or steak.

Makes: ¾ cup
Prep time: 5 minutes
Total time: 5 minutes

Ingredients
¼ cup crumbled blue cheese
¼ cup mayonnaise
½ cup yogurt
Milk to thin if necessary
1 tablespoon finely minced parsley

Directions
1. Combine all ingredients.
2. If necessary, add a splash of milk to thin the dressing.

SIDEBAR

STORAGE:

Refrigerate: 1 to 2 weeks

COCKTAIL SAUCE

SIDEBAR

SERVE WITH:

The classic way to serve cocktail sauce is with shrimp, crab, lobster, and seafood cocktails. I love the flavor so I add it on other foods such as meatloaf, even hotdogs and hamburgers.

STORAGE:

Refrigerate: 6 months

Classic cocktail sauce is so easy to make that there is no need to buy it. Making it gives you the flexibility to make it with as much spice as you like, and I like it to have a bite.

Serves: 4
Prep time: 5 minutes
Total time: 5 minutes

Ingredients

½ cup chili sauce (by Heinz); you can also use ketchup.
2 teaspoons horseradish sauce; more if you like (I like using Gold's Horseradish sauce.)
½ teaspoon Worcestershire sauce
1 lemon, juiced
Dash of hot sauce, such as Tabasco; the amount depends on how spicy you like it.

Directions

1. In a small bowl combine the chili sauce, horseradish, Worcestershire sauce, lemon juice to taste, and hot sauce.
2. Mix well.
3. Adjust the seasonings to your taste.

BARBECUE SAUCE

There are lots of uses for Barbecue sauce. It is easy to make and adjust the flavors to your liking. It's delicious on chicken beef, and pork, good used in stews and soups to add great flavor to what you are cooking.

Makes: 2 cups of sauce
Prep time: 10 minutes
Total time: 20 minutes

Ingredients
½ teaspoon garlic powder
2 tablespoons honey
1½ cup brown sugar; use less to make it less sweet
1½ cup ketchup
½ cup red wine vinegar
½ cup water
1½ tablespoon Worcestershire sauce
2 teaspoons dry mustard
2 teaspoons paprika, smoked
2 teaspoons salt
1½ teaspoon pepper
2 dashes of hot sauce or more to taste

Directions
1. Combine all ingredients and bring to a simmer. Lower heat and cook for 8 to 10 minutes until the sauce thickens.
2. Refrigerate in a resealable container and use it as you please.

SIDEBAR

NOTES:

Years ago a good friend/caterer Joanna made barbecue sauce at a party we were having. She placed the sauce into a resealable jar with a lid she'd pierced with lots of little holes. When the food was ready she just shook the sauce on the meat. So easy and simple.

STORAGE:

Refrigerate: 2 weeks

FOOL-PROOF GRAVY

SIDEBAR

VARIATIONS:

Mushrooms—Slice 2 cups mushrooms and sauté them with oil and butter until they have reduced and browned. Add the mushrooms to the gravy before serving.

Herbs—Add fresh herbs to the liquid as you make your homemade broth. Remove before serving.

After you've made this a few times you'll see how easy it is—you'll no longer need the recipe.

One last thought: if you want to make gravy and you don't have any giblets, you can use a combination of low-salt broth and low-salt poultry bouillon. Remember, you want your broth to have lots of flavor.

I remember asking my mother-in-law, June Santiago, to please make the gravy as we lifted the turkey out of the oven. "Yes," she answered. But I noticed her quizzical expression so I quickly added, "I don't know how. I tried," I continued, "but ended up with a lumpy mess."

I watched as she whisked everything together, resulting in a smooth flavorful gravy. Easy.

It took me a few tries. Instead of making the traditional roux (flour and butter), I make a flour slurry to thicken the gravy. It does the trick every time without any lumps.

Homemade Broth

Start making the broth when you put the turkey in the oven so it is ready when the bird comes out. What is great about doing this is there is very little fat.

Makes: at least 2 cups

Ingredients

Giblets—that's everything that is packed in your poultry's cavity.
4 to 6 cups turkey or chicken broth
3 to 4 tablespoons or cubes of low-salt turkey or chicken bouillon

Directions

1. Place the giblets, in a pot with 4 to 6 cups of chicken or turkey broth, depending on how much gravy you want to end up with.
2. Bring to a boil, lower temperature and simmer for 1 hour. (Add more broth if it gets too low.) Taste; you want the flavor to be strong. If needed, add the bouillon.
3. Remove 1 cup of liquid and refrigerate. You want it cold when you make your gravy.

Fool-proof gravy continued

TO MAKE THE GRAVY

Ingredients

Flour, approximately 4 to 5 tablespoons, depending on quantity of liquid
You may need a fat separator.
1 pint-size jar with a tight-fitting sealable lid

Directions

1. When chicken or turkey is ready and resting on cutting board covered with foil, place roasting pan on your burners over high heat. If the pan doesn't have much liquid left you'll have lots of crispy drippings stuck to the bottom. That's where all the flavor is.
2. Deglaze pan by adding a cup of that wonderful broth you made and scrape the bottom of the pan, releasing all bits.
3. If pan has lots of liquid left, bring it to a boil and as above, scrape the bottom to loosen all morsels.
4. If pan gravy contains lots of fat, use a fat separator.
5. Pour gravy into separator, wait a few minutes for fat to come to the top. Pour gravy into roasting pan or a separate pot.
6. Add enough broth so you have 3 cups, bring it to just under a boil.
7. Make a flour slurry, to thicken the gravy:

   In a jar with a tight-sealing lid, pour the cup of reserved cold broth and add flour. Seal the jar tightly and shake vigorously to eliminate all the lumps. Open jar to be sure the slurry is well combined. If necessary, stir with a spoon and seal jar and shake again.
8. Slowly pour the slurry into the broth, whisking continuously. Add as much as needed to get the desired consistency. (If you need more slurry than you have, make more and add it.)
9. There is never too much gravy; remember, you can reheat it for leftovers.

SIDEBAR

NOTES:

To keep the gravy warm:

Keep it in the pot on the lowest heat and whisk from time to time to break up any skin that forms on top. (Tip: Add some butter on top. It will prevent a skin from forming on top of the gravy.)

I've started pouring the gravy into an insulated container so it stays hot without my worrying about it.

Note: If you want a very smooth gravy or (heaven forbid) there are lumps, all you need to do is pour the gravy through a sieve. The results will be perfect—it's foolproof.

Deglaze (page 36)
Flour slurry (page 60)

BOLOGNESE SAUCE

This recipe is full of flavor. I developed it through trial and error and have continued to make it because it's that good. I once made too much for a party our daughter was giving. We sent everyone home with extras. The next day I got calls from the parents saying how good it was and would I share the recipe. Need I say more?

Serves: 8
Prep time: 40 minutes
Total time: 1 hour 15 minutes to 2 hours 15 minutes

Ingredients
1 large onion, chopped
3 cloves garlic, chopped
1 tablespoon herbes de Provence
Tomatoes, skinless, two 28-oz cans
Tomato paste, 1 tablespoon or more
3 medium-size zucchinis, cubed
Add low-salt beef bouillon to taste
Salt and pepper
1 tablespoon soy sauce
½ lb ground beef
½ lb ground pork
4 spicy turkey sausages removed from the casing
½ lb ground lamb
Parmesan cheese
2 lbs Penne pasta
Garlic bread

Directions
1. In a large skillet, heat oil and cook chopped onion and garlic until they soften and become translucent.
2. Add 1 tablespoon herbes de Provence.
3. Drain juice from the tomatoes and chop them with kitchen scissors while the tomatoes are still in the can and add to the skillet.
4. Add the diced zucchini and simmer 20 minutes.

SIDEBAR

NOTES:

The addition of zucchini adds lots of body, helps thicken the sauce, and adds a vegetable without adding any zucchini flavor.

I made this when my son was young, he didn't want to eat vegetables. He couldn't taste the vegetable, so we were both happy.

I like meaty sauces so I will often brown ground beef, spicy turkey sausage removed from the casing, and lamb or veal together and add the meat to the sauce.

Bolognese sauce by definition is a rich meat sauce. If you want to make a tomato without meat this recipe will work. Omit all the meat and make it with just the vegetables. As with any recipe when you make changes you will need to taste and make adjustments to the resulting flavor.

BOLOGNESE SAUCE - continued

5. Add tomato paste to thicken the sauce. Continue simmering 15 minutes.
6. Taste the sauce and add beef bouillon cubes or the equivalent.
7. Add soy sauce.
8. Add salt and pepper.
9. With and immersion blender, emulsify the sauce.
10. In a sauté pan, brown the beef, pork, turkey sausage, and lamb- but leaving some chunks to create texture.
11. Once browned strain the meat, removing all the excess fat.
12. Combine meat and place it in the cooked tomato sauce.
13. At this point, you can serve the sauce, but you can also continue simmering the sauce for another hour to develop the richness of the sauce.
14. There should be lots of meat and chunks.

SIDEBAR

SERVE WITH:

Pasta or other dishes when you want a rich meaty tomato sauce. Try it with a penne pasta with a green salad and a crusty loaf of bread.

ENTERTAIN:

There is nothing like a good pasta dish. The fact that you can make this sauce ahead and freeze it means it is ready to use when you need it. This is one of the characteristics that makes it great for when you're entertaining.

STORAGE:

Refrigerate: 5 days
Freeze: 4 to 6 months.

I always make more than I need so I have it in the freezer when I need it.

herbes de Provence (page 49)

WHITE CLAM SAUCE

SIDEBAR

SERVE WITH:

A simple salad and a loaf of crusty bread

Soy Sauce (page 41)

What makes this sauce so good is the abundance of clams. I always start with a can of baby clams and add fresh clams to that base. If I can't get fresh, I make it with only the canned clams and it's delicious—maybe not as pretty but the taste is great.

Serves: 6
Prep time: 15 minutes
Total time: 25 minutes

Ingredients

1 tablespoon kosher salt added to the water to flavor the pasta
2 tablespoons butter
1 tablespoon olive oil
6 cloves garlic minced—I use a garlic press
1 cup white wine
1 can whole baby clams; drain the juice, roughly chop clams; reserve both
1 bottle clam juice
½ cup water if needed
Fish or chicken bouillon, low-salt, 1 tablespoon or 1 cube (optional)
4 tablespoons of chopped fresh parsley
2-dozen whole littleneck clams
Dash red pepper flakes or cayenne pepper
1½ lb dry linguini pasta
1 teaspoon soy sauce (optional) this adds a touch of savory flavor

Directions

1. Fill a large pot with water and 1 tablespoon salt, bring to a boil, lower to a simmer until you're ready to cook pasta.
2. Under cold running water, scrub the clams and set aside.
3. In a saucepan, melt butter and olive oil.
4. Add minced garlic and lower temperature to avoid browning garlic, cook 2 minutes.
5. Add ¾ cup wine, clam juice left in can, and bottle of clam juice as well as the 3 tablespoons of chopped parsley.
6. Simmer on medium-low heat. Let sauce slowly reduce by half.
7. Add baby clams to sauce.

WHITE CLAM SAUCE continued

8. You want sauce to be full of flavor since it will be diluted by the pasta.
9. Taste, add salt and pepper, red pepper flakes or cayenne, and more bouillon if necessary.
10. In a separate pan add ¼ cup wine, ½ cup water, and clams over medium-high heat. Cover and cook until steam opens up all the clams. Discard any clams that do not open.
11. Remove clams and keep warm.
12. Pour the liquid remaining in the pan into a measuring cup. Let it sit for a minute to let any sand discharged by the clams settle on bottom. Being careful to leave the sediment on the bottom, add liquid to sauce.
13. Add the pasta to the boiling water and cook al dente, a little firm. Drain.
14. Serve pasta in bowls and pour sauce over linguine.
15. Add fresh clams and remaining parsley on top of pasta. Serve.

SIDEBAR

"A good cook is like a sorceress who dispenses happiness."

—Elsa Schiaparelli

VEGETABLES

VEGETABLES

ABOUT VEGETABLES

Thank goodness for vegetables!

ABOUT VEGETABLES

Vegetables are incredibly versatile and nutritious. They are full of fiber, minerals, and vitamins. For a healthy diet, it is recommended that we eat five or more portions a day, so it makes sense that we learn how to prepare them.

They are numerous in variety and delicious eaten raw or cooked.

The foundation of many recipes throughout the world starts with an assortment of vegetables used to build the flavor base, when cooking stews, soups, or sauces.

In France the combination of finely chopped carrots, onions, and celery is known as Mirepoix. The Italians call it soffritto. In Louisiana Creole cooking it is known as the holy trinity. The Spanish call it sofrito. And the Germans suppengrun.

See the following chart for the ingredients and proportions you'll need to make your vegetable base.

AROMATICS BASES BY COUNTRY OF ORIGIN		
France	Mirepoix	2 parts onion 1 part carrot 1 part celery Dice ingredients
Germany	Suppengrun	2 parts carrots 1 part leek ¼ celery root Small bunch parsley Roughly chop all ingredients
Italy	Soffrito	1 part onion 2 to 3 parts carrots 2 to 3 parts celery Mince ingredients
Louisiana, Creole	Holy Trinity	2 parts onion 1 part green pepper 1 part celery Mince ingredients
Spain	Sofrito	1 onion 2 cloves garlic 1 green pepper 3 tablespoons olive oil 5 to 6 ripe tomatoes Mince all ingredients

VEGETABLES CAN BE COOKED USING DIFFERENT TECHNIQUES.

- **Grill**—intensifies flavor, crispy and smoky
- **Raw**—enjoy them as is or with a sauce or dip
- **Bake**—allows vegetables to become tender and stay moist
- **Roast**—intensifies flavor, crispy and smoky
- **Steam**—cooks vegetables without adding any flavor
- **Poach**—use wide pan, add veggies, add flavored liquid just to cover, cook until tender, liquid is flavorful
- **Boil**—bring water to boil, add veggies, back to boil, lower heat, simmer until tender
- **Simmer**—add liquid or broth, cook until tender, reduce liquid so it becomes a sauce
- **Braise**—oil, butter, melt, cut just enough veggies to cover bottom, pan brown 3 to 4 minutes, turn at 2 minutes, deglaze, finish with butter
- **Stew**—stew—cut veggies, add liquid to cover, cook until tender (to make a stew or soup)

VEGETABLES continued

FRESH VEGETABLES CAN BE FROZEN

BEFORE FREEZING—

Cut your vegetables to a usable size.
Blanche.
Dry your vegetables.
Place in a plastic bag.
Remove as much air as possible before closing.
Label and date.
Freeze.

FREEZING—

Is a great way to take advantage of the wonderful flavors of the summer harvest. Before freezing vegetables, they should be blanched in order to prevent them from going bad.

BLANCHING—

Dip vegetables into boiling water for a minute or two until they turn bright green. Denser vegetables will need to stay in the boiling water longer than greens. Once removed, they need to be immediately dunked into an ice bath for the same amount of time to stop the cooking process. The benefit of blanching is that it keeps the bright color of vegetables, helps them retain their nutrients, and stops the enzymes that cause vegetables to decay.

BAKED POTATOES

Considering how delicious and versatile baked potatoes are, they are incredibly simple to make. Your goal is to get the skin crispy and have the inside light and fluffy. Coating the skin with olive oil and salt and then baking the potato in a hot oven is all it takes.

Serves: 1 potato per person
Prep time: 5 minutes
Total time: 1 hour 5 minutes
Preheat oven to 450°

Ingredients
1 potato per person; Russet potatoes are best for baking.
Olive oil
Salt to taste
Butter or sour cream

Directions
1. Wash potatoes well under running water.
2. Pierce each potato with a fork or skewer into the center of the potato. This lets the steam out to prevent it from exploding in the oven.
3. To create the crispy skin, rub the outside of each potato with olive oil and sprinkle with salt.
4. Place your potatoes in the middle of your preheated oven directly on the metal racks.
5. Bake for 1 hour, depending on the size of the potatoes and how many you are baking.
6. To check if the potatoes are done, squeeze them using a kitchen towel to see if they are soft or poke them with a fork.
7. Serve the potatoes with butter, sour cream, or your favorite toppings.

SIDEBAR

VARIATIONS:

Potato skins are delicious and full of vitamins.

Twice-baked potatoes:
After following the recipe, cut open the potato lengthwise, remove the cooked potato into a bowl and blend with cheese and/or bacon, herbs and chives to create a filling.
Place back into oven 350° to heat and brown.

Sweet potatoes are also delicious baked; they are so sweet they almost taste like dessert.
Keep in mind that they take a little longer to cook.

Remember to pierce the skin to let the steam out.

GRATIN DAUPHINOIS
SCALLOPED POTATOES

This dish is creamy, cheesy, and delicious. The magic is the garlic mixture that intensifies the flavor and makes these potatoes really special. My mother taught me the secret of pre-cooking the potatoes before putting the dish together. It allows it to cook a lot faster while still being scrumptious.

Serves: 6
Prep time: 60 minutes
Total time: 1 hour 40 minutes
Preheat oven to 400°
3-quart oven proof baking dish

Ingredients
6 to 8 Yukon gold potatoes, depending on size
6 to 8 garlic cloves
Salt and pepper
1 tablespoon chopped parsley
2 tablespoons olive oil—maybe more
1 cup Gruyere cheese, grated (Do not use pre-grated cheese; it won't melt properly.)
1 cup heavy cream

Directions
1. Wash potatoes, peeling is optional, slice potatoes so they are very thin, between ¼" and ⅛". I like using a food processor or a mandolin. If you prefer, you can use a knife and slice them by hand.
2. Place in a pot of boiling salted water and cook; drain when they start to soften. They will continue to cook in the oven, so you want them to be underdone.
3. Smash garlic cloves, add salt to make a paste. I use a wood bowl with a pestle to make my paste, but you can do it with the flat side of a knife or the back of a spoon.
4. Add 1 tablespoon olive oil along with pepper and continue to blend the paste; add 1 tablespoon of chopped parsley, continue blending paste while adding remaining olive oil. If it is

SIDEBAR

NOTES:

I always place a baking sheet under the dish in the oven to catch any spills during cooking.

If you want to avoid using heavy cream, make a roux with milk instead and substitute for heavy cream.

ENTERTAIN:

We make this dish for dinner parties or holidays. It is so good that I like to freeze the leftovers.

VARIATION:

Substitute 2 potatoes with turnips; it's a great flavor addition.

STORAGE:

Refrigerate: 3 to 4 days
Freeze: 3 to 4 months

Garlic Paste (page 50)
Roux (page 60)

SCALLOPED POTATOES continued

very thick, add more oil. You want it to be the consistency of heavy cream.

5. Butter the bottom and sides of your pan.
6. Place your first layer of potatoes on the bottom of the dish.
7. Add ⅓ of the garlic mixture, dotting the potatoes.
8. Add ⅓ of the grated Gruyere on top.
9. Pour in ¼ cup of the heavy cream.
10. Continue adding 2 more layers, as above, finishing with the Gruyere.
11. Place dots of butter on top of the cheese and pour the remaining cream over the potatoes.
12. Place into the center of a 400° oven and cook for 40 minutes. It will get bubbly on the sides and the top will start to brown.
13. If it hasn't browned yet, turn the temperature up to 500° or place the dish under the broiler until it starts to brown—about 2 minutes. Do not let it burn.
14. If you find it is browning too quickly, cover the top with aluminum foil and finish cooking.

    Serve.

SIDEBAR

SERVE WITH:

Stews, roasts, or spiral ham

STOP GUESSING!

Once frozen, everything looks the same.

Don't forget to date; label everything you freeze.

CAULIFLOWER AU GRATIN

This dish is made in an oven-proof 2-quart dish and finished off by browning the cheese that is sprinkled on top. Cauliflower is the main ingredient, but you can substitute another vegetable: broccoli, summer squash, or a combination of vegetables. If you want to make this into a main dish, add cooked shredded chicken, garlic, onion, and a selection of herbs. The simplicity of this dish makes it flexible and easy to make.

Serves: 4
Prep time: 30 minutes
Total time: 55 minutes
Preheat oven to 400°

Ingredients
1 small to medium head of cauliflower
2 tablespoons butter
2 tablespoons flour
1 cup milk
¼ teaspoon salt and ¼ teaspoon white pepper
1 cup grated Gruyere cheese. Do not used pre-grated cheese, it won't melt correctly.

Directions
1. Cut off and discard hard stem of the cauliflower and break up head into 2" pieces.
2. Butter bottom and sides of oven proof dish.
3. Bring a large pot of salted water to a boil and insert cauliflower. Let cook until just tender—about 7 to 10 minutes. Drain and place back into pot.
4. In a medium saucepan make a roux. Melt butter over medium-high heat.
5. Add flour and mix for about 2 minutes until you have a bubbly paste, but do not let it brown.
6. While stirring, slowly add milk, letting it thicken as you continue to add more milk.

SIDEBAR

VARIATIONS:

You can make this recipe with other vegetables, such as potatoes, broccoli, zucchini, or a combination of vegetables.

STORAGE:

Refrigerate: 4 to 5 days
Freeze: 4 to 5 months

ENTERTAIN:

This is a great side dish that is delicious with meats or fish. It's agreat alternative to potatoes. Because it freezes so well, it's perfect to serve for a dinner party and all you have to do is reheat it.

Roux (page 60)

CAULIFLOWER AU GRATIN continued

SIDEBAR

7. As it thickens, add salt and fresh pepper, stirring to combine.
8. Cook sauce 2 to 3 minutes to allow sauce to thicken, and for the flavor of the flour to cook out.
9. Add ⅔ of grated Gruyere cheese, stir to combine, and cook for 2 minutes, letting cheese melt into the sauce.
10. Pour sauce over cauliflower and blend well.
11. Pour mixture into ovenproof baking dish.
12. Top with remaining Gruyere and dot with small pieces of butter.
13. Place dish in a 400° oven for 25 minutes or until it is bubbly on the sides and top is brown. If dish hasn't browned, raise heat or turn on broiler until it is golden—about 1 or 2 minutes so don't walk away or it may burn.

VEGETABLES
STEAMED & SEARED

I've discovered that by combining these two methods of cooking, the resulting vegetables become tender by the steam and browned and flavorful due to the searing. It's simple, quick, and works perfectly on a variety of vegetables. I start by adding a small amount of water to the vegetables in a sauté pan. Cover the pan and let them steam until the vegetables are just starting to become tender. I then remove the pan from the heat, drain any remaining liquid. Place the pan back on medium-high heat, letting the moisture completely evaporate before adding oil and seasonings. Let the vegetables brown and finish cooking before serving.

Asparagus, carrots, green beans, leeks, fennel, onions, and zucchini are good choices. You can cook them individually or combine them for a flavorful assortment. Keep in mind that some vegetables are denser than others and will take longer to cook.

Serves: 4
Prep time: 5 minutes
Total time: 15 minutes

Ingredients
2 cups asparagus, remove the ends and cut into 1½" pieces.
½ cup water
1 tablespoon olive oil
2 tablespoons butter, divided
1 clove garlic, crushed

Directions
1. Place asparagus in a large sauté pan (don't overcrowd the pan), add ½ cup water over medium-high heat, and cover.
2. When they turn bright green and just start to soften, take off the stove and drain any remaining water.
3. Place pan and vegetables back on medium-high heat. Let any moisture left in the pan evaporate before adding olive oil and butter.

SIDEBAR
VARIATIONS:

STEAMED & SEARED continued

SIDEBAR

4. Let vegetables start to brown before turning. Your vegetables will finish cooking as they are searing.
5. Once they've started to brown, add the garlic, salt and stir as they finish cooking.
6. Add the remaining butter; toss
   Serve.

DID YOU KNOW?

Asparagus stems will snap off when you bend them at the end.

PAN-SAUTÉED SPINACH

SIDEBAR

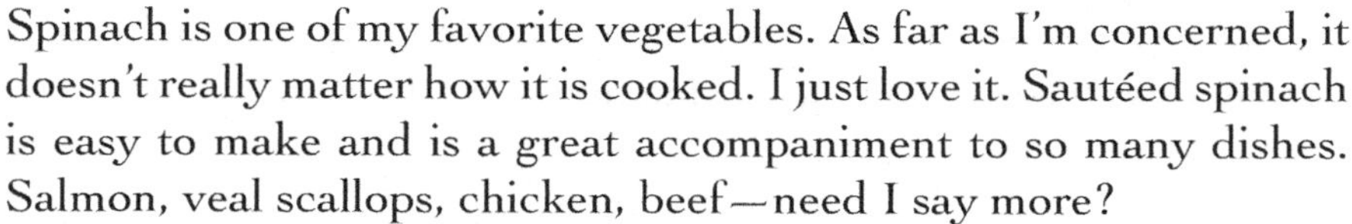

Spinach is one of my favorite vegetables. As far as I'm concerned, it doesn't really matter how it is cooked. I just love it. Sautéed spinach is easy to make and is a great accompaniment to so many dishes. Salmon, veal scallops, chicken, beef—need I say more?

Serves: 4
Prep time: 2 minutes
Total time: 5 minutes

Ingredients
1½ tablespoons olive oil
3 cloves garlic, crushed
1½ lbs baby spinach leaves should result in about 2 cups of cooked spinach

Directions
1. Heat the oil in a large skillet, add the garlic, cook for 1 minute to release its flavor but do not let it burn.
2. Fill the pan with as much spinach as will fit. Stir as the spinach begins to cook and melt. Continue adding the spinach leaves as long as there is room. Add a little water to help cook spinach.
3. Season with salt and pepper.
4. Cover and cook 2 minutes.
   Serve immediately.

SAUTÉED VEGETABLES
CABBAGE

This is a surprisingly easy way to cook cabbage, and it's delicious. I serve it with soy butter sauce that adds just the right flavor.

Serves: 4
Prep time: 5 minutes
Total time: 25 minutes

Ingredients
1 small head of cabbage or ½ of a large head cut into 1½-inch pieces
1 cup broth or water
4 tablespoons butter
1 tablespoon soy sauce

Directions
1. Place cabbage into your skillet, add 1 cup of water, and bring to a boil.
2. Reduce heat, cover, and simmer for about 5 minutes.
3. Stir, then cover and continue cooking until cabbage is fork tender at its thickest part. About 5 minutes.
4. Once cabbage is done, do not let it brown.
5. Remove cabbage from pan, set aside.
6. Discard any liquid left in the pan and place back on the heat letting pan dry out completely.
7. Melt butter over medium-low heat.
8. Remove from heat and add soy sauce to the butter. Combine well and return cabbage to pan, tossing to coat with sauce. Serve.

SIDEBAR

VARIATION:

Add 4 oz of sliced mushrooms to the pan before you add the cabbage. Cook for 3 to 4 minutes and then add the cabbage as above.

Soy Sauce butter (page 99)

MASHED POTATOES

This is my husband, Mark's, recipe for mashed potatoes. In our home he is the one in charge of making these for every holiday and all those times in between when we have them. They are made with butter and heavy cream, meaning they are FULL of flavor.

Serves: 8
Prep time: 25 minutes
Total time: 1 hour 10 minutes

Ingredients
4 to 5 lbs Yukon gold potatoes, about 12 medium peeled and quartered
3 cloves garlic, peeled
1 medium yellow onion, peeled and quartered
1 pint heavy cream; or half and half if you prefer
2 sticks of butter cut into pieces
Salt to taste

Directions
1. Place peeled and quartered potatoes in a large pot of salted water. Make certain the potatoes are well covered.
2. Add onion and garlic to the pot.
3. Bring water to a boil and reduce to a simmer. Cook until the potatoes are tender. 35 to 45 minutes.
4. While potatoes are cooking, combine heavy cream and pieces of butter. Either using a microwave or the stove, heat cream on low until the butter has melted. Do not boil. Reserve.
5. Check if potatoes are tender by inserting point of a knife or skewer in potatoes to see if they are cooked all the way through.
6. Drain and place the potatoes, onion, and garlic back into the pot.
7. Pour in ⅓ of the cream mixture and, using a hand mixer, start blending to combine.
8. Continue adding cream mixture while beating potatoes until potatoes are light and fluffy.
   Serve.

SIDEBAR

NOTES:

My husband likes to say that this unique combination of heavy cream and butter results in 0 calories! One thing is for certain the mashed potatoes are delicious.

Do not use an immersion blender; the potatoes will become gummy. They should be smooth, yet still have some texture.

STORAGE:

Refrigerate: 3 to 4 days
Freeze: 3 to 4 months

You can freeze these mashed potatoes. When you thaw them you'll need to whip them again with a little cream.

Roasted Garlic (page 191)

VEGETABLE PURÉE

SIDEBAR

Experimenting is the best way to discover your favorite flavors.

This is a delicious and unexpected alternative to mashed potatoes. It's a great way to serve vegetables, adding color and flavor to your plate. There are a lot of vegetables that can be cooked and made into a delicious purée. Experiment with different combinations and even a little fruit.

DIFFERENT VEGETABLES TO USE IN PURÉES	
Cauliflower	Celery root
Pumpkin	Butternut squash
Beet	Carrots
Turnip	Carrot / turnip
Parsnip	Butternut squash / apple
Rutabaga	Potatoes
Cabbage	Sweet potatoes

BASIC PURÉE RECIPE
Serves: 6
Prep time: 15 minutes
Total time: 1 hour

Ingredients
6 cups diced vegetables
1 onion
2 cloves garlic
½ cup half and half or heavy cream
4 tablespoons butter melted
Salt and pepper

Directions
1. Peel and dice the vegetable(s) you've chosen.
2. Place the vegetables in boiling water and cook until soft, 20 to 30 minutes.
3. Using a blender, food processor, or an immersion blender, purée the vegetables, adding the butter and cream until you've achieved your desired consistency.
4. Season with salt and pepper to taste.

ROASTED ROOT VEGETABLES
PURÉE

Starting with vegetables that you've roasted adds a great flavor to the purée.

Serves: 6
Prep time: 30 minutes
Total time: 1 hour 15 minutes
Preheat oven to 400°

Ingredients

Cut-up vegetables—7½ cups
1 head of garlic
Olive oil to coat slightly
Salt and pepper, ¼ teaspoon each
½ cup half and half or heavy cream
2 tablespoons butter

Directions

1. Cut all vegetables into even-size pieces and place in a large bowl. If you are using roasted garlic, keep it whole, cutting off the top third, exposing the cloves. Wrap in aluminum foil and place in the oven with the other vegetables.
2. Add just enough olive oil to lightly cover vegetables. Add salt and pepper, tossing to combine.
3. Spray 2 sheet pans with oil and spread all vegetables on pans, leaving as much room as possible between vegetables to allow them to roast.
4. Stir occasionally.
5. Halfway through cooking, move top pan to lower shelf and vice versa to help them brown evenly.
6. The vegetables should be tender and well browned when done—about 40 minutes.
7. Place all vegetables into a large pot.
8. If using garlic, when it has cooked through, open foil and squeeze softened garlic into pan with other vegetables and purée using immersion blender to emulsify vegetables.
9. On low heat, mix in the butter, cream, and adjust seasonings.

SIDEBAR

NOTES:

Root vegetable suggestions:
Sweet potatoes
Beets
Parsnips
Turnips
Carrots
Onions
Garlic
Celery root

This can be made ahead of time and re-heated in a double boiler or in a microwave.

VARIATIONS:

You can add sour cream or creme fraiche to make the purée creamier.

Roasted Garlic (page 191)

CARROT TURNIP PURÉE

This is a good combination. It is worth trying even if you aren't familiar with turnips. They add a good balance to the carrots.

Serves: 8
Prep time: 15 minutes
Total time: 45 minutes

Ingredients
10 large carrots—about 2 lbs or 3½ cups, chopped
2 large turnips—about a 1 lb or 2½ cups, chopped
2 onions—about 1 lb or 1½ cups, chopped
1 tablespoon Spike seasoning. Use more if needed.
½ cup half and half
4 tablespoons butter
Pepper to taste

Directions
1. Peel and cut all vegetables into 2" pieces.
2. In a large saucepan, add the vegetables, cover with water, and bring to a boil. Lower to a simmer and cook until all the vegetables are tender. 20 to 30 minutes.
3. Drain.
4. Use an immersion blender to purée the vegetables in the pot. (If you use a blender, you may need to add some of the half and half to help the blender purée the vegetables.)
5. On low heat, mix in the butter, half and half, and season with Spike and pepper to taste.

This can be made ahead of serving and heated in a double boiler or in the microwave.

SIDEBAR

NOTE:

Spike is a special blend of 39 flavorful herbs used instead of salt to add flavor to your food.

It is available at health food stores.

The label on the jar says "Spike Salt Free Magic Gourmet Natural Seasoning is a carefully selected, balanced blend of 39 flavorful herbs, exotic spices and vegetables that will turn every meal into a gourmet delight without the salt or calories!"

ROOT VEGETABLES
ROASTED

Roasting is a great way to cook vegetables. The inside stays moist while the outside browns and caramelizes.

Serves: 6 (Since the vegetables reduce when they cook, I estimate 1 cup of raw vegetables per person.)
Prep time: 10 minutes
Total time: 55 minutes
Preheat oven to 425°

Ingredients

Select an assortment of root vegetables: carrots, potatoes, sweet potatoes, onions, butternut squash, beets, or fennel—enough to fill 1 or 2 baking sheets without crowding
Olive oil—enough to drizzle lightly
Salt and pepper to taste

Directions

1. Cut your vegetables into even-size pieces about 1½".
2. Place root vegetables in a large bowl, add oil and salt and pepper, and mix well.
3. Lay your vegetables out onto 1 or 2 baking sheets without crowding.
4. Place in oven.
5. As the vegetables start to brown, turn them occasionally, making certain they brown on all sides.
6. You want vegetables to be fork tender and well browned.
7. It should take 30 to 45 minutes. Leave them in the oven longer if they still need to brown.

SIDEBAR

NOTES:

Softer vegetables like squash will cook faster than denser ones like potatoes. If you mix them you need to watch the softer vegetables so they don't burn while the denser vegetables cook. If they start to burn, remove them from the oven set aside and cover while the other vegetables finish cooking.

STORAGE:

Refrigerate: 4 days
Do not freeze.
These are best fresh.

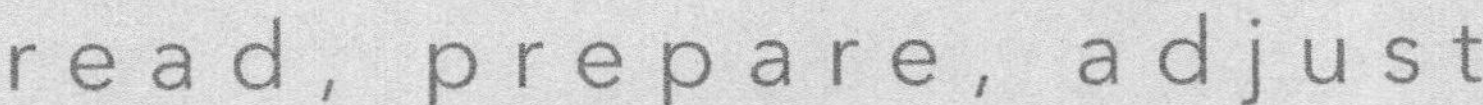

ROASTED POTATOES

These crispy roasted potatoes are simply delicious. Make more than you think you'll need because everyone asks for more.

Leftovers are easy to reheat. Pop them in your toaster oven at 400° and serve them with eggs for breakfast.

Serves: see below
Prep time: 5 minutes
Total time: 35 minutes
Preheat oven to 400°

Ingredients

6 to 8 baby potatoes per person, cut in half
Olive oil, enough to lightly coat the potatoes
Herbes de Provence or crushed rosemary
Salt and pepper

Directions

1. Place cut potatoes on a baking sheet.
2. Coat lightly with olive oil.
3. Season with herbes de Provence or rosemary, salt and pepper.
4. Place in upper third of oven.
5. After 15 minutes, start turning the potatoes over so they brown evenly on all sides.
6. Cook until potatoes are tender and well browned; it can take as long as 60 minutes. Keep checking that they are browning on all sides.

SIDEBAR

STORAGE:

Refrigerate: 4 days
Do not freeze.
These are so easy to make and are best fresh.

VARIATIONS:

Add:
Sliced onions
Brussels sprouts quartered
or sliced carrots

ENTERTAIN:

These are great for entertaining because they are full of flavor.

SERVE WITH:

This side dish is great with just about any main course.

herbes de Provence (page 49)

POTATOES & CARROTS
ROASTED

This is a good combination. I'm not certain why but the flavor of the potatoes and carrots works really well. But I have to say the addition of the burnt butter sauce makes it even better.

Serves: I plan on 4 baby potatoes and carrots per person.
Prep time: 10 minutes
Total time: 50 minutes
Preheat oven to 375°

Ingredients

4 small (baby) potatoes per person, cut in half
4 small carrots per person; if they are larger than the potatoes, cut them in half.
1 tablespoon olive oil
Salt and pepper
1 stick unsalted butter, cut into slices

Directions

1. Coat vegetables with olive oil and season with salt and pepper.
2. Place on a sheet pan in oven and cook until vegetables start to brown and are tender, about 40 minutes.
3. In a saucepan, place butter and stir as it melts.
4. Once butter starts to spit, lower heat to a simmer.
5. Stir as it starts to separate. When it browns, remove from heat.
6. Pour butter into a pitcher or measuring cup. When vegetables are done, pour burnt butter over vegetables and serve.

SIDEBAR

Burnt butter (page 98)

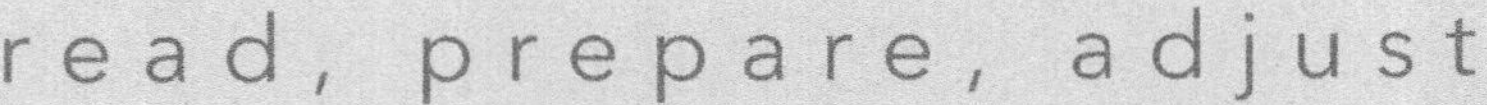

TOMATOES PROVENÇALE
OVEN-BAKED TOMATOES

SIDEBAR

SERVE WITH:

Oven-roasted tomatoes are good on sandwiches.

Combine a baked tomato with a slice of smoked Gouda, black forest ham, and multi-grain bread.

Oven-roasted tomatoes are delicious served with roast chicken or lamb.

Their intensity of flavor adds great contrast to other dishes.

While tomatoes are in season you can preserve that amazing taste to enjoy when summer is long gone. I halve the tomatoes and bake until they brown and dry out. They are a little like sundried tomatoes without being as chewy or leathery with, in my opinion, a lot more flavor. The heat concentrates the flavors and caramelizes the natural sugars, creating a tomato that is almost like candy and just as addictive. They are so good that I find myself popping them into my mouth and savoring that great taste.

Serves: Depends on quantity of tomatoes you use
Prep time: 25 minutes
Total time: 2 hours 15 minutes
Preheat oven to 325°

Ingredients
Tomatoes medium, buy enough to fill 1 or 2 baking sheets. The type is up to you. I like using plum tomatoes.
Sheet pan
Silicone matt, parchment paper, or aluminum foil
Olive oil, enough to lightly coat the pan and sprinkle tomatoes
Salt

Directions
1. Slice the tomatoes in half.
2. Gently squeeze to drain off the juice and seeds.
3. Place the tomatoes on a sheet pan.
4. Season lightly with salt and drizzle with a touch of olive oil.
5. Place pan into the 350° oven.
6. While cooking, periodically check tomatoes to make certain they do not burn. They should dry out and brown but not burn. If they start to darken before they have dried out, lower the temperature. It should take about 1½ hours but that varies on the size of the tomato and how much moisture they contain.
7. Note: tomatoes do not need to be turned over.
8. Let them cool completely.

OVEN-BAKED TOMATOES continued

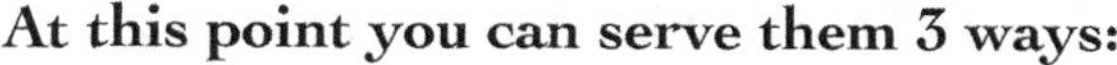

At this point you can serve them 3 ways:

As is—If you want them to be a little juicier, you can take some tomatoes out of the oven a little ahead of the others.

Freeze them—When you need them, take a couple out of the-freezer bag, slice or dice them, and pop them into stews or soups.

Make tomato paste—To create a paste, put dried tomatoes into a food processor or heavy-duty blender. Spoon out paste into an ice cube tray and freeze. Place in plastic bag.

When you want to add a burst of tomato to your dish, open your freezer and pop a cube or two in the sauce, soup, stew, or whatever you happen to be cooking.

SIDEBAR

STORAGE:

Refrigerate: 1 week
Freeze: 4 to 5 months

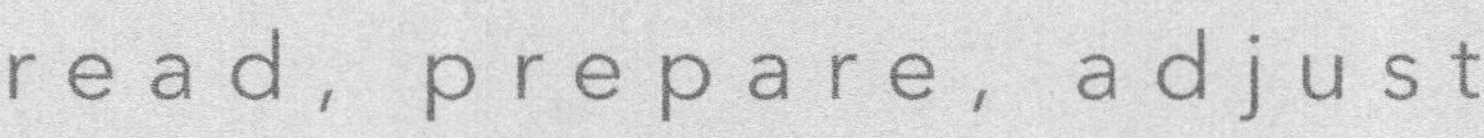

TOMATO SALAD

> "It's difficult to think anything but pleasant thoughts while eating a homegrown tomato."
> — Lewis Grizzard

There is nothing quite as special as a sun-ripened tomato, hanging on the vine, so full that it drops off the stalk into your hand. Sliced and seasoned with a little salt and eaten without pause—the experience is pure hedonism. So when it's tomato season don't hesitate to indulge.

About tomatoes: **Do not refrigerate tomatoes**; they will lose their flavor and turn mushy. Make a point to not to buy tomatoes that have been refrigerated.

Salting tomatoes is the best way to bring out their flavor. Salt causes the juice of the tomatoes to come out, giving you even more tomato flavor.

Serve with a good bread and, in true French fashion, sop up all the extra tomato juice—it's so good!

This recipe will work with any type of tomato as long as it is ripe.

Serves: 4
Prep time: 5 minutes
Total time: 30 to 60 minutes

Ingredients
4 medium to large ripe tomatoes
Salt
½ cup vinaigrette
1 bibb lettuce; cleaned and dried (keep the leaves whole)
1 tablespoon chopped parsley or basil
1 loaf of crispy French bread

SIDEBAR

NOTES:

To cut tomatoes either use a very sharp knife or a serrated knife. You need to slice through the skin and a dull knife won't; instead it will crush it. Not what you want.

You can make this salad with or without lettuce; either way it is delicious.

Vinaigrette page 100

TOMATO SALAD continued

Directions

1. Slice the tomato in half and then slice the halves into ⅛ to ¼" slices. Place in bowl.
2. Sprinkle with a little salt. Continue slicing, adding to bowl and salting each layer.
3. Let the tomatoes sit on the counter for a minimum of 30 minutes and up to 3 hours.
4. Periodically turn the tomatoes over in their juice.
5. To serve, add ½ cup of vinaigrette to the tomatoes, stirring to mix well.
6. Divide the lettuce leaves between the 4 plates. Add the slices on top (equivalent of 1 tomato) on the lettuce.
7. Drizzle with plenty of sauce and sprinkle with parsley or basil. Serve.

SIDEBAR

DID YOU KNOW?

Tomatoes will lose their flavor if you refrigerate them.

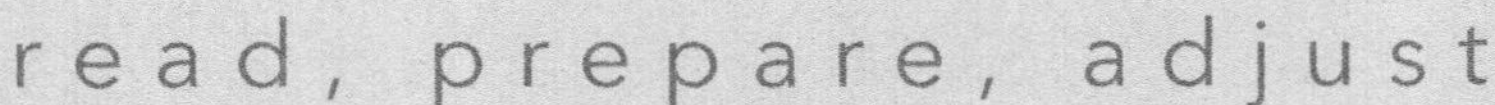

GREEN SALAD VINAIGRETTE

SIDEBAR

In France, green salad is traditionally served after the main course. The acidity of the salad dressing is a great way to cut the heaviness of the main course and cleanse your palate. It is usually served with a selection of cheese. After that, dessert is served and only after dessert is coffee served. Whenever you decide to serve it, a simple green salad is delicious.

Serves: 6
Prep time: 10 minutes
Total time: 10 minutes

Ingredients
Salad greens: 1 lb of mixed greens should give 1½ cups per person. A good combination is Boston, romaine, red leaf, and frisé.
½ cup assorted chopped herbs adds great flavor to your salad; consider parsley, basil, mint, dill, and arugula

Directions
1. Separate the lettuce, discarding the outer bruised or wilted leaves. Wash in cold water and dry in salad spinner. If you're not using, immediately wrap the greens in a dish towel. (Flour sack kitchen towels are my favorite.) Refrigerate.
2. When ready to serve, break up the leaves and place in a salad bowl.
3. Roughly chop herbs; add to the bowl.
4. Just before you are ready to serve, add your vinaigrette and toss the salad.
5. Add a small amount, toss, taste, and add more dressing only if it needs it.
6. Adding too much vinaigrette will cause your greens to become soggy.

Vinaigrette (page 100)

POTATO SALAD
JOHN TAUSSIK'S

Mayonnaise-based potato salads have never been my favorite; the flavor was always lacking—until I had this potato salad. Its flavor is amazing. When I first had it at my friend's house I couldn't figure out if the flavor was from a combination of mayonnaise and creme fraiche, or was it maybe whipped cream? I was wrong on both counts. "Vinegar," said John Taussik, the creator of this recipe. I never imagined that vinegar could transform the mayonnaise to make it so light and aromatic.

Serves: 6 to 8
Prep time: 30 minutes
Total time: 45 minutes

Ingredients
48 oz bag of small (baby) potatoes (they can be large and just cut up to smaller sizes).
1 cup mayonnaise
¼ cup malt vinegar
8 to 10 cornichons chopped fine
½ small red onion, chopped fine

Directions
1. Put potatoes in a pot of water, bring to a boil, then turn off heat and leave them in water about 15 minutes; test if they are tender with a fork. Strain potatoes but do not rinse.
2. Let cool but not completely, add the dressing while still warm.
3. Cut bigger potatoes in half or in quarters.
4. Combine 1 cup mayonnaise with ¼ cup malt vinegar and mix well.
5. Add chopped cornichons and red onion.
6. Mix in with potatoes so it is well combined.
7. If you need more of the mayonnaise mixture, you can add more, but make certain you maintain the same proportions.

SIDEBAR

STORAGE:

Refrigerate: 4 to 5 days

The use of malt vinegar is essential to create the taste that makes this potato salad so wonderful.

VARIATIONS:

French potato salad is a simple and great tasting alternative.

Boil potatoes until tender but not too soft.

Let them cool about 10 minutes, peel and slice thin.

Season with vinaigrette, and sprinkle with chopped parsley. Refrigerate 30 minutes and serve

Vinaigrette (page 100)

WATERCRESS SALAD

APPLES, ENDIVES, NUTS, & BLUE CHEESE

SIDEBAR

SERVE WITH:

I love the contrast of flavors in this salad. It is perfect served as a lunch salad or after a main course to finish the meal.

I love the combination of contrasting flavors in this salad. It is perfect as a lunch salad or for dinner to contrast the main course. You can alter the ingredients but I find it perfect as is.

Serves: 4
Prep time: 15 minutes
Total time: 20 minutes

Ingredients
2 to 3 Granny Smith apples, peeled, cored, and sliced into ½" slices
⅓ cup blue cheese, crumbled
3 tablespoon chopped walnuts
1 small endive
1 bunch watercress, washed and thick ends cut off

Dressing:
1 tablespoon mustard
2 to 3 tablespoons white wine vinegar
⅛ teaspoon salt
⅛ teaspoon ground pepper
½ cup extra-virgin olive oil

Directions
1. Whisk the mustard and vinegar to combine.
2. Add oil very slowly as you whisk so the dressing emulsifies.
3. Place the apples, blue cheese, and walnuts in a bowl and add 3 tablespoons of dressing mix to cover all the ingredients.
4. At serving time, cut off the end of the endive and then cut into thirds lengthwise.
5. Add the endive leaves and watercress to the apple mixture and blend, adding more dressing to just coat.
6. Toss well and serve on individual plates.

QUICK COLESLAW

A simple fresh coleslaw recipe is always good. This recipe is easy and delicious. I particularly love how fresh and crispy this salad is when I make my own.

Serves: 6
Prep time: 15 minutes
Total time: 1 hour 15 minutes

Ingredients
3 cups shredded green cabbage
2 cups shredded purple cabbage
1 cup shredded carrots
1 cup finely chopped parsley
Dressing
1 cup mayonnaise
¼ cup apple cider vinegar
1 tablespoon Dijon mustard
Salt and pepper to taste

Directions
1. In a large bowl combine all the salad ingredients.
2. In a separate bowl mix the dressing.
3. Place the dressing onto cabbage salad and toss to coat.
4. Refrigerate 1 hour
   Serve.

SIDEBAR

VARIATION:

A great alternative is to omit the mayonnaise dressing and substitute an oil and vinegar dressing. Adding chopped walnuts or sunflower seeds adds a nice crunchy texture to the salad.

STORAGE:

The fresh crispiness of the vegetables is what makes this salad so good and a reason to make it yourself.

You'll start losing that after 4 days refrigerated.

NOTES:

The proportion of ingredients is 3-green cabbage, 2-red cabbage, and 1 carrot. If you want to increase or decrease the quantity keep the proportions. What I love about this coleslaw is its crispiness and freshness and therefore is best served the day you make it.

Lemon dressing (page 103)
Vinaigrette (page 100)

Cooking Through a Child's Eyes—
Magic in the kitchen

The first time I saw magic happen in the kitchen I was six years old and wanted to help my mother cook. I'd follow her every step and move, clinging like her shadow, struggling to see what she was doing. Inevitably, she'd turn around and trip over me. It wasn't optimum for either of us, so when she told me we were going to bake a special cake and I could help, I beamed with joy.

"We're making a marble cake and there is a surprise at the end," she promised.

I'd never seen a marble cake and I had no idea what marble was, but helping her in the kitchen and getting a surprise too was better than I'd hoped.

"Get up on the chair so you're tall enough to help me," Maman told me. "We're going to start by making the cake batter." My job was to drop the eggs into the bowl of flour. I also needed to pour the milk in. "Be careful, pour it in slowly," she explained. "I have to blend it in while you're pouring." Once the mixture was soft and smooth, we poured the batter into two different bowls.

"Why?" I kept asking.

"That's what the recipe says," she responded. "You need to be patient. You'll see at the end."

We poured chocolate powder into one of the bowls and mixed it in, so the batter was now a rich chocolate brown color. In the other bowl, we dripped some vanilla and blended it in as well.

"Watch this," Maman said, as she poured some of the vanilla batter down one side of the baking pan and then the chocolate on the other side until they met in the middle. She continued pouring, alternating between the chocolate and the vanilla. She picked up a spatula and sank it into the batter, swirling it through from one end of the pan to the other. "That's it," she said as she opened the oven and put the

pan in. "Now we have to wait for it to bake and then cool down before I can cut and you can have a slice."

Off I went to play until I heard Maman call, "C'est prêt." I ran into the kitchen excited to see the results.

The cake was sliced and set on a plate. "How did it get that way?" I asked, amazed.

Maman tried to explain that marble meant that the different flavors stayed separate.

I stared at the cake slice in total amazement. "Why didn't it get all mixed up?" I asked.

Maman smiled as she saw the expression of bewilderment on my face. "That's what makes this cake so special," she said, trying to explain—but I stopped listening because I knew it was magic.

There is no question in my mind that what happened was magical. Cooking is full of mystifying moments that are thrilling. I realize that those moments can be explained but that's not the point. Viewing the world through the naiveté of a child is what allows us to be bowled over by how truly extraordinary life is. Isn't that what magic is—the power to make impossible things happen?

"Cooking with kids is not just about ingredients, recipes, and cooking. It's about harnessing imagination, empowerment, and creativity."

—Guy Fieri

"Cooking requires confident guesswork and improvisation —experimentation and substitution, dealing with failure and uncertainty in a creative way."

—Paul Theroux

6.

COOKING METHODS

learning how to cook

ABOUT COOKING METHODS

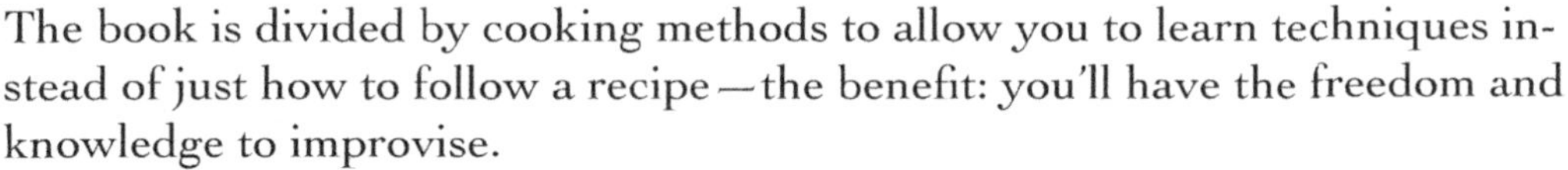

The book is divided by cooking methods to allow you to learn techniques instead of just how to follow a recipe—the benefit: you'll have the freedom and knowledge to improvise.

METHOD	DEFINITION
Baking	Using an enclosed space to surround food with heat and cooking from the outside in.
Boiling	A liquid is used to cook food.
Braising	Start by browning protein then finish cooking with small amount of liquid until moist and tender.
Grilling	Cooking on open fire or on very high heat.
Roasting	Placing proteins in your oven cooking with high dry heat.
Sautéing	Cooking food quickly with fat over high heat.
Soups	A liquid food usually containing vegetables, protein, or grains.
Stews	Cooking proteins and usually vegetables immersed in a liquid—cooked until very tender.

BAKING

How to use your oven

BAKING

ABOUT BAKING

How to use your oven

BAKING AND COOKING—IS THERE A DIFFERENCE?

Baking and cooking both occur in an oven, a closed space, with dry heat. The heat completely surrounds the food and it cooks from the outside in. When you add dry heat to food, you're heating the moisture within the food, causing it to evaporate. At that point the food goes through a chemical reaction known as the Maillard effect. That is what gives the food you are cooking its color, aroma, and its great taste.

WHAT YOU SHOULD KNOW:

- You need to preheat your oven to the required temperature before you start to cook or bake.
- Occasionally, you will need to cover what you are cooking to keep the steam in allowing the dish to cook without losing any moisture.

Baking cakes, breads, cookies, etc. is a process that needs to be precise; the ingredients must be measured exactly. Because chemical reactions occur in the oven, you need to follow the recipe exactly in order to get the intended result.

I learned this the hard way, I wanted to serve biscuits to accompany the southern lunch I planned to serve my cousins who were visiting from France. I followed the directions, or so I thought, but instead of fluffy biscuits I got flat hard pucks. When my husband makes biscuits, they come out flaky and perfect. My solution? Easy: he makes the biscuits in our house.

And then there was the time I was trying to make cookies and instead of

Mailliard Reaction (page 68)

following the recipe exactly I approximated. If one teaspoon is good, a little good, a little won't work. When I took the cookies out of the oven I had these puffy dry little cakes instead of moist cookies.

Cooking isn't nearly as precise. Making a casserole, meatloaf, or a protein such as fish or poultry you do not need to follow the recipe exactly. You can be inventive, make changes, and even improvise and still get great results.

THEY SAY:

"Baking is a science.

Cooking is an ART."

It is often said that you are either a baker or a cook; that is how different the two skills are. I am much more comfortable approximating and inventing than I am following directions exactly. That being said, you can learn the other skill. I can bake but I have to read and reread the recipe to make certain I understand and then I have to set out all my ingredients, measured exactly so that I am ready to start and there is no chance I'll go astray. (This process is also known as mise en place.)

It is just as difficult for the baker to stop following the recipe exactly and start tasting and improvising as they cook. This method results in a dishes that can be adjusted to satisfy your taste buds.

Mise en place (page 75)

BEST QUICHE EVER!

I've evolved this recipe over the years. After trying to make it less caloric, I realized that the fat is essential to making a great quiche. Trust me on this, this quiche is amazing and worth every calorie. Some things just need to be enjoyed. When I want to make something great for friends or family, this is it. The key to this recipe is to use full fat ingredients. Even whole milk has too much water to get the great results this recipe creates.

I made this quiche when my sister-in-law was visiting from France, and she loved it. She even asked how I'd made it and she's a great cook. That says everything you need to know about this recipe. Try it; you won't regret it!

SIDEBAR

SERVE WITH:

The quiche is filling. I serve it with a green salad and vinaigrette dressing.

Serve it with a fruit dessert: assorted fruit salad or sliced orange salad sweetened with a little sugar or honey.

STORAGE:

Refrigerate: 4 to 5 days.
Quiche can be frozen for 3 to 4 months.

Serves: 8
Prep time: 25 minutes
Total time: 1 hour 15 minutes
Preheat oven to 375°

Ingredients

2 cups heavy cream
1 cup Gruyere, grated
1 cup Swiss cheese, grated
6 eggs
1 cup cooked bacon
Optional: Instead of using bacon, use 1 cup ham that is diced into ¼" pieces.
Salt and pepper
Fresh herbs or herbes de Provence

Directions

1. Start by making your pastry dough following the directions and rolling it out and place it into the pie plate and refrigerate for 1 hour.
2. In the pastry shell spread out your bacon or ham. Add grated cheese almost to the top of the crust.

Pastry Dough (page 321)

BEST QUICHE EVER! continued

3. Mix the heavy cream and eggs until well blended. Pour the mixture into the shell over the cheese mixture; it should go almost to the top.
4. Use a fork to mix the cheese and meat to combine—it is important to make certain everything is well blended.
5. Place in preheated 375° oven and bake for approximately 50 minutes. (The time may vary depending on your oven. Check at 45 minutes to gauge how close it is to being done.) The quiche is done when the center is set. (When you shake the pan, the center is no longer liquid, though it may still jiggle a bit.)
6. Do not let it overcook. Keep checking.
7. Remove from the oven and let it sit 20 to 30 minutes. This lets the custard set up before cutting and serving it.

SIDEBAR

ENTERTAIN:

This quiche is perfect for entertaining. Make it for brunch or dinner with a simple salad.

This isn't your normal quiche; the filling is rich and luscious making it a delicacy worth savoring.

VARIATIONS:

This recipe can be made vegetarian by omitting the bacon and ham.

Adding vegetables to the mixture is problematic because it makes the quiche watery and runny.

Whatever vegetables you use, cook them first and remove all the excess water before adding them to the quiche.

Try using asparagus, mushrooms, onions, zucchini, and spinach. Slice them and sauté until they release their liquid. Discard liquid before adding vegetables to the quiche and cooking.

CHICKEN POT PIE

Chicken pot pie is an easy way to satisfy your need for comfort food without a lot of work. You can use store-bought roast chicken or any leftover chicken you have. This is comfort food that you'll want to make often.

Serves: 6
Prep time: 35 minutes
Total time: 1 hour 10 minutes
Preheat oven to 425°

Ingredients

1½ lbs boneless skinless chicken breast, about 3 cups diced or shredded chicken
1 tablespoon olive oil
2 tablespoons butter
4 cloves garlic, crushed
2 medium carrots cut into ½" rounds
1 large yellow onion, roughly diced
2 celery stalks sliced ½" rounds
2 red potatoes, peeled, cooked, and diced in ½" cubes
1 bay leaf
2 cups low-salt chicken broth
2 teaspoons or cubes low-salt chicken bouillon
1 tablespoon fresh parsley
Salt and pepper
3 tablespoons flour
Puff pastry, buy frozen. Take out 1 hour before to let it thaw.
1 egg

Directions

1. If you need to cook chicken, season with salt and pepper.
2. Place in 350° oven for 35 minutes; once cooked, let cool and shred or dice.
3. Heat oil and butter in a large sauté pan, add onions, carrots, and celery, cook for 5 to 8 minutes medium heat until they start to soften, and cook garlic another 5 minutes.

SIDEBAR

ENTERTAIN:

This is a great dish to serve for a small dinner party. You can play with the ingredients, spices and herbs to make your own mixture:
mushrooms, sliced asparagus, pearl onions, or you could add ginger and snow pea pods.

Have fun making it.

STORAGE:

Freeze: Okay to freeze without the crust. The pastry will get soggy.
You have 2 choices:
Freeze the pot pie with the uncooked crust.
Freeze the filling alone.
When you're ready thaw the filling and add the pastry.
Follow the recipe starting at step 12.

CHICKEN POT PIE continued

4. Add ½ cup chicken broth to pan to scrape up anything stuck to bottom of the pan.
5. Add remainder of chicken broth, cook until vegetables are tender—about 10 minutes.
6. Add potatoes.
7. Taste sauce and add chicken bouillon if it needs more flavor.
8. Add parsley and salt and pepper to taste.
9. Make a flour slurry.
10. Add slurry to sauce, letting it thicken over medium heat. You want the sauce to be thicker than heavy cream.
11. Add chicken to vegetable mixture. Let simmer on low heat.
12. Dust flour on clean work surface. Place puff pastry on work surface and dust top with flour. Roll out to ¼" thick. Make certain pastry will cover your baking dish with 2" overhang.
13. Place chicken filling into an oven-proof 3 qt casserole dish. (9" x 13")
14. Beat egg with 1 tablespoon water and brush it on edge of your dish.
15. Place puff pastry on top of the dish and press down on the edge to seal.
16. Cut 2 slits, vent holes, into top of crust and brush egg wash over entire top of pastry dough.
17. Place in preheated oven and bake until pastry is golden brown and puffed up—about 20 to 25 minutes.
18. Take out of oven and let sit 10 minutes before serving.

SIDEBAR

TIPS:

You can use leftover chicken or store-bought roast chicken.

SERVE WITH:

A simple green salad

Green Salad (page 144)
Roast Chicken (page 238)
Flour Slurry (page 60)

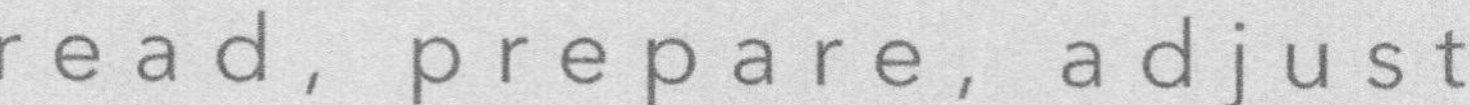

MEATLOAF

This recipe for meatloaf is a little different than other meatloaf recipes because it doesn't have any beef in it. Instead, it is made with a combination of lamb, turkey, and spicy turkey sausage. It is surprisingly flavorful and moist. The other important part of this recipe is the use of ice cubes to keep the meat fat very cold; this helps the meatloaf stay very moist.

Serves: 8
This recipe makes 1 large loaf that serves 8, or you can divide the meat to make 2 loaves; each serving 4. I've even divided it into 4 loaves that serve 2 each.

Prep time: 20 minutes
Total time: 1 hour 20 minutes
Preheat oven to 375°

Ingredients
3 eggs, slightly beaten
1 cup seasoned breadcrumbs
½ cup Parmesan cheese
1 tablespoon herbes de Provence
3 cloves garlic, minced
1 onion, chopped very fine
½ teaspoon ground pepper
1 teaspoon chili hot sauce (optional)
1 lb ground lamb
1 lb ground turkey
1 package of turkey sausage—I like to use the spicy sausage; it adds flavor but not too much spice.
½ teaspoon salt
½ teaspoon pepper
3 to 5 ice cubes

SIDEBAR

NOTES:

The trick to creating a juicy meatloaf is to keep the meat very cold (actually you are keeping the fat cold so that during the cooking the fat melts and keeps the loaf moist and juicy. There are two ways I do that:

First, keep the meat refrigerated until you are ready to use it.

Second, before you start mixing all the ingredients, add four or five ice cubes to the bowl. It works well to keep the meat cold without actually getting mixed into the meat. When you are done the ice cubes will be sitting on the bottom of the bowl making it easy to remove and yet keeping the meat ice cold.

Remove the sausage casing. Use point of a knife to slice the casing on each sausage and then slip it off.

Herbes de Provence (page 49)

MEATLOAF continued

For the sauce:

1½ cups tomato ketchup (I like Heinz chili sauce's flavor.)
⅓ cup mustard
3 tablespoons brown sugar
2 tablespoons white wine vinegar

Directions

1. In a large bowl, add onion, garlic, herbs, breadcrumbs, Parmesan cheese, chili hot sauce, salt, pepper, and eggs. Stir to combine.
2. Remove sausage casing. Add meat and ice cubes.
3. In your bowl mix all ingredients until blended; do not over mix. The ice will be left on bottom of the bowl.
4. Line a sheet pan with foil, parchment paper, or a silicone baking sheet.
5. Shape meat into 1, 2, or 4 loaves.
6. For sauce, combine chili sauce, mustard, brown sugar, and vinegar.
7. Coat loaves with sauce.
8. Place into oven and bake for 1 hour. The meat should reach an internal temperature of 155°. Do not overcook. Keep in mind that the larger the meatloaf, the longer it will need to cook. The smaller ones will be done sooner. The best way to not overcook them is to check the internal temperature before the cooking time is up.
9. Remove from oven, tent loaves, and let rest for 10 minutes.
10. Heat remainder of the sauce and serve meatloaf with extra sauce.

DON'T PANIC!

Some recipes are long. But they are not difficult. They are explained in detail to make it easier for you to follow.

SIDEBAR

SERVE WITH:

Mashed potatoes (page 133)
Sautéed green beans.

ENTERTAIN:

This is comfort food. Since this meatloaf recipe is different from traditional ones, it's good choice for entertaining.

Anything you can make ahead of time so you aren't spending the evening in the kitchen is perfect for entertaining.

For dessert, stay with the theme of comfort food and serve it with an apple dessert:
apple pie,
a baked apple,
apple tart.
Top it off with vanilla ice cream. Yum!

STORAGE:

Freeze: 3 to 4 months
Meatloaf freezes very well so this is a great recipe to make more than you need and freeze the extra for another night.
Refrigerate: 5 to 6 days

SHEPHERD'S PIE

This is a great dish to make when you have leftover mashed potatoes. I often make extra mashed potatoes so I can make this dish. Though made slightly differently, this is comfort food in many countries. In France it is called Hachis Parmentier. In England shepherd's pie is typically made with lamb or mutton. Wherever it is made it is delicious.

Serves: 6
Prep time: 25 minutes
Total time: 1 hour
Preheat oven to 400°

Ingredients

1 package of hot turkey sausage, casing removed
1 lb hamburger meat
Beef bouillon—low-salt, the equivalent of 2 to 3 cubes
1 teaspoon soy sauce
3 cups mashed potatoes; this is a good use of leftover mashed potatoes
1 cup grated Gruyere cheese
3 tablespoons butter
Salt and pepper

Directions

1. Cook ground beef, remove excess fat.
2. Remove sausage casing and break it up to combine with ground beef and cook.
3. Add 1 beef bouillon, let it melt and blend in, taste and add more if necessary.
4. Cook through completely.
5. Butter the bottom of gratin dish.
6. Start by spreading all the meat mixture over the bottom of dish. Place the mashed potatoes over the meat mixture.
7. Add Gruyere on top and dot with slivers of butter.
8. Place in oven for 30 minutes.
9. Brown the top. If necessary, raise the temperature to broil, cook 1 to 2 to minutes—do not walk away it can burn easily.

SIDEBAR

SERVE WITH:

This is a one-dish meal and the only thing you need to serve with it is a salad.

ENTERTAIN:

This is a great family dinner. Why not treat guests like family; they'll be happy you did.

STORAGE:

Refrigerate: 4 to 5 days
Freeze 3 months.

NOTES:

I use Shady Brook turkey sausage because they have a lot of flavor. They come in Hot Italian and Sweet Italian They both are very good. The hot isn't spicy; just flavorful when mixed in with other ingredients; don't be afraid to try it. If you can't find Shady Brook try other brands to find one you like.

Adding soy sauce (page 41)
Sausage remove casing (page 164)

LASAGNA

This recipe is a mix of my mother-in-law, June Santiago's, recipe and my husband, Mark's, interpretation. It's different from most lasagnas in that it leaves out the ricotta cheese. Instead it uses cottage cheese. I wasn't convinced until I tasted it. It's great, very light yet full of flavor. I highly recommend it.

This makes a large pan of lasagna. When it is more than we need, we freeze it. It freezes really well and is always welcomed when we don't have time to cook. This recipe has a lot of meat, making this lasagna a very tasty and hardy meal.

Serves: 12
Prep time: 35 minutes
Total time: 3¼ hours
Preheat oven to 375°

Ingredients
1 package 5 Italian sausages, hot or sweet, remove casing
1 or 2 lbs ground beef
1 large 24-oz container of cottage cheese
1 lb mozzarella—DO NOT USE FRESH; there is too much water.
8 sheets fresh pasta or 12 dried lasagna noodles cooked al dente and coated with olive oil to prevent from sticking
Salt and pepper to taste
Tomato sauce recipe (page 92, 94), omit meat

Directions
1. Start by making the sauce.
2. Place meat in a large skillet and cook ground beef and sausage until it has cooked through and starts to brown. Drain meat of any extra oil and set aside.
3. For dry lasagna noodles, place them in a large pot of salted boiling water, cook until they are al dente. Drain and cool in cold water. Drain again and coat with oil to keep noodles separated. If using fresh use as is.

SIDEBAR

SERVE WITH:

A large Caesar salad and lots of garlic bread.

NOTES:

If you want to make less just divide the recipe in ½ to make enough for 6 people.

Tomato sauce should be thick and noodles well drained, so lasagna isn't too liquid.

ENTERTAIN:

We like to serve this when family comes for a visit and it's a full house. It's a great make-ahead dinner.

STORAGE:

Refrigerate: 6 days
Freeze: 4 to 6 months
Once thawed, place in oven-proof covered dish. Add ¼ to ½ cup water,
Place in a preheated 350° oven for 20 to 30 minutes until hot.

Sausage remove casing (page 164)
Bolognese sauce (page 112), omitting the meat.
Tomato sauce (page 92)

LASAGNA continued

SIDEBAR

4. Assemble lasagna:
5. A metal roasting pan is ideal for cooking your lasagna or a 5-qt baking dish (11" x 15").

Putting the lasagna together

a. Put a full ladle of tomato sauce in the pan-enough to cover bottom of pan.
b. Cover bottom of pan with pasta.
c. Cover pasta with more sauce.
d. Add meat on top.
e. Place dollops of cottage cheese on top of meat.
f. Add mozzarella.
g. Pour on more tomato sauce.
h. Cover entire layer with sheets of pasta.

Repeat layers: meat, cottage cheese, mozzarella, tomato sauce, pasta, until pan is full, ending with mozzarella on top.

6. Cover pan with foil and place in preheated 375° oven.
7. Cook for about 1½ hours to 2 hours until the sides of the pan are bubbling.
8. Remove foil, raise temperature to 450°, and let lasagna brown about 10 minutes.
9. Let sit 15 minutes for the lasagna to set and cool. Serve.

MAC & CHEESE

This isn't your box macaroni and cheese; don't let that turn you off. This one is versatile, delicious, and all grown up. Have fun customizing it and making it yours.

Serves: 6 to 8
Prep time: 23 minutes
Total time: 1 hour
Preheat oven to 350°
Use a 3-qt ovenproof baking dish

Ingredients
8 oz elbow macaroni, cooked and drained
2 tablespoons olive oil (divided)
4 tablespoons unsalted butter for the roux
¼ cup flour
3 cups whole milk
1 teaspoon dried mustard
2 cups Gruyere cheese grated*
3 cups sharp cheddar grated*
Enough butter to coat bottom and sides of casserole dish
1½ cups breadcrumbs
4 tablespoons butter melted for the breadcrumbs

Directions
1. Cook macaroni and drain, drizzle with a small amount of olive oil to keep it from sticking together.
2. Make a roux. Melt butter in a saucepan over medium heat.
3. Add flour and dry mustard, mixing until you have a thick paste without letting it brown.
4. Start slowly adding milk while whisking to incorporate. Finish adding the milk and keep whisking until the sauce is smooth.
5. Sauce will start to thicken. Continue cooking 2 to 3 minutes, without browning; lower heat if necessary.
6. Add cheese, 2 cups at a time—blending to make certain it's completely combined before adding more. When all cheese is added, sauce will be smooth and thick.

SIDEBAR

SERVE WITH:

Simple salad with a lemon dressing (page 103).
Add pound cake for dessert (page 315), top it with lemon curd or fruit coulis.
Doesn't that sound great!

NOTES:

***Important**: do not use pre-shredded cheese. It is coated to keep it from clumping and will not melt properly.

Roux (page 60)

MAC AND CHEESE continued

SIDEBAR

STORAGE:

Refrigerate: 4 to 5 days
Freeze: 4 months

ENTERTAIN:

This is a great dish to serve guests. You can make it early and warm it up when you need it. Dress it up, so to speak, with lots of extras.
Try: bacon, lobster, ham, bacon bits, mushrooms, chicken, shrimp, turkey meat, or hamburger. Make sure to cook the ingredients before adding them.

No matter what you choose, it's delicious.

7. Add any other cooked ingredients you want. Such as: bacon, ham, chicken, or lobster meat.
8. Salt and pepper to taste.
9. Butter casserole dish.
10. Combine sauce with pasta and pour it into casserole dish, spreading it out evenly.
11. Mix melted butter with breadcrumbs and scatter over the mac and cheese.
12. Place the dish in the upper third of hot oven and bake 30 minutes.
13. When the breadcrumbs are brown and cheese is bubbling, the dish is done.
14. Remove from oven and rest 10 minutes.
    Serve.

BAKED FISH

This is a simple recipe for fish fillets that is easy and versatile. You can change the flavor by changing the herbs you use, adding a bit of spice (paprika instead of cayenne pepper), or by adding a dash of white wine. It's up to you and your taste buds. Don't forget to write down the changes you made so you can repeat what you did.

The best types of fish for baking are: salmon, bluefish, mackerel, halibut, snapper, tilapia, cod, and sole.

Serves: 6
Prep time: 5 minutes
Total time: 30 minutes
Preheat oven to 350°

Ingredients
Fillet of fish, ⅓ to ½ lb per person (2 lbs for 6 people)
Salt and pepper
¼ cup butter
2 tablespoons lemon juice
⅛ teaspoon dried dill
⅛ teaspoon of paprika

Directions
1. Grease baking dish with oil.
2. Place the fish fillets, skin side down, in the greased baking dish.
3. Season with salt and pepper.
4. Melt the butter and mix with the lemon juice and paprika.
5. Pour over the fillets.
6. Place in preheated oven and bake for 20 to 25 minutes until the fish easily flakes with a fork and is opaque.

   Serve.

SIDEBAR

SERVE WITH:

Rice (page 185)
Sautéed greens, like kale or spinach
A simple salad to finish

STORAGE:

Best served immediately.
Do not freeze.

DON'T FORGET

Write down any changes you make to the recipe, so you can repeat them.

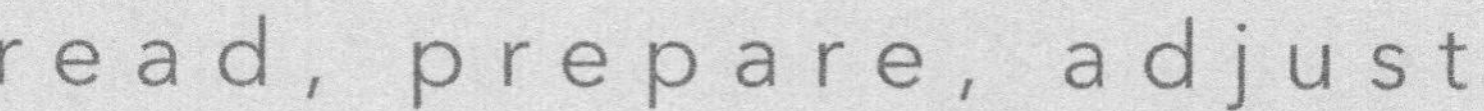

BAKED SALMON

EVA & JUDY TAUSSIK

This is a great salmon recipe! Not only is it good, but it is so easy to make you won't believe it. I got the recipe from my friend Judy, who got it from her mother-in-law, Eva Taussik. It gets passed down from generation to generation—that is how good this recipe is. You'll understand why when you make it.

Serves: 4 (Plan on serving ⅓ to ½ lb of fish per person.)
Prep time: 10 minutes
Total time: 1 hour 16 minutes
Preheat oven to 350°

Ingredients

2 to 2½ pounds to serve 4 to 5 people
Olive oil, enough to coat the fish
Cooking spray
¼ to ½ cup of white wine depending on how much salmon you are cooking
1 small onion sliced thin (optional)
2 lemons—1 lemon thinly sliced and I lemon juiced
Dill, chopped
Salt and pepper

Directions

1. Place large piece of aluminum foil down on a sheet pan and spray oil on the foil.
2. Place onion on foil and fish on top, skin side down.
3. Coat top of fish lightly with olive oil.
4. Add seasonings—dill, lemon juice, and lemon slices on top of salmon.
5. Bring sides and ends of foil up to create a container to hold in liquid.
6. Salt and pepper.
7. Add enough wine to cover bottom.
8. Seal foil—if foil isn't large enough, place another piece on top and close sides so salmon is completely enclosed. Leave some space for steam to build up as it cooks.

SIDEBAR

SERVE WITH:

Herb couscous
Steamed asparagus
A cucumber salad

Try a **yogurt dill sauce**:
1 cup Greek yogurt
1 teaspoon lemon zest
1 teaspoon lemon juice
2 tablespoons chopped dill
Blend and refrigerate before serving.
Also try serving it with cucumber dill sauce

ENTERTAIN:

This dish is perfect to serve for a dinner party or lunch. It's easy to make and can be prepared ahead of time.

You can dress the salmon up by layering thin slices of peeled cucumber over the top of the fish, overlapping to look like fish scales.

STORAGE:

Salmon is delicious served either hot, warm, or cold.
Refrigerate: 2 days
Fresh fish is always best.

BAKED SALMON continued

9. Cook between 45 minutes to 1 hour, depending on size of salmon.
10. Remove from oven. Carefully open foil, being mindful of the hot steam.
11. Check if salmon is cooked by testing with a fork to see if fish flakes easily.
12. If it needs to cook more, reseal the foil and let it sit 5 minutes.
13. Or open the top of the foil and put it back into the hot oven for a few minutes.

DID YOU KNOW

If fish is fresh it doesn't smell fishy.

SIDEBAR

Cucumber dill sauce (page 104)

COD EN PAPILLOTE

Cod is a white fish that is thick and moist. It works well when cooked with a sauce. Cooking en papillote means you create a parchment paper envelope in order to cook your fish in a moist environment. If you don't have parchment paper, you can use foil to create the envelope.

Serves: 2
Prep time: 25 minutes
Total time: 1 hour
Preheat oven to 425°

Ingredients
2 red potatoes
1 lb cod; you can also use arctic char or salmon.
4 cloves garlic, crushed
1 tablespoon chopped dill plus ½ teaspoon for garnish
1 teaspoon chopped parsley
1½ tablespoons olive oil, divided
1 bottle, 8 fluid oz clam juice
2 tablespoons butter
1 lemon, divided, ½ lemon to squeeze, ½ sliced
8 slices of fennel cut thin

Directions
1. Thinly slice potatoes (peeling is optional).
2. Place them in salted boiling water and cook until almost done—drain and keep in cold water until ready to use.
3. In a sauté pan heat 1 tablespoon olive oil, garlic, and chopped herbs. Cook slowly until they soften; do not let them burn. If necessary, move the pan off the heat to slow down the cooking.
4. Add 1 tablespoon clam juice to deglaze the pan, scraping the bottom of pan to loosen all bits; add the remaining clam juice; bring to a boil. Lower to medium heat and continue cooking, reducing to ¼ cup without burning.
5. Add butter and remove from heat.
6. Season fillets with salt and pepper on both sides.

SIDEBAR

NOTES:

Creating a paper envelope is a way to cook fish but an envelope can be used for other foods such as chicken and vegetables.

The recipe is written for 2. If you want to serve 4, you can double the recipe.

COD EN PAPILLOTE continued

7. With the parchment paper you are going to make two individual packets. See folding directions in sidebar.
8. Add a small amount of olive oil on the bottom of the parchment paper, place half of the potatoes down on the paper, add salt and 1 teaspoon sauce.
9. Place the fish over the potatoes and cover with half of the sauce 2 slices of lemon and squeeze a little lemon juice on top.
10. Add slices of fennel and top with ¼ teaspoon of chopped dill.
11. Fold over and close the parchment en papillote as indicated and place on the baking sheet.
12. Make your second packet (repeat steps 8 through 11) and also place on the baking sheet.
13. As this bakes, the parchment envelope will puff up by the steam in the sealed envelopes. Bake for 20 minutes.
14. Often the packet is placed on a dinner plate, cutting it open, being careful to not burn yourself with the escaping steam, and serve.
15. Since the fish releases a lot of liquid, I prefer to open the packets and place the ingredients on plates, spooning as much sauce on the fish as you like.

SIDEBAR

NOTES:

En papillote -
Take a sheet of parchment paper about 13" square and fold in half.
Cut it into what will be a large heart shape when opened up. Make the heart as large as you can.

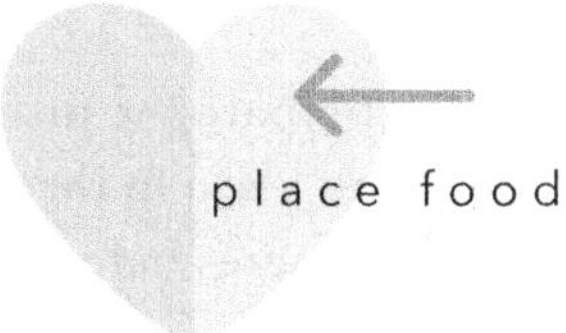

Open up the folded heart and place your ingredients on half staying close to the fold.

Fold the top half over. Starting at top, fold the edge over making a sharp fold; keep folding and overlapping the previous fold.
Continue to the bottom fold, creating a tail to fold under to seal the packet.

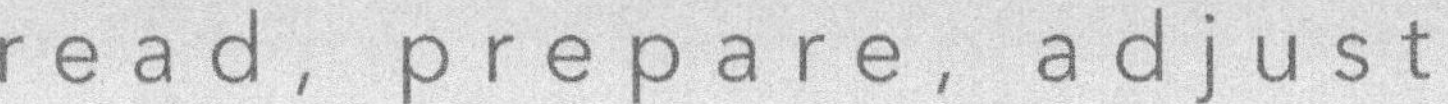

BAKED RED SNAPPER

This baked fish recipe is just as good made with trout, halibut, grouper, tilapia, or perch.

SIDEBAR

SERVE WITH:

Serve with boiled potatoes, butter, and chopped parsley. A green salad with lemon dressing.

ENTERTAIN:

This is a good recipe to serve for a dinner party.

You can prepare the dish ahead of time and place in the oven 40 to 50 minutes before you are ready to serve.

Boil the potatoes, make your sauce, and dress the salad before serving.

STORAGE:

Best served immediately.
Do not freeze.

Beurre manié (page 59)

Serves: 4
Prep time: 10 minutes
Total time: 60 minutes
Preheat oven to 425°

Ingredients

1 small bulb fennel, sliced thin
1 medium onion, sliced thin
¾ cup white wine
1½ lbs snapper fillets
Salt and pepper
½ to 1 cup low-salt chicken broth if necessary
1 tablespoon butter
1 tablespoon beurre manié

Directions

1. Lay sliced fennel and onion on bottom of a roasting pan or large cast-iron skillet.
2. Add wine to the pan.
3. Season snapper fillets with salt and pepper, place skin side down on top of sliced vegetables.
4. Place pan into your preheated oven for 40 to 50 minutes until fish is flaky and tender. Remove fillets onto a separate plate and cover with foil.
5. To make the sauce: Pour liquid from roasting pan into a saucepan, add broth to make ¾ cup liquid.
6. Over medium heat, simmer sauce and reduce to ½ cup; add 1 tablespoon butter and whisk to blend.
7. If you need to thicken sauce, add beurre manié and stir over medium-high heat until sauce is blended and starts to thicken.
8. Adjust seasonings.
9. Place some sliced fennel and onion on each plate; top with the fillet and the sauce.

"A recipe has no soul. You
as the cook must bring
soul to the recipe."

—Thomas Keller

The Coffee-Shop Grilled Cheese

Attitude affects the pleasure of food

"How about lunch?" I ask my father. "It'll have to be quick," he responds. "I have an appointment later." This was impromptu; I was happy with what I could get; after all I'd just walked in to his office, unexpected. As we go down the elevator, he asks if his local lunch spot is okay.

I follow his lead as we enter a nondescript coffee shop bustling with the lunch crowd. He motions to the counter where two adjacent seats are available. The waitress places water and menus in front of us and exchanges hellos with my father. "Are you having your usual, grilled Swiss?" He smiles and says, "Yes." "I'll have the same," I second, not wanting to bother with the menu.

A few minutes later, our sandwiches are in front of us. I pick mine up with my fingers, as I've grown accustomed to doing. He, on the other hand, picks up his knife and fork. First he takes a little mustard and puts it on the side of the plate and then slices off a small piece of pickle. He then places them both on a part of the sandwich that he has just cut, then delicately puts it into his mouth and savors the flavors. As I observe him, I realize that he is having a meal that is as wonderful to eat as it is to watch.

I wipe my greasy hands on my napkin and look down at my plate. I haven't even taken the time to taste what is in my mouth. Watching my father eat his grilled cheese sandwich had given me more enjoyment than eating my own.

Never being one to not try something that looks good, I pick up my knife and place a little mustard on my plate, copying everything he has just done. I taste what I have just put into my mouth, the flavors merge and contrast each other with every bite—I am delighted. We continue our conversation, and I notice I sit a little straighter as though I am in a fine restaurant, fully enjoying the pleasure I am experiencing.

BOILING

Cooking in a rolling liquid

ABOUT BOILING

Cooking in liquid without the use of fats or oils

A method of cooking food by immersing it in liquid—water, broth, or milk—and bringing it to a boil (212°) or placing it in the already boiling liquid to cook. Eggs, pasta, rice, grains, beans, vegetables, and some meats (corned beef) are foods that cook well and quickly this way.

One of the advantages is that there is no need for fats or oils for this type of cooking method.

DID YOU KNOW?

When rice and beans are combined they create a complete protein that contains the eight amino acids that are the building blocks to life.

GRAINS
PASTA, BREADS, RICE, AND CEREALS

SIDEBAR

ABOUT GRAINS AND HOW TO COOK THEM

Grains are either whole grains or refined grains.
Whole grains contain the entire grain kernel including the bran (fiber and vitamin b), the germ (oils, vitamins, minerals, and anti-oxidants), and the endosperm (carbohydrates and protein).
Refined grains are milled to remove the bran and the germ, giving the grain a finer texture, but at the same time the process removes some of the nutrition and because of that vitamins are added back in after processing.

HOW TO COOK GRAINS

1. Remember to use a heavy saucepan with a tight-fitting lid.
2. Rinse the grains thoroughly.
3. See the grain-to-water ratios in the following chart.
4. Bring the water to a boil, add the grain, and return to a boil.
5. Reduce the heat, cover, and simmer for the indicated time.
6. Once all the water is absorbed, fluff the grain with a fork, replace the cover, remove from the heat, and let sit for about 15 minutes.
7. When cooking grains for salads, reduce the cooking times slightly so they retain a chewy texture.

ABOUT BEANS

Beans, though larger than grains are also edible seeds. They are an important source of fiber, vitamins, and minerals and are an essential part of our diets.

DIFFERENT METHODS TO SOAK AND COOK BEANS

SOAK OVERNIGHT—Cover the beans with 2" of water, add salt, and soak 4 to 8 hours, drain and rinse.

QUICK SOAK—Add 2" of water above beans, add salt, bring to a boil, remove from heat, let soak for 1 hour and rinse.

HOW TO COOK BEANS continued

SIDEBAR

NO SOAKING—If I forget to presoak and the beans are small, I just put them into the pot with everything I am cooking and cook them longer than I normally would. Cook them until they are tender but not mushy. It can take an hour or two depending on the type of bean.

SLOW-COOKER—Cover the beans with 2" of water, add salt and any spices you plan to use. Cook on low for 4 to 6 hours.

PRESSURE COOKER—This is the quickest way to soak the beans before cooking. As with the other methods, cover the beans with 2" of water, add salt and spices to the pot. Be careful not to overfill the pot. Manufacturers recommend adding 1 tablespoon of vegetable oil to the water. This prevents the foam from clogging the vent. (Small beans on high pressure will cook for about 15 minutes. Larger beans will take about 40 minutes.)

Lentils are small, they do not need to be soaked before cooking. They are done when tender.

HOW TO COOK BEANS
1 cup of dried beans will equal about 3 cups cooked beans.

Adding salt when you cook beans helps them cook faster. Contrary to popular lore, salt doesn't toughen the beans; it simply flavors them.

1. Rinse the legumes and discard any foreign objects.
2. Cover the beans with at least 2" of water and bring to a boil.
3. Remove any sludge on the surface of the water.
4. Reduce the heat to a simmer and continue cooking the beans until they are tender. The amount of cooking time will vary by the size of the bean. When they are tender, they are done. Lentils can take 15 to 20 minutes, garbanzo beans 2-plus hours.

HOW TO COOK GRAINS continued

SIDEBAR

Beans freeze well so don't hesitate to make more than you need. Beans are economical and are a good choice if you want to keep your food budget down.

The following chart describes grains, how to use them, and how to cook them. I found this information in a copy of the 2017 Farmer's Almanac. The Almanac has been in publication since 1818 and is a wonderful resource for the weather, moon cycles, natural remedies, gardening, seasonal fruits and vegetables, and trivia. It's a great resource.

AN IMPORTANT NOTE ABOUT RICE:

There have been studies that show that rice contains arsenic. It is absorbed through the earth and the water. Rinsing the rice is important.

If you know you want to make rice, it is a good idea to soak it from 8 to 48 hours drain and cook as normal. Another method of cooking rice that will help remove the arsenic is to cook 1-part rice to 6 to 10-parts water. Once the rice is done, drain the excess water.

These techniques will help eliminate some of the arsenic in the rice.

HOW TO COOK GRAINS

GRAIN	USES	TO COOK
Amaranth	Mild, digestible. Caution: This grain becomes sticky when cooked. Mix it with corn, scallions, and cooked pinto beans. Do not salt until thoroughly cooked.	1 cup amaranth to 2½ cups water; simmer 25 to 30 minutes.
Barley, pearled	Lightly milled to retain all of the germ and at least ⅔ of the bran, barley can be used in salads with red onions, cucumber, and feta and in soups, stews, and chilies. Try barley as a stuffing for peppers, tomatoes, or poultry and in low-fat "meat" loaf.	1 cup barley to 3 cups water; simmer 45 to 60 minutes.
Buckwheat groats (kasha)	Not part of the wheat family, buckwheat can be eaten by many on a wheat-free diet. It can be roasted in a skillet with an egg for extra flavor. Cook with noodles as a stuffing for cabbage, or serve with squash.	1 cup groats to 2 cups water; simmer 20 minutes.
Bulgur (quick-cooking)	This is cracked wheat that has been partially cooked and dehydrated. It is most often combined with olive oil, garlic, mint, parsley, paprika, and lemon to make tabbouleh. Try it with pine nuts, cinnamon, and lemon as a stuffing for tomatoes or green peppers.	1 cup bulgur to 2 cups water; simmer 5 minutes. Or combine 1 cup bulgur with 1½ cups boiling water and let stand for 20 minutes.
Couscous	These quick-cooking wheat berries have been ground, steamed, and dried to form tiny pellets. Use as a light bed for spicy vegetables and stews or in a risotto with curried vegetables.	1 cup couscous to 1½ cups water; simmer 5 minutes.
Millet	This is a mild, digestible grain often used by people on wheat-free diets. Serve as a bed for sautéed vegetables and chickpeas, as a stuffing with applesauce, or sprinkled into soups, stews, or risotto.	1 cup millet to 3 cups water; simmer 20 to 25 minutes.

HOW TO COOK GRAINS continued

GRAIN	USES	TO COOK
Oats, rolled	Eat as cereal (try adding currants and toasted nuts), or use in grain burgers, in cookies and quick breads, and as a thickener in soups.	1 cup oats to 3 cups water; simmer 10 to 15 minutes.
Quinoa	Light, nutty flavor and higher in protein than other grains, quinoa (actually the fruit of an herb) is excellent in grain salads, as a stuffing for zucchini or tomatoes, or in enchiladas or fajitas. It is also great with salsas and chutneys.	1 cup quinoa to 2 cups water; rinse several times before cooking; simmer 20 minutes.
Rice	Rice is a wonderfully versatile grain, good plain, added to vegetable casseroles, and used to stuff peppers and tomatoes. Use short-grain, which is sticky, for puddings and layered vegetable dishes; use medium-grain as a side dish and in Korean, Japanese, and Italian dishes; use long-grain for stews, curries, paellas, and salads.	1 cup rice to 2 cups water; simmer 15 to 20 minutes for white rice; 40 to 60 minutes for brown rice.
Rice (wild)	This seed of aquatic grass is high in B vitamins. Combine with other grains, use with smoked turkey as a salad, or serve with apples and squash.	1 cup wild rice to 3½ cups water; simmer 60 minutes.
Wheat berries	Combine cooked, hard red winter wheat berries with bean sprouts, carrots, tamari, sesame oil, and scallions for salad; or blend into stuffing with celery, mushrooms, thyme, and sage; or serve as a side dish with butter, salt, pepper, and chopped fresh parsley.	1 cup wheat berries to 3 cups water; simmer 1½ to 2 hours. Do not salt.

Chart taken from the 2017 Farmer's Almanac

HOW TO COOK PASTA

SIDEBAR

DRIED PASTA

Serves: 1 lb of dried pasta will serve 4 people

Directions

1. In a large pot, boil 4 quarts of water; add 1 tablespoon kosher salt.
2. Once the water is boiling, add 1 lb of dried pasta.
3. Stir the pasta in the water to prevent it from sticking (using a pasta fork helps keep the pasta separated).
4. Taste the pasta to see if it is done. Don't follow the directions on the box; instead, use your taste buds. When the pasta tastes the way you like it, it's done.
5. Before you drain the pasta, reserve 1 cup of pasta water.
6. Don't rinse the pasta; it will hold the pasta sauce better.
7. The reserved pasta water is good if you need to thin your sauce.

FRESH PASTA

Serves: 1¼ lbs of fresh pasta serves 4 people (You need slightly more fresh pasta than you do dried.)

Directions

1. Fresh pasta takes less time to cook than dried pasta.
2. In a large pot, boil 6 quarts of water with salt added.
3. Add the pasta to the boiling water and stir to prevent from sticking together.
4. Cook for 1 to 3 minutes and taste the noodles to see if they are cooked the way you like them.

PASTA, PARMESAN & BASIL

This is a simple sauce that is a combination of flavors at their best. You can serve a small amount as a starter or a full serving as a main dish. This recipe is proportioned to be served as an entrée.

Serves: 4
Prep time: 5 minutes
Total time: 10 minutes

Ingredients
1¼ lb of fresh pasta
1 tablespoon olive oil
3 tablespoons butter
3 tablespoons Parmesan cheese
1 tablespoon basil, cut chiffonade, (Roll the leaves together and slice thinly.)
2 cloves garlic, chopped fine
Salt and pepper to taste

Directions
1. Cook the pasta and drain.
2. In a saucepan melt the butter and oil, add the garlic to soften.
3. Mix the garlic butter into the pasta.
4. Combine all the other ingredients and toss thoroughly.
5. Salt and pepper to taste.

This dish should be served as soon as it is done.

SIDEBAR

VARIATIONS:

The simplicity of this recipe makes it good to experiment with. Try using other spices: sage, parsley, thyme, or other combinations. Finish with lemon zest.
Try using just garlic and Parmesan.

If you have leftovers, try pan frying them.
Place noodles in an ovenproof dish,
Sprinkle Parmesan on top.
Dot the entire top with slivers of butter.
Place in 400° oven until the noodles are hot and crispy. It makes a great side dish.

Chiffonade (page 67)

RISOTTO

This is a classic Italian dish that is mouthwatering. In order for risotto to become as creamy and tasty as it does, you can't rush the process. It's important that you stir the rice as you allow the liquid to completely absorb before adding more broth. It takes time and your attention, but trust me, the result is well worth the effort.

Serves: 4
Prep-time: 10 minutes
Total time: 45 minutes

Ingredients

4 cups chicken stock
1 tablespoon olive oil plus 2 tablespoons butter
½ cup shallots or onion, diced small
1½ cups **Arborio** rice Do not rinse the rice. (This is a must as it will not work with any other rice.)
½ cup dry white wine
2 tablespoons butter cut into slices
¼ cup grated Parmesan cheese
1 tablespoon parsley minced
Salt and pepper

Directions

1. Heat the stock, then lower heat to keep it simmering.
2. Reserve one cup of broth to use at the end.
3. In a heavy-bottomed skillet, add oil and butter, add onion or shallots. Cook until translucent over medium heat, 2 minutes.
4. Add rice to the pan, stir making certain to coat rice with oil, cook for 1 minute.
5. Add wine to pan and stir until absorbed.
6. Add ½ cup of the simmering broth, continue to stir until the broth is absorbed.
7. Continue this process until the liquid is absorbed and rice is almost tender; it should have a slight bite in the center.
8. Remove from heat. Rice will be very creamy but not mushy.
9. Stir in butter, Parmesan cheese, and parsley.
10. Stir in the final cup of broth and season with salt and pepper.

SIDEBAR

VARIATIONS:

Risotto is delicious with added ingredients. Add them to the rice when you are almost finished cooking the risotto. Your additives should be cooked before adding them in.
Some suggestions:
Mushrooms, asparagus, chicken, sausage, shrimp, scallops, lemon, and tomato.

ENTERTAIN:

This dish is delicious served at any dinner. The negative is that it does need to be made at the last minute and it takes all your attention.
An alternative is to pat the cold risotto into cakes and pan fry them to create a krispy coating.

STORAGE:

Risotto is best eaten the moment it is done but if you have leftovers, you can reheat them in the top of a double boiler, letting the steam warm it up.

NOTES:

Arborio rice is a MUST. Using other types of rice will not work.

PASTA CARBONARA

This is a rich and delicious pasta recipe. You can serve this dish as an appetizer, it will serve 8. If you make it as a main course, a simple green salad is a perfect accompaniment.

Serves: 4
Prep-time: 10 minutes
Total time: 45 minutes

Ingredients
1 lb thick-cut bacon, cut into ½" pieces
3 cloves garlic, minced
1 lb pasta
Reserve 2 cups of hot pasta water
1¼ cup Parmesan cheese
3 eggs
2 egg yolks
1 tablespoon chopped parsley
Salt and pepper

Directions
1. Start heating a large pot of water with 1 teaspoon of salt to a boil. Cook the pasta, when al dente, drain and set aside. Reserve 2 cups of hot pasta water.
2. While the water is heating, place the bacon in a large skillet; cook, stirring until browned, set aside. Remove excess fat, leaving just 2 tablespoons of fat in the pan.
3. Mix the eggs and egg yolks in a bowl, add Parmesan, stir to combine.
4. Add garlic to the pan and cook just long enough to release the flavor. Turn off the heat.
5. Pour the drained pasta into the skillet stirring to coat pasta.
6. Add ½ cup of the hot pasta water to the egg mixture, stir and pour into the skillet, stirring to combine with the pasta.
7. Add the bacon; mix and add as much pasta water as needed to create a sauce.
8. Add the parsley, salt, and pepper.

SIDEBAR

STORAGE:

This pasta dish is best served just after cooking.

If you have leftovers, add a little water, cover, and microwave long enough to heat through.

RICE PILAF

Rice pilaf is a tasty accompaniment to main dishes. It is easy to make, has more flavor than plain rice, and can be easily altered by the spices you use or the additions you make. Mushroom, nuts, or chopped greens are a few ideas for additions.

Serves: 4
Prep time: 15 minutes
Total time: 30 minutes

Ingredients
Butter
Oil
1 Spanish onion, diced small
1½ cup rice
3 cups chicken broth
Salt and pepper to taste
1 tablespoon chopped parsley

Directions

1. Add butter and oil into a large deep skillet. Cook until hot and the butter starts to bubble, then lower temperature to medium high. Add onion, cook so the onion softens but doesn't brown. About 8 minutes.
2. Add the rice and stir, letting the oil coat the rice completely. About 2 to 3 minutes.
3. Add the broth and lower the heat to a low simmer. Cover and let the rice cook for 15 minutes until the broth is absorbed and the rice is tender. Let cook another 2 minutes if there is still liquid at the bottom of the pan.
4. Stir the rice, taste, adjust seasoning, add the parsley, and serve.

SIDEBAR

VARIATIONS:

Use different spices to change the flavor. Try adding chopped nuts or sesame seeds to the pan at the same time you add the rice.
Chopped fresh baby spinach leaves 10 minutes before the rice is finished cooking.

WHITE BEAN SPREAD

White bean spread is delicious eaten with raw vegetables, pita bread, or as a spread for a sandwich. Use it as a sauce on brown rice to create a good vegetarian base. Keep in mind that the sauce should be full of flavor since it gets diluted by what you eat it with. I make it with a mix of both cannellini and chickpeas because it creates a thicker texture that I like, but you can use just cannellini beans if you want. I love this recipe as it is, but don't hesitate to play with the seasonings to create slightly different flavors. For instance add a little rosemary to get great flavor.

Serves: 6 to 8
Prep time: 10 minutes
Total time: 10 minutes

Ingredients

1 15-oz can white cannellini beans, drained
1 15-oz can chickpeas, drained
2 tablespoons olive oil
3 cloves garlic
3 tablespoons lemon juice, use more to taste
¼ cup parsley, chopped
⅛ teaspoon cayenne pepper
Salt and pepper

Directions

1. In a blender or a food processor, place the beans, oil, garlic, cayenne, and lemon juice.
2. Blend until well combined.
3. Pour into a bowl and stir in parsley and cayenne.
4. Refrigerate and serve with cut-up vegetables, pita bread, or crackers.

SIDEBAR

VARIATIONS:

Use 3 cloves roasted garlic instead of fresh to add flavor.

To **roast garlic**, take a head of garlic, remove loose outer layers, leaving the rest of the skin. Cut off the top third of garlic head. Drizzle with olive oil. Wrap in foil. Place in center of 400° oven for 45 minutes. Open foil to see if the center cloves are soft. Let cool. Remove the cloves individually by pushing from the bottom.

STORAGE:

Refrigerate: in air-tight container 2 weeks
Freeze: 3 months

LENTILS AS A SIDE DISH

Lentils are commonly eaten in France as either a side dish or as a simple salad. This is a good alternative to add to meals. Try the lentil salad as a side served with a fresh tomato salad for a summer lunch.

Serves: 6
Prep time: 5 minutes
Total time: 25 minutes

Ingredients
1 cup dry lentils
3 cups water
½ teaspoon of salt (Add only at step 3.)
3 tablespoons butter
2 tablespoon lemon juice
1 tablespoon chopped parsley

Directions
1. Wash lentils, removing any foreign items (stems or small stones)and drain.
2. In a large pot, place lentils and water. Bring to a boil and reduce heat to a simmer.
3. Cook 10 minutes and add ½ teaspoon of salt; continue cooking another 10 minutes until the lentils are tender.
4. Drain.
5. Add butter, lemon juice, and parsley; stir to combine.
   Serve.

Lentil Salad
1. Cook the lentils as above.
2. Cool.
3. Toss with vinaigrette dressing.
   Serve.

(See sidebar for additives.)

SIDEBAR

NOTES:

Lentil salad is a good base to add other flavors. Here are a few suggestions:

cherry tomatoes,

parsley,

crumbled feta cheese,

diced peppers,

chopped olives,

Chopped red onion,

As with all dishes you make once you've prepared it you need to taste and adjust the flavors.

POACHED FISH

Poaching is a good way to cook fish or poultry. The result is moist and flavorful protein that cooks in its own sauce. It all starts by creating a liquid that is full of flavor. Immerse the fish or poultry in the broth and let it cook in the liquid. Remove the protein and continue to boil the liquid to intensify the taste and serve as a sauce.

Serves: 2
Prep time: 10 minutes
Total time: 20 minutes

Ingredients
¾ lbs fish such as sole, Arctic char, halibut, salmon, mahi mahi
1 small onion or 2 shallots, diced
1 carrot, diced
½ cup white wine
2 cups clam juice
1 cup water
1 teaspoon herbes de Provence
1 bay leaf
1 tablespoon lemon juice
1 tablespoon chopped parsley

Directions
1. Salt and pepper both sides of fish or poultry.
2. In a large skillet, add broth, wine, onion, carrot, the lemon, bay leaf, and herbs. Bring to a simmer, add the fish.
3. If necessary, add water so the broth covers the fish.
4. Do not boil the liquid; keep it at a simmer. It should cook in about 10 minutes. Check that the fish is opaque and flaky or the chicken is cooked through.
5. Remove the fish using a slotted spoon and place in center of a plate. Set aside and cover.
6. Bring the broth to a boil and reduce by half. Remove the bay leaf.
7. Taste seasonings, add more lemon if needed, and pour the broth over the fish and sprinkle with parsley and serve.

SIDEBAR

VARIATIONS:

To poach chicken breasts:
Use chicken broth instead of clam juice. Check that the chicken is done with an instant-read thermometer. The internal temperature should be 165°.

NOTES:

To add more flavor to the broth I add Better Than Bouillon Fish stock.

If you have any left over poaching broth freeze it to use as a base for sauce to use at another time with a different fish dish.

"Cooking and shopping for
food brings rhythm and meaning
to our lives."

—Alice Waters

BRAISING

This method turns inexpensive meats into mouthwatering dishes.

ABOUT BRAISING

This method turns inexpensive meats into mouthwatering dishes.

The type of heat that is used in braising meat is long, slow, and wet. The best meats for this method of cooking are the less expensive tougher cuts, such as short ribs, pork or lamb shoulder, chuck, chicken thighs and legs, roasts, briskets, and rounds. Braising is done in a large pot, 3 to 6 quarts, that can be used on the stovetop and in an oven, often referred to as a Dutch oven.

Serves: plan on ⅓ to ½ lb of meat per person
Prep time: 20 minutes
Total time: 3 hours 20 minutes
Preheat oven to 300°

Ingredients
Meat
Vegetables
Liquid: broth, wine, beer, or water
Seasonings: salt, pepper, spices, herbs

Directions

1. Use a whole chunk of meat as opposed to stews where the meat is cut up.
2. In a Dutch oven, sear the meat on all sides. Do not omit this step, as it develops the rich flavors.
3. Remove from pan and set aside.
4. Sear the vegetables; I use a mirepoix (chopped onions, carrots, and celery.)
5. Deglaze with broth, wine, beer or water. This is an important step. You want all those burnt bits in your sauce since that's where the flavor is.

Mirepoix (page 120)

BRAISING continued

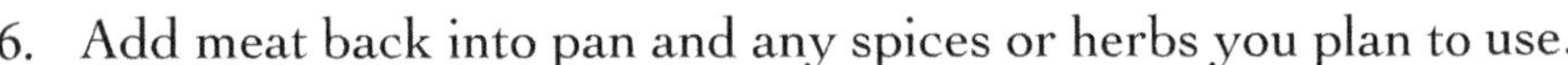

6. Add meat back into pan and any spices or herbs you plan to use.
7. Add enough liquid to rise no more than 2 to 3 inches up the side of the meat.
8. Bring to a boil.
9. Cover the Dutch oven and place it into a preheated 300° oven.
10. Cook for 2½ to 3 hours.
11. An hour into cooking, check that there is enough liquid left. Add more liquid if less than 1" is left.
12. Meat needs to be very tender—so it falls apart with a fork. Remove from the oven and place on stovetop.
13. Take out meat and vegetables and set aside.
14. Remove fat by skimming the surface.
15. If the sauce needs to thicken, let simmer. Add a thickner if necessary.
16. Adjust flavor and serve.

DON'T FORGET!

You can get bonus materials and extra videos, by going to:
french-secrets.com/pages/book

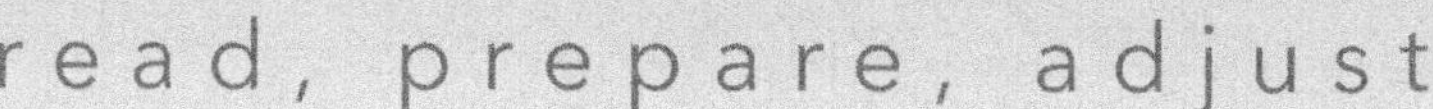

BRAISED FISH

SIDEBAR

SERVE WITH:

Serve with white rice.
Add a spoonful of rice at the bottom of a bowl. Place the fish on top and pour the sauce over the fish and serve.

Mirepoix (page 120)

This is a great way to cook moist fish that is full of flavor. Be flexible with the vegetables you add to change the flavor. A diced tomato and a splash of hot sauce will give you a great burst of flavor. Halibut or Chilean sea bass are good alternative to the cod.

Serves: 4
Prep time: 20 minutes
Total time: 40 minutes
Preheat oven to 325°

Ingredients
2 tablespoons olive oil
1 onion cut in half and sliced thinly
4 cloves garlic, thinly sliced
1 small bulb fennel; trim off the top, cut bulb in half, slice thinly
Reserve 1 tablespoon chopped fennel fronds
2 bottles clam juice
1¾ lb cod, cut into 4 pieces, salt and pepper both sides
1 teaspoon fennel seeds, crushed

Directions
1. Using an ovenproof deep-frying pan or Dutch oven with a lid, heat oil, add onion slices, cook until softened without browning, 4 minutes. Stir while cooking.
2. Add garlic and fennel seeds, cook 2 minutes.
3. Add the sliced fennel and clam juice, cook on simmer for 10 minutes to develop the sauce and continue stiring.
4. Nestle the cod into the vegetables, cover and place in the oven.
5. Cook 15 to 20 minutes until the fish is opaque and flakes.
6. Place each cod fillet in individual bowls.

BRAISED FISH continued

7. Place the pot back on stove and add 2 tablespoons butter, stirring to blend and create a sauce.
8. Place the vegetables and the sauce in the bowls with the cod, top with fennel fronds.
   Serve.

SIDEBAR

SUCCULENT VEAL
MOPPET'S VEAL

This is one of those great recipes that is as good for a dinner party as it is for a weeknight dinner. And the best part is that it is easy to make. Ever since my friend Moppet Reed shared this recipe with me, it has become one of my favorite, tried-and-true recipes.

For entertaining, this is a no stress dinner. Everything can be done ahead so you are ready and waiting when your guests arrive—that's the way I like to entertain.

Veal tends to shrink a lot so I always make more than I think I need. My experience is that people always want seconds so I buy 3 to 4 veal slices per person.

Serves: 4
Prep time: 30 minutes
Total time: 1 hour 30 minutes

Ingredients
2 or more lbs of veal scaloppini (pound it so it is thin)
¼ cup flour
Salt and pepper
Olive oil, enough to lightly cover the bottom of your pan
½ cup heavy cream
Beef broth, low-salt, enough to cover the veal
2 tablespoons of cream sherry; optional
Beef or chicken bouillon, low-salt
Beurre-manié
Kasha, enough for 4 servings (see sidebar)

Directions
1. Make ¼" slice on the edge of the veal in a few spots and pound flat. (The cuts help veal stay flat when it cooks.)
2. Combine flour, salt, and pepper in a plastic bag and toss the veal to coat evenly.

SIDEBAR

SERVE WITH:

I like serving this veal dish with kasha, a buckwheat grain; it is low in fat, wheat, and gluten free and has a wonderful nutty flavor.

Wolff's makes a good medium-grain kasha that I've been using for years and love. The kasha takes about 15 minutes to cook.

Serve with carrot and turnip purée on the side (page 136).

SUCCULENT VEAL continued

3. Heat oil, place veal into a large sauté pan, and brown until veal naturally separates from pan, 3 to 5 minutes. Flip and brown the other side. Do not crowd the pan.
4. In the same pan lay out veal; it is okay to layer the veal so it fits. Cover with chicken or beef broth. Bring to a boil, lower heat to a simmer. Continue cooking for 45 minutes to 1 hour. Make certain veal is very tender, fork tender.
5. If you do not plan to serve immediately, cool veal and refrigerate.
6. When you are ready to serve, bring veal to room temperature and then heat the veal on your stovetop at medium heat, letting it simmer until hot. Remove veal from pan and place in a large serving dish, cover with foil.
7. To make sauce, add 2 tablespoons of sherry, if using, and simmer for 2 minutes.
8. Taste sauce and adjust seasonings by adding bouillon and salt and pepper.
9. Before serving, add ½ cup of heavy cream to sauce. The sauce should be thick enough to cover back of a spoon. If it needs thickening, add beurre manié, stirring to combine as it thickens.
10. Pour the sauce over the veal.
    Serve.

SIDEBAR

ENTERTAIN:

This is a great dish for a dinner party since it can be made ahead and reheated.

STORAGE:

Refrigerate: 4 to 5 days
Freeze: 3 to 4 months

beurre manié (page 59)

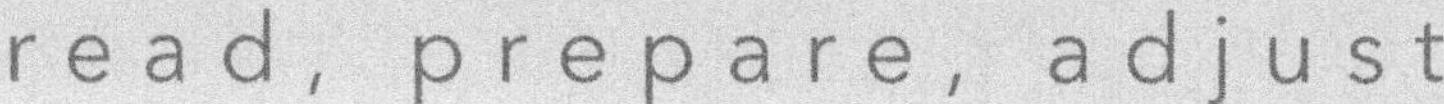

24-HOUR LAMB

This is an amazing recipe. When we're in France lamb is our go-to dish. It isn't that there aren't lots of other dishes we love to eat but there is something about the way they cook lamb that is unforgettable.

Just outside of Maussane Les Alpilles in Provence, France, is a restaurant called Aux Ateliers Chez Franck et Flo. They serve a 24-hour lamb dish that is so tender and flavorful you can't get enough of it. When people come to visit us, in Maussane, that is the first place we take them to have 24-hour lamb and we generally go back to have lamb once again before they leave.

The problem is when we get back to the States, there is no 24-hour lamb! When you crave something, you find a way to satisfy that craving. We were determined to figure out how to make it—and with a little trial and error we did.

It is hard to believe that cooking lamb at 160° Fahrenheit for 24 hours will create such amazing results that are every bit as good as the lamb we eat in France. And it's easy!

Use a boneless leg of lamb or boneless lamb shoulder. If you can't find it boneless, ask your butcher to remove the bone. Lima beans are traditionally served with lamb. Cooked this way, they take on the flavor of the sauce the lamb is cooked in and are delicious.

Serve with fingerling potatoes or mashed potatoes.

Serves: 6 to 8
Prep time: 50 minutes
Total time: 24 hours
Preheat oven to 160° Fahrenheit

Ingredients
4 to 6 lbs boneless lamb shoulder or leg of lamb
(The lamb will get smaller as it releases it juices.)

SIDEBAR

NOTES:

The length of time the lamb cooks causes it to releases a lot of liquid. Because of this buy a larger piece than you think you will need. We served 8 lbs to five people and, to my disappointment, there were no leftovers—just five very happy people.

Note: 160° Fahrenheit is not a mistake

STORAGE:

If you have any leftovers refrigerate 4 days

Freeze: You can but I don't recommend it.

Deglaze (page 36)
Garlic paste (page 50)
Mashed potatoes (page 133)
Beurre manié (page 59

24-hour lamb continued

1½ teaspoon salt
1 teaspoon pepper
1 tablespoon rosemary, finely chopped
2 tablespoons finely chopped garlic
6 cloves garlic, thinly sliced
4 sprigs rosemary
1 cup chopped onions
1 cup beef or chicken broth
1 teaspoon soy sauce
1 tablespoon chopped parsley
16 oz baby lima beans
12 to 18 fingerling potatoes cut in ½
Beurre manié

Directions

1. Make a garlic paste with salt, pepper, rosemary, and olive oil.
2. Open up the lamb and spread the garlic paste over the inside of the meat.
3. Roll the lamb back up and tie it closed with kitchen twine.
4. Season the outside of the lamb with salt and pepper.
5. In a Dutch oven, starting with the fat side down, brown the lamb well on all sides. You want the lamb to fit snugly.
6. Add the remaining garlic and rosemary around the lamb.
7. Cover the pot and place in the oven for 14 hours.
8. Add onions, stock, (potatoes if using), cover and return to the oven for another 6-plus hours.
9. Last 4 hours add lima beans.
10. The lamb will be very tender.
11. Remove the lamb and lima beans from the sauce with a strainer and cover.
12. Place the pan on the stove, bring the sauce to a boil and simmer until it intensifies and reduces.
13. If the sauce needs to be thickened, add beurre manié and whisk it in.
14. Slice the meat and place in the center of the platter, surround by the lima beans and the potatoes.
    Enjoy.

SIDEBAR

NOTES:

BRAISED CHICKEN
WHITE WINE

The way the chicken is cooked in this recipe creates a delicious sauce. This is also a great recipe to cook a day or two ahead of time and reheat when you are ready to serve it.

Serves: 6
Prep time: 35 minutes
Total time: 1 hour 30 minutes
Preheat oven to 400°

Ingredients
1 tablespoon oil
8 oz bacon cut into 1" slices
8 oz small white pearl onions—I use frozen pearl onions.
8 cloves garlic, crushed
1 cup carrots, sliced into ½" rounds
½ cup flour
Salt, pepper
4 lbs chicken thighs, bone in and skin on
2 tablespoons olive oil
Fresh rosemary
Bay leaves
1 cup white wine
1½ cups low-salt chicken broth
Bouillon low salt, 1 to 2 tablespoons as needed

Directions
1. Cook bacon until crispy, about 5 minutes. Remove from pan, set aside.
2. Add onions, garlic, and carrots to pan and cook until they begin to soften and brown, about 10 minutes. Remove from pan, set aside with bacon.
3. Mix flour, salt, and pepper in a bowl. Coat the chicken pieces in flour mixture and shake off excess.
4. You need about 2 tablespoons of olive oil in skillet; add more if necessary. Heat on medium-high heat. When hot, add chicken pieces, skin side down. Do not crowd pan. Cook without

SIDEBAR

SERVE WITH:

Rice, mashed potatoes, or wide noodles.
Salad

ENTERTAIN:

Because this dish can be cooked a day or two ahead of time it is perfect for when you have guests.

STORAGE:

Freeze: divide into portion sizes 5 to 6 months.

Reheat in a 350° oven covered for about 30 minutes until the chicken is hot.

BRAISED CHICKEN continued

turning for about 5 minutes until chicken releases naturally from pan. Flip chicken and repeat cooking until browned, another 5 minutes. Set chicken aside.

5. Remove all but 2 tablespoons of oil. (If there isn't enough, add more.)
6. In the skillet, arrange chicken, skin side up. Add vegetables and bacon. Add rosemary leaves, bay leaves, and wine to pan.
7. Add enough stock to go ¾ of the way up the side of the chicken; make sure you don't cover the chicken.
8. Bring to a boil, place pan in oven without cover.
9. Cook until the chicken is cooked through, about 40 minutes.
10. Remove pot from oven (be careful not to burn yourself). Remove chicken and vegetables from broth and set aside; cover with foil.
11. Discard herbs. Simmer sauce over medium-high heat, letting it evaporate until sauce thickens enough to coat back of a spoon. Add a thickener if necessary.
12. Season to taste. Add low-salt bouillon if sauce needs more flavor.

SIDEBAR

Thickeners (page 59)

BRAISED BEEF

This recipe is made with beef but you could just as easily use lamb, veal, or chicken. Adjust the flavors, to your tastes.

Serves: 6
Prep time: 35 minutes
Total time: 3 hours 35 minutes
Preheat oven to 350°

Ingredients
5 lbs boneless beef chuck (pot roast)
3 tablespoons high-heat oil
2 onions, sliced
3 garlic cloves, crushed
1 teaspoon cumin
1 teaspoon paprika
Salt and pepper
Black pepper
1 cup red wine
¼ cup water
Beurre manié

Directions
1. Cut the beef into 2″ chunks.
2. Using high-heat oil, brown beef chunks over high heat in skillet. Remove and set aside in a bowl. Do this in stages so you do not crowd pan.
3. Cook onions in same skillet until cooked through and translucent.
4. Add minced garlic, cook 1 or 2 minutes, remove from pan and set aside.
5. In bowl, place dried spices and blend.
6. Add onion mixture to the meat, blend well. Place everything in Dutch oven.
7. Add red wine and water to pot. Bring to boil, cover, place in

SIDEBAR

SERVE WITH:

Mashed potatoes or wide pasta. If you prefer, serve it with a simple salad.

ENTERTAIN:

Meats that cook at low temperatures, for a long time, are imbued with flavors and moisture that surrounds them. The result is meat that is moist, flavorful, and very tender.

Who wouldn't want to enjoy that for dinner?

STORAGE:

Refrigerate: 4 to 5 days
Freeze: 3 to 4 months

NOTES:

Trying to brown too much meat at a time will cause the meat to steam instead of brown. The process of caramelizing the surface is what gives food its great flavor.

beurre manié (page 59)
high-heat oil (page 44)

BRAISED BEEF continued

oven, and cook for 3 hours at 350°.

8. Check while meat is cooking to make certain there is enough liquid in pot. If there is less than 1", add 1 cup water.
9. You want the meat to be cooked through and fork tender so it falls apart.
10. Remove meat and place in covered bowl.
11. If sauce needs to be thickened, continue cooking at a simmer and reduce. To thicken more, add beurre manié, stir, and cook until thickens. About 2 to 3 minutes.

    Serve.

SIDEBAR

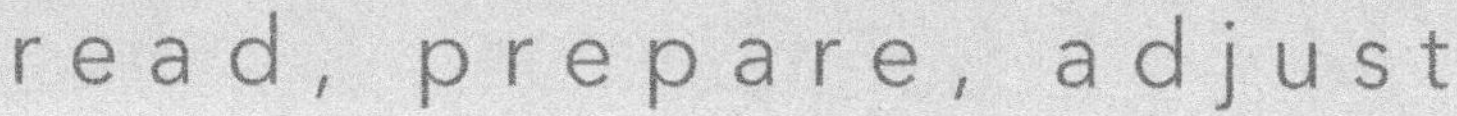

BRAISED LAMB
WITH ROSEMARY AND GARLIC

SIDEBAR

ENTERTAIN:

This is a great dish for a spring dinner with family or friends.

STORAGE:

Refrigerate: for 4 to 5 days
Freeze: 3 to 4 months

NOTES:

This recipe is best if you allow it to marinate for 4 to 12 hours to allow the flavors to be at their best.

If you don't leave enough time, don't worry, it will still be good.

Garlic paste (page 50)
Deglaze (page 36)

The combination of lamb, garlic, and rosemary is a classic combination that is delicious. Make a paste out of the garlic and rosemary to insure that the aroma permeates the entire piece of meat, resulting in huge flavor.

Serves: 8 to 10
Prep time: 1 hour 15 minutes, plus time to bring meat to room temperature
Total time: 3 hours 35 minutes
Preheat oven to 450°
Optional: Best if, after seasoning the lamb, you let it sit refrigerated for 4 to 12 hours.

Ingredients
6 cloves garlic
1 tablespoon fresh rosemary leaves, chopped
½ tablespoon oregano
½ teaspoon pepper
½ cup olive oil
6 lbs boneless leg of lamb, butterflied
Kitchen twine
1 small onion, diced
1 fennel bulb, diced
2 large carrots, diced
4 cloves garlic, sliced thin
¾ cup red wine
Water
Bouillon, beef or chicken low-salt, add to taste
Soy sauce; if necessary, add to taste

Directions

1. Place the 6 garlic cloves, chopped rosemary, oregano, and pepper into a food processor or use a mortar and pestle. Mix until you start to get a thick paste. Add the oil in a stream while mixing so the paste thickens.

BRAISED LAMB continued

2. Open up the lamb, sprinkle with salt. Spread ½ the rosemary paste over the inside of the lamb.
3. Roll lamb, starting from short end, and place it seam side down.
4. Starting in the center, use kitchen twine to tie a knot every 2 inches.
5. Cover the outside of the lamb with remaining rosemary paste.
6. Optional: place on a plate, cover tightly with plastic wrap and refrigerate for 4 to 12 hours, letting the flavor get absorbed into the meat. If meat is cold, bring to room temperature (about1 hour) before cooking.
7. In a Dutch oven, heat 2 tablespoons oil on high heat, add lamb, let brown on all sides. About 5 to 7 minutes per side. Set aside.
8. In pan add 2 tablespoons olive oil and onion, fennel, carrots, and remaining 4 garlic cloves over medium heat, stirring until vegetables start to soften and brown. About 20 minutes.
9. Add wine, bring to simmer and remove from heat.
10. Place lamb back into pot. Pour in water until it reaches halfway up the side.
11. Cook lamb uncovered in the oven for about 1 hour.
12. Using an instant-read thermometer, check that meat has reached 140° at its thickest point.
13. Remove from oven and let lamb rest for 20 minutes.
14. Taste the braising liquid, adjust the flavors. Add bouillon if necessary. If sauce needs to reduce, continue to cook on medium heat. If the sauce needs to be a bit more savory, add 1 or 2 tablespoons soy sauce.
15. Slice the lamb and place it in serving platter. Cover with braising liquid and surround with the vegetables.
    Serve.

SIDEBAR

Difference between broth and bouillon (page 40-41)
Soy sauce (page 41)

SHORT RIBS

SIDEBAR

SERVE WITH:

Mashed potatoes (page 133)
Potatoes Dauphinoise (scalloped potatoes) (page 125)
Wide egg noodles or
Risotto (page 188)

ENTERTAIN:

This is also a great dish to make when you want to entertain: no cooking necessary the day of the party. I love that!

STORAGE:

You can make and refrigerate this dish 2 to 3 days ahead of serving. This gives the meat extra time to take on the flavor of the sauce.

Refrigerate: 4 to 5 days
Freeze: 3 to 4 months

Short ribs are delicious, especially when they've cooked long and slow over medium heat. The other plus about this recipe is that it can be made ahead of time and kept refrigerated for 2 to 3 days. That's perfect for entertaining; no cooking on the day of the party. As a matter of fact, the dish gets better by waiting a few days before serving.

Note: If you can, refrigerate this overnight before you finish it. This allows the fat to solidify so you can easily remove it in the morning. The resulting sauce will be flavorful without being fatty.

Serves: 8
Prep time: 40 minutes
Total time: 3 hours 10 minutes
Preheat oven to 350°

Ingredients
8 beef short ribs
¼ cup flour for coating the ribs
Salt and pepper (kosher salt and crushed pepper)
3 tablespoons olive oil
1½ cups roughly chopped onion
2 medium carrots, sliced 1" pieces
2 ribs celery, 1" pieces
1 leek cleaned, trimmed, and sliced into 1" pieces
1 fennel bulb—Remove the top with the fronds, slice and cut into 1" pieces.
6 cloves garlic, crushed
Sprig fresh rosemary
Sprig fresh thyme
2 bay leaves
Flat-leaf parsley
1 bottle red wine
8 cups beef stock
2 tablespoons soy sauce

SHORT RIBS continued

Directions

1. Lightly coat half the ribs in flour and salt and pepper.
2. In Dutch oven heat oil over medium-high heat. Add 4 short ribs, brown on all sides, about 5 minutes each side. Repeat with last 4 ribs. Remove short ribs and set aside.
3. Add all vegetables, including herbs, into Dutch oven over medium heat and cook until they soften and begin to brown.
4. Add wine, short ribs, and broth back into pan and bring to a boil. Cover and place into center of your oven and cook for 2½ hours.
5. While cooking, open pan and stir, making sure ribs are covered with sauce to keep moist.
6. Remove from oven; let cool and refrigerate overnight.
7. The next day, remove fat that has solidified on top.
8. Reheat dish, remove ribs and set aside, cover to keep warm.
9. Using an immersion blender, emulsify the vegetables to add flavor and thicken the sauce. Bring sauce to a boil, lower to simmer if necessary and let it reduce.
10. Taste to adjust flavors.
11. Place the short ribs back into the sauce.
    Serve.

SIDEBAR

NOTES:

Refrigerate the dish overnight. When it is cold, all the fat will congeal on top, making it easy to remove before finishing the dish.

This step is well worth the effort: your ribs won't be fatty and that makes a huge difference to the flavor.

"I'm not a chef. But I'm passionate about food - the tradition of it, cooking it, and sharing it."

—Zac Posen

GRILLING

Grilling is the oldest way of cooking.

ABOUT GRILLING

Grilling creates a charred smoky crust that adds a unique flavor.

Grilling food occurs directly over a heat source. The intense heat will sear the food, creating a caramelized crust on the surface. The heat cooks the food quickly and is usually done outside using charcoal, gas, or wood as the fuel source. A grill is great to cook steaks, chicken, hamburgers, hot dogs, sausage, fish, shrimp, kabobs, chops, vegetables, fruits, and even pizza. Using a meat thermometer is the most precise way to know when your meat is done.

HOW TO START A CHARCOAL GRILL

Use a chimney starter.

Fill it with coals.

Pour a generous amount of lighter fluid on the coals and light.

Or add newspaper in several spots within the chimney. Light the coals or the newspaper.

When flames reach top of the chimney and coals are covered with white ash, turn chimney over and spread out coals; it should take about 15 minutes.

Your coals are ready to use.

HOW TO USE A GAS GRILL

1. Make certain the grill is clean.
2. Check to see if you have enough fuel for the grill.
3. Gas grills need to be preheated.
    a. Open the cover
    b. Turn the gas on high
    c. Light the gas
    d. Close the cover and preheat for 10 to 15 minutes
4. Once it's ready, adjust the heat to what you need to cook.
5. Use cover as necessary to hold in heat.

COOKING TEMPERATURES

Doneness	Internal Temperature	Meat Firmness to the touch	Cooking Time
STEAKS			
Rare	120°	Soft	2 to 3 minutes
Medium rare	130°	Less soft	7 minutes
Medium	140° - 145°	Just firm	9 minutes
Medium well	150° - 155°	A bit firmer	11 minutes
Well	160°	Firm	13 minutes
CHICKEN			
Done	165° - 190°		
PORK			
Done	145° - 160°		
LAMB	130° - 145°		

Once meat has reached internal temperature let it sit 15 - 20 minutes before slicing. This will result in juicier meat.

NOTE:

Using newspaper to light coals in your chimney takes a bit more time and care than lighter fluid, but it works and is good to know in a pinch.

GRILLED FISH STEAKS

This is a basic recipe for grilled fish, that's flexible. Use your imagination to alter the flavor. It is as easy as changing the ingredients in the marinade to give the fish a different flavor.

Serves: 4
Prep time: 35 minutes
Total time: 45 minutes

Ingredients

2 lbs fish steaks (1½" to 2" thick) halibut, swordfish, tuna, or salmon steaks

Marinade

- ½ cup olive oil
- ¼ cup lemon juice
- Pinch cayenne pepper
- 1 tablespoon white wine vinegar
- ½ teaspoon of assorted herbs such as chopped parsley, thyme, basil, cilantro or rosemary
- Salt and pepper

Serve with lemon wedges.

Directions

1. Coat fish on both sides with marinade and let it sit refrigerated for at least 30 minutes.
2. Brush grill with high-heat oil.
3. Determine when grill is the right temperature; if using coals, they will be covered with white ash.
4. Place fish on grill about 5" from coals.
5. Cook 4 to 5 minutes. With a wide spatula, flip the fish and cook another 4 minutes.
6. Check to see if fish is done by inserting tip of a knife into thickest part of fish to make certain that it is opaque and flaky.
7. Remove to a platter.
8. Heat remaining marinade and serve with the fish.

SIDEBAR

NOTES:

If using a grill pan, preheat oven and grill to 450°.

Tuna is a fish that is normally not cooked through. It is delicious and moist when the center is left raw or somewhat raw. How you serve it is up to your taste buds.

Starting your grill (page 218)
High-heat oil (page 44)

GRILLED SCALLOPS
WITH GARLIC BROWN BUTTER

This recipe is simple, quick, easy, and delicious. Try it using shrimp; it's just as good.

Serves: 4
Prep time: 10 minutes
Total time: 20 minutes

Ingredients
4 sea scallops per person; sea scallops are the large ones
4 wood skewers (soak for 10 to 20 minutes in water to prevent them from burning)
Olive oil—enough to coat the scallops and the grill
Salt and pepper
4 tablespoons butter
1 clove garlic minced
2 lemons
Pinch of cayenne pepper (optional)
1 tablespoon chopped parsley

Directions
1. Dry scallops before threading onto skewers.
2. Brush on a little olive oil and season both sides with salt and pepper.
3. In a saucepan melt butter and let cook until it starts to turn brown.
4. Remove from heat, add minced garlic, juice from ½ lemon, cayenne pepper, and half the parsley. Set aside.
5. Prepare your grill.
6. Brush grill with oil and let it get very hot.
7. Place skewers on grill. Turn after about 3 minutes; when scallops are ready to turn, they will release naturally; do not pull if they don't release on their own; wait, they will.
8. Do the same on reverse side. The scallops are cooked when on the sides you can see that they are opaque all the way through.
9. Coat scallops with garlic burnt-butter sauce and serve on skewers or take them off.
10. Add a wedge of lemon to each plate. Sprinkle remaining parsley.

SIDEBAR

SERVE WITH:

Rice or orzo (a grain made of pasta slightly larger than rice) with lots of chopped fresh parsley.

Pass the extra burnt butter sauce.

NOTES:

Works also on very hot grill pan.

VARIATIONS:

Mix your skewers with shrimp as well as scallops.
Substitute large shrimp for the scallops.

Starting a grill (page 218)
Burnt butter (page 98)

GRILLED SHRIMP

You can cook this either on your grill or on a grill pan in your oven. This recipe is simple and full of flavor. It's a great way to prepare shrimp. Every time we make it, we're surprised how good it is.

Serves: 4 (To serve 2, divide the shrimp quantity by half but keep the marinade quantities the same.)
Prep time: 10 minutes
Total time: 15 minutes
If using grill pan in your oven, preheat both to 450°

Ingredients
1 clove garlic, chopped
½ teaspoon salt
¼ teaspoon cayenne (if you prefer a bit more spice, add ½ teaspoon)
½ teaspoon paprika
2 tablespoons olive oil
1 teaspoon lemon juice
24 jumbo shrimp, remove shell except tail and devein
2 teaspoons chopped parsley or coriander

Directions
1. Mix together garlic, salt, cayenne, paprika, olive oil, and lemon juice in a bowl large enough to hold the shrimp.
2. Add shrimp and mix to coat well.
3. Refrigerate for ½ hour to 4 hours.
4. Brush grill with oil to prevent sticking.
5. Place shrimp on skewers and put on hot grill, cook 2 minutes; turn shrimp over and cook another 2 minutes. Shrimp will turn bright pink on outside and opaque on inside. Do not overcook or they will dry out.
6. For grill pan: place in upper third of oven, preheat to 450°.
7. Oil pan before adding shrimp (skewers are optional). Cook 2 minutes per side until they are bright and opaque all the way through.
8. Serve with parsley or coriander.

SIDEBAR

SERVE WITH:

NOTES:

If using wood skewers make certain to soak in water for 10 to 20 minutes before using them so they do not burn.

Marinate shrimp for 30 minutes to 4 hours to get maximum flavor.

To devein the shrimp:
Use a small sharp knife and cut down the back of peeled shrimp. Remove the back vein under running water.

STORAGE:

Refrigerate: 1 day

Risotto (page 188)
Couscous (page 184)
Rice (page 184)
Simple salad (page 144)

GRILLED FISH FILLETS

Grilling fish fillets can be scary. If it isn't done right the fish can stick to the grill and become a big mess. Here are a few basic rules to make it easier.

Serves: ½ lb per person
Prep time: 25 minutes
Total time: 35 minutes

For best results, choose a fish that is firm such as salmon, sword fish, tuna, halibut, and mahi mahi.

General rule for 1" of thickness, cook fish for a total of 8 to 10 minutes.

Ingredients
Plan on ½ lb of fish per person
High-heat oil to coat fish generously
Salt and pepper

Directions
1. Bring fish to room temperature before grilling.
2. Make certain you clean your grill well.
3. Coat the grill with oil (I use tongs to hold a paper towel with oil on it and coat the grill a few times while it is heating up.)
4. Heat the grill to high temperature.
5. Coat the fillets well with high-heat oil and season with salt and pepper.
6. Place the fillet skin side down and cook for 4 minutes until the skin separates naturally from the grill. Do not pull, wait until it does separate.
7. Flip the fish over and cook for the final 4 to 5 minutes, again until the fish separates naturally from the grill.
8. The fillets should be opaque and flaky.
9. Use 1 or 2 spatulas to remove the fish from grill. Serve.

SIDEBAR

NOTES:

If your outdoor grill isn't available, grill the fillets on your grill pan in the oven. Follow the recipe.

If you do not want to flip the fish, cover it loosely with foil until the fish is done.

High-heat oil (page 44)

GRILLING STEAK

SIDEBAR

SERVE WITH:

Grilled vegetables, and potatoes are a great accompaniment to a grilled steak.

See chart to determine meat's doneness (page 218-219)

Types of steaks to grill:
flat iron,
rib eye,
T bone,
fillet mignon,
porterhouse,
New York strip,
prime rib, skirt,
sirloin, and round steak

Serves: ¼ to ½ lb per person
Prep time: 25 minutes
Total time: 40 minutes

Ingredients
Steaks
Salt
Pepper

Directions
1. Let steak reach room temperature before cooking about 30 minutes. Generously salt and pepper both sides of the steak.
2. Check chart (page 219) to see how long to grill steak for your desired doneness.
3. Place the steak on the grill to sear until it turns golden brown and releases on its own; it will be slightly charred, about 3 minutes depending on how rare you want your steak.
4. Flip and cook until it releases from the grill on its own.

GRILLING CHICKEN
THE EASY WAY

When you cook chicken on a grill, it takes time for it to reach an internal temperature of 165°; with poultry, the meat needs to be cooked through without any sign of pink, the juices need to run clear. The best way to shorten the cooking time on the grill is to precook the chicken in the oven until it is almost done and then finish it on the grill so it has the charred flavor that makes grilling so delicious. You can season the chicken with just salt and pepper or with a marinade such as BBQ sauce. You will get more flavor if you let the marinating chicken sit refrigerated for 2 to 8 hours. Before precooking, bring the chicken to room temperature.

Serves: ½ lb per person
Prep time: 10 minutes
Total time: 75 minutes
Preheat oven to 350°

Ingredients
½ lb of chicken per person with the bone in and skin on.

Directions
1. Season the chicken pieces with salt and pepper.
2. If using a marinade, coat the chicken and if possible, refrigerate for 2 to 8 hours. Bring to room temperature before cooking.
3. Place the chicken on a sheet pan in your oven for about 30 minutes. Turning after 15 minutes.
4. If using a marinade, baste the chicken while cooking.
5. Remove from oven.
6. Liberally coat the grill with oil.
7. Place the chicken on your hot grill and cook for 10 to15 minutes; turn over and cook for 10 more minutes.
8. If using a marinade, be sure to coat chicken while it is on the grill and again when you flip chicken.
9. You want the chicken to get that wonderful flavor food gets when grilled.

SIDEBAR

ENTERTAIN:

Precooking chicken before putting it on the grill cuts the grilling time, so you can spend more time with your guests.

BBQ sauce (page 109)

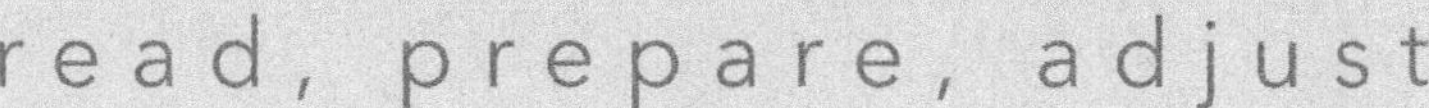

MAYONNAISE CHICKEN

SIDEBAR

STORAGE:

Refrigerate: 3 to 4 days

I'm not a big fan of mayonnaise, so to be honest, when my husband suggested we try a recipe he'd just read in the *New York Times* cooking site, I wasn't convinced. When I thought about it, mayonnaise is just egg yolks, olive oil, and a little lemon juice; there is no reason it wouldn't be good when grilled. The mayonnaise created a crispy crust on the outside while leaving the meat moist and tender.

There is one detail that you have to keep in mind. The mayonnaise causes the coals in your grill to smoke a lot. So much so that our neighbor came over to make sure our house wasn't on fire. I really appreciated his concern but when I explained that it was the mayonnaise marinade on the chicken that was causing the smoke and suggested that he try the recipe because it was really good, I'm not certain that he really believed me.

I did a little research about the use of mayonnaise as a marinade. Everyone who wrote about it loved it. You can use it as a marinade for any meat with great results.

Serves: 4
Prep time: 10 minutes
Total time: 45
Marinade: 30 minutes
Cook time: 15 minutes

Ingredients
8 small to medium chicken thighs (skin on and bone in)
½ cup of mayonnaise
Salt and pepper

Optional: 2 tablespoons of dry mustard

MAYONNAISE MARINADE continued

SIDEBAR

Directions

1. Salt and pepper both sides of the chicken.
2. Coat the chicken with the mayonnaise and let it sit for 30 minutes before grilling.
3. Place the chicken skin side up on a hot grill and cook about 15 minutes.
4. Flip the chicken skin side down and grill for another 15 minutes.
5. The chicken will be done when the juices run clear.
6. If you are cooking on a gas grill, cover the chicken as it cooks. It will cook faster—about 10 minutes per side.

GRILLED SPICY PORK
SKEWERS

This marinated grilled pork is delicious and can be served as a main dish or as appetizers. Marinate the pork for at least 5 hours for it to develop its flavor.

Serves: 8 servings
Prep time: 20 minutes
Total time: 30 minutes
Marinade: 5 to 8 hours in refrigerator
Preheat oven to 400° if using grill pan

Ingredients

2 lbs pork shoulder, skinless, boneless
½ small red onion, thinly diced
5 garlic cloves, coarsely chopped
1 tablespoon hot pepper sauce
2 tablespoons brown sugar
1 tablespoon ginger
½ cup soy sauce
3 tablespoons rice vinegar
½ teaspoon kosher salt
12 to 16 8" metal skewers or wooden skewers (Soak wood skewers in water for 15 minutes to prevent them from burning.)

Directions

1. Freeze pork until firm around edges, about 60 minutes; this makes slicing pork into thin strips easy. Remove from freezer and slice pork so it is ⅛ to ¼" inch thick. If your piece of pork is wide, slice it so strips are about 1" wide. The length doesn't matter. If the meat softens, place back into freezer to harden so you can continue to cut thin slices.
2. Meanwhile, combine onion, garlic, red pepper sauce, brown sugar, ginger, soy sauce, vinegar, and salt in a large resealable plastic bag. Place pork in the marinade being sure to coat each piece fully. Close and chill for 5 hours. Turn the bag over occasionally during the 5 hours.

SIDEBAR

SERVE WITH:

Try a nutty grain like brown rice or make a modern slaw salad.

Green and red, cabbage with carrots.

Green and red pepper and thinly sliced cilantro. Mix ½ cup rice vinegar, 2 tablespoons sugar, 2 tablespoons sesame oil, and salt. Refrigerate 2 hours before serving.

NOTES:

If using wood skewers, soak in water for at least 15 minutes to prevent burning.

You can prepare the meat and skewers ahead and cook them at the last minute.

Pre-freezing the meat in order to slice it thin is a great technique. Try it on other meats and poultry. Do not let the meat freeze more than 60 minutes or it will be too hard to slice.

Use either gloves or a dish towel to protect your fingers from the cold when slicing.

GRILLED SPICY PORK continued

3. Prepare grill for medium-high heat. Or place grill pan in the upper ⅓ of oven.
4. Remove pork from marinade and thread onto skewers.
5. Place the marinade in a pot; bring to a boil, reduce heat, and simmer until pork is ready.
6. Put the pork skewers on hot grill; letting them brown, turn over to brown all sides, about 4 minutes total.
7. Remove from the grill or grill pan.
8. Serve with the extra marinade on the side.

SIDEBAR

STORAGE:

We don't usually have any left-overs , but if you do refrigerate for 3 to 4 days.

My suggestion: use cold in a salad or sandwich.

Brown Rice (page 185)
Cole slaw (page 147)

"Cooking is about creating
something delicious
for someone else."

—Ayumi Komura

A GREAT WAY TO RELIEVE STRESS

There is nothing like a good meal at the end of the day to get rid of the stress headache of the day's tasks.

The other night I made Cornish game hens. Instead of following my usual recipe, I decided to spice them up a bit. It was so easy and the result was amazing!

All I did was pick some herbs—rosemary, sage, chives, and parsley. I added crushed garlic and inserted some of that assortment into the hen's cavities. The rest I placed under the breast skin. Sounds harder than it is. All you have to do is slide a finger between the skin and the breast meat, separating them to create a pocket on both sides of the breast bone. That's where I insert the herbs, the crushed garlic, and salt and pepper.

Once the skin is crispy, the meat is cooked through, and when you take a bite to taste all that infused flavor, you'll be delighted.

Best of all, the day's stress is now replaced by the pleasure of a good meal—that was super easy.

Try this technique with roast chicken; you'll get the same great results.

ROASTING

Dry heat is used to caramelize the outside while the inside stays moist.

ABOUT ROASTING

ABOUT ROASTING

Creates a crispy exterior while the center stays moist and succulent.

Roasting is done using dry hot heat that surrounds the food as it cooks, browning the outside of your food while the inside stays moist and juicy. The benefit of this method is that it creates a lot of flavor. Sauces are the perfect complement to roasted foods. They give you the ability to turn a simple dish into something really special.

Roasting works well with the following ingredients:

beef
chicken
lamb
pork
fish
shellfish
vegetables

Directions

1. Preheat oven to 350°.
2. Bring your food to room temperature and season with salt, pepper, and any spices you choose.
3. Place in a roasting pan and in center of preheated oven.
4. Cook 20 minutes per pound plus 20 minutes. If you are roasting vegetables, roast until they are cooked through and evenly browned, turning as they cook.
5. For chicken, meat thermometer should reach 180° to 190° at thickest part of thigh without touching bone. The juices must be clear.
6. If you are making gravy from the pan drippings, adjust flavors and thicken if necessary.

ROASTING TEMPERATURES Use these temperatures as a guide		
Beef	140°	Rare
	160°	Medium
	170°	Well
Rump Roast	150° to 170°	
Veal	170°	
Lamb	140°	Rare
	160°	Medium
	170°	Well
Poultry	180° to 190°	Done

Chicken is safe to eat at 165° but I don't think it is fully cooked until no pink is left and that only happens at 180° to 190°. That is the temperature I cook my poultry at.

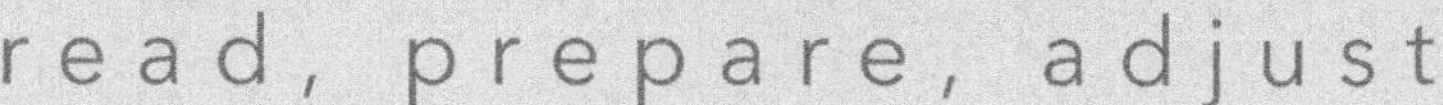

CORNISH GAME HENS

Cornish game hens are produced from a cross between two breeds of chickens: the Cornish and White Plymouth Rock. The offspring are little chickens that weigh about two pounds each and are low in fat. Because of their size, they cook faster than regular chickens. The skin gets crispy while the meat stays moist. They are a great alternative to the larger roasting chickens.

Serves: 4
Prep time: 20 minutes
Cook time: 1 hour
Total time: 1 hour and 20 minutes
Preheat oven to 400°

Ingredients

2 Cornish game hens—The hens are usually sold in a package of two. I plan on ½ a hen per person but if you have big eaters, serve 1 per person.
3 tablespoons melted butter
1 lemon, sliced
3 sprigs rosemary
2 cloves garlic, crushed
Olive oil, enough to coat bottom of the pan
2 medium potatoes, sliced into ¼" rounds
Salt and pepper

Directions

1. Using a brush, coat skin with melted butter, then sprinkle with salt and pepper.
2. Place lemon slices, garlic, and 1 sprig of rosemary into cavity of each hen.
3. Coat potatoes with olive oil and season with salt and pepper. Place on bottom of roasting pan, adding last sprig of rosemary on the bottom of the roasting pan. Place hens on top.
4. Put in center of oven for 50 minutes to 1 hour. You want the

SIDEBAR

SERVE WITH:

Roasted vegetables
Roasted potatoes

STORAGE:

Refrigerate: 4 to 5 days
Freeze: 3 months

ENTERTAIN:

This is a good dish to make for guests.

Gravy (page 110)
See story (page 232) for another way to add flavor to the hens
Roasted vegetables page 137
Roasted potatoes page 138

CORNISH GAME HENS continued

internal temperature to at least reach 165° but I prefer between 180° to 190° so the juices are clear and the meat by the bone is no longer pink.

5. If skin isn't brown or crispy raise temperature to 500° for the last few minutes of roasting.
6. To crisp the bottom of the hens, turn them over and brown for last 10 to 15 minutes of cooking.
7. While you make the gravy, tent bird with foil and rest for 10 minutes to let juices redistribute before carving and serving.

SIDEBAR

ROAST CHICKEN
MY GO-TO RECIPE

Mastering a good roast chicken is a must for cooking basics. If you serve a perfectly roasted chicken to guests, I assure you they'll be thrilled. If at first you don't succeed, try again. You won't regret taking the time to master this recipe.

Serves: 4
Prep time: 15 minutes
Total time: 1 hour 45 minutes
Preheat oven to 450°

I like to use a roasting pan that is slightly larger than the chicken. My preference is a cast-iron skillet because it does a better job browning the chicken than other pans. If you want to add vegetables, your pan will need to be large enough to include them.

Ingredients
3 to 4 lbs chicken. Use the best quality chicken you can buy.
Olive oil, enough to coat the chicken
Salt and pepper
1 lemon, sliced
3 sprigs of thyme
3 sprigs rosemary
2 large yellow onions, peeled and cut into ½" thick rings
Optional: add carrots, fennel, and potatoes into 2" chunks
½ cup melted butter
½ teaspoon dried thyme
3 cloves crushed garlic
⅓ cup white wine
1 tablespoon lemon juice

Directions:
1. Remove gizzards from the chicken's cavity and make broth (page 241).
2. Pat the chicken dry.

SIDEBAR

NOTES:

Do not wash the chicken; current wisdom says washing the chicken spreads more bacteria than it removes.

The biggest mistake people make is to undercook their chicken. If there is any sign of pink, it isn't cooked enough.

STORAGE:

Refrigerate: 4 to 5 days
Freeze: 3 months
Any leftover chicken can be shredded, frozen, and used at a later time for chicken pot pie (page 162) or chicken noodle soup (page 274).

ENTERTAIN:

Who doesn't like a good roast chicken for dinner?

Gravy (page 110)
Roasted root vegetables (page 137)
Roasted potatoes (page 138)

ROAST CHICKEN continued

3. Rub with olive oil and season with salt and pepper inside and out. Add a few slices of lemon, a sprig of thyme and rosemary into cavity.
4. Lay the onion slices and the other sprigs of thyme and rosemary on the bottom of the roasting pan; place the chicken, breast side up, on top.
5. Add any other vegetables you want to use around the chicken.
6. Place chicken in lower third of preheated oven, bake for 20 minutes.
7. Reduce heat to 350° and finish cooking, 1hour and 10 minutes.
8. If the skin is getting too brown, cover it with foil.
9. Melt the butter, add salt and pepper, crushed garlic, dried thyme, lemon, and white wine, simmer on very low heat for about 5 minutes.
10. For the last 15 minutes of cooking, brush the marinade on the chicken. If there is any leftover, pour it over the vegetables and finish cooking.
11. Make certain that the chicken is cooked through. With a knife, pierce the skin between the leg and thigh to make certain juices run clear and joint moves freely.
12. Use an instant meat thermometer; at thickest part, it should reach at least 165° but preferably 180° to 190° so it cooked through.
13. Remove the chicken to a carving board with a well, or a serving plate to catch the juices. Tent the chicken with aluminum foil and let rest 20 minutes before cutting.
14. Remove all the vegetables from the pan and set aside.
15. Reserve any juices to make your gravy.

SIDEBAR

NOTES:

To make chicken broth:
Place gizzards, 1 onion, 1 carrot cut in half, bay leaf, thyme, and parsley into pot. Add 4 cups water or broth; bring to a boil and let it simmer until it reduces by half. Strain and discard all solids.
Keep the broth on low heat until you are ready to use it.
If necessary, add low-salt chicken bouillon to punch up the flavor. You want the resulting broth to be full of flavor but not salty.

VARIATIONS:

For another way to season chicken see story (page 232)

ROAST BEEF

SIDEBAR

SERVE WITH:

Roast meats are delicious served with potatoes, either
mashed (page 133)
scalloped (page 125)
roasted (page 138)

NOTES:

If you don't have a V shape rack. You can raise the meat off the bottom of the pan with chunks of vegetables.

VARIATIONS:

Serve with cream sauce

On medium heat add 1 tablespoon butter, add 2 cloves minced garlic, ½ teaspoon sage

Deglaze pan add ½ cup wine reduce by half

Add ½ cup chicken broth evaporate by half

Whisk in crème fraiche

Add parsley, serve

If you want add mushrooms

Slice mushrooms and sauté when brown add to cream sauce.

Roasts are a great way to cook meat. The advantage is that it is the meat that is the main focus, as opposed to stews when the meat becomes part of the other ingredients. I like using a V-shaped roasting rack to roast meats so the hot air can travel around the meat, roasting it on all sides.
Best cuts of beef for roast beef. rib eye, sirloin, tenderloin, beef boneless chuck, and Chateaubriand.

Serves: 4 to 6
Prep time: 15 minutes
Total time: 1 hour 45 minutes
Preheat oven to 450°

Ingredients
3 to 3 ½ lb round roast
4 cloves garlic
1 tablespoon rosemary
1 tablespoon thyme
½ teaspoon cayenne pepper
2 teaspoons kosher salt
1 teaspoon pepper
2 tablespoons olive oil

Directions
1. Bring the meat to room temperature.
2. Crush garlic, rosemary, thyme, cayenne, salt, and pepper.
3. Slowly add oil to make a paste.
4. Cover the roast with the paste.
5. Place roast in a V-shaped roasting rack in a roasting pan in the oven for 20 minutes.
6. Lower the temperature to 325° and continue cooking 20 minute per pound. For medium, the internal temperature should be 145°.
7. Remove from oven, tent with foil, and let rest for 20 minutes. Serve.

ROAST LAMB

When I was growing up, my mother always made roast lamb with baby lima beans. The beans would cook on the bottom of the pan absorbing all the juices from the lamb. It is delicious and simple to make.

SIDEBAR

Serves: 4 to 6
Prep time: 15 minutes
Total time: 1 hour 25 minutes
Preheat oven to 375°

Ingredients
3½ to 4 lbs leg of lamb, bone removed
6 cloves garlic
2 tablespoon rosemary
2 teaspoons kosher salt
1 teaspoon pepper
2 tablespoons olive oil
1 16-oz container of frozen baby lima beans

Directions
1. Bring the lamb to room temperature.
2. Create a paste with chopped garlic, rosemary, salt, and pepper. Add olive oil, blend well to create thick paste.
3. Cover the entire lamb with garlic paste mixture.
4. Pour the lima beans into the bottom of roasting pan, add 1 cup of water.
5. Place the lamb on top of beans and place in the middle of oven.
6. Cook for 30 minutes. Open the oven and stir the beans making sure to coat with the sauce. Return to oven to continue cooking another 30 minutes.
7. Using an instant-read thermometer, check temperature
   Rare 140°
   Medium 160°
   Medium well 170°
8. Let rest, covered for 15 minutes and slice.
9. Place the lima beans and any sauce on serving plate with the sliced lamb on top.

Garlic paste (page 50)

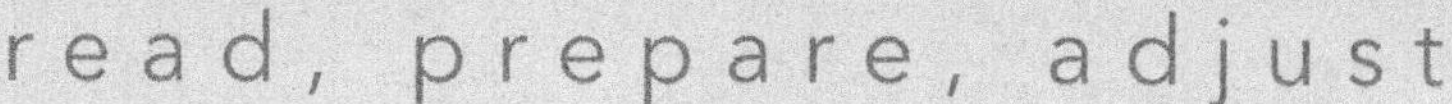

PORK TENDERLOIN

Pork tenderloin is a lean meat that is easy to cook. Adding a sauce to finish the tenderloin adds flavor and moisture to the meat. I prefer roasting the tenderloin using a cast-iron pan. The pan is heavy and maintains the heat, making it perfect for braising and oven roasting.

Serves: 3
Prep time: 8 minutes
Total time: 33 minutes
Preheat oven to 425°

Ingredients
1 one-lb pork tenderloin
Salt and pepper
4 garlic cloves, crushed
Herbs of your choice; parsley, rosemary, sage, and thyme go well with pork.

Directions
1. With a towel, pat dry the room-temperature tenderloin.
2. Season entire meat with salt and pepper.
3. On stovetop, heat an ovenproof heavy bottom frying pan—or cast-iron skillet.
4. When pan is hot, add 1 tablespoon high-temperature oil.
5. Add tenderloin, cook about 2 to 4 minutes per side; let meat naturally release from pan before turning. Brown on each side.
6. Add your combination of dried herbs and crushed garlic to pan and place in oven.
7. Cook for about 15 minutes.
8. The pork is done when internal temperature is 145°.
9. Carefully remove pan from oven, remembering that it is hot.
10. Place meat on a plate, tent with foil to rest for 5 to 10 minutes.
11. On your stovetop, deglaze pan with broth and follow directions to make a sauce of your choice.

SIDEBAR

SERVE WITH:

Roasted vegetables
Roasted potatoes

STORAGE:

Refrigerate: 4 to 5 days
Freeze: 3 months

VARIATIONS:

Serve with cream sauce

On medium heat add 1 tablespoon butter, add 2 cloves minced garlic, ½ teaspoon sage

Deglaze pan add ½ cup wine reduce by half

Add ½ cup chicken broth evaporate by half

Whisk in crème fraiche

Add parsley, serve

If you want add mushrooms

Slice mushrooms and sauté when brown add to cream sauce.

Gravy (page 110)
Deglaze (page 36)
Roasted vegetables (page 137)
Roasted potatoes (page 138)

JOSÉ'S ROAST PORK

José, my father-in-law, lived with us at the end of his life. He loved food and often told me stories about what a great cook his mama was, as he described the foods of his youth. Unfortunately, I didn't know how to cook the comfort foods he craved; I made the foods I knew—quiche, coq au vin—they were good, but not what he wanted, and this was a bone of contention between us.

When he still could, he would go to the grocery store and buy the ingredients he needed to show me how to make his favorite recipes. Some were delicious and others I could have skipped; oxtail soup isn't my favorite but seeing the delight on his face made it worth it.

His stories helped me understand the importance food plays in bringing back family memories and in our comfort level. Each recipe he made was accompanied by a story, and as he told me the details, his eyes would sparkle. Now, when I make one of his recipes, I think of him. I'm grateful that he took the time to share.

Serves: 6 to 8
Prep time: 30 minutes—optional: let marinate for 1 hour
Total time: 1 hour 40 minutes
Preheat oven to 350° if using a grill pan

The flavor of this marinade is the perfect complement to pork.

Ingredients
3 lb pork loin
8 large garlic cloves
1 tablespoon salt (kosher)
1 teaspoon ground pepper, fine
3 tablespoons olive oil
Optional: kitchen twine

Directions

1. I use a wood mortar and pestle to make the paste. Add garlic

SIDEBAR

STORAGE:

Refrigerate: 4 to 5 days
Freeze: 3 months

SERVE WITH:

Roasted vegetables
Roasted potatoes

Roasted vegetables (page 137)
Roasted potatoes (page 138)
Garlic Paste (page 50)

JOSÉ'S ROAST PORK continued

SIDEBAR

NOTES:

Making a piping bag is an easy way to fill the slits you made in the pork: Put the paste into a small re-sealable bag.
Press the garlic paste to the bottom corner of the bag to create a piping bag. Cut the small tip off the point and use that to insert into the slits and squeeze the paste into them.
This works better than trying to slide the paste in with a knife or spoon.

to bowl and pound with the pestle to crush. You can also do this in a small food processor or on a chopping board with the flat part of a knife.

2. Add some salt and continue pounding and crushing the garlic until it starts to break down, add rest of salt and pepper and continue to mix until it become a paste.
3. With mixture in a bowl, slowly add olive oil, stirring until it emulsifies and becomes a thick paste.
4. If you can, unfold pork and spread garlic paste on inside and roll it back up using kitchen twine to tie meat back together.
5. If your pork is in one piece, take a knife and poke slits about 2" deep all over the pork loin and fill with the garlic mixture. (see sidebar)
6. Coat outside with remaining marinade.
7. Optional: if you have time, roll the pork in a large sheet of plastic wrap and twist each end. Refrigerate for an hour or more before cooking. Unwrap the plastic and let pork warm to room temperature.
8. Cook tenderloin on a grill pan or sheet pan in oven, turn frequently to brown the entire piece of meat.
9. Continue cooking until a meat thermometer inserted into the center reads 160°, about 1 hour. Remove from heat and tent with aluminum foil and let stand 5 to 10 minutes before slicing.

SLOW-ROASTED FISH

I use cod for this recipe, but you could use salmon, halibut, or flounder to get the same great results.

Serves: 4
Prep time: 20 minutes
Total time: 45 minutes
Preheat oven to 350°

Ingredients
2 lbs cod fillet; I plan on ½ pound per person.
Olive oil, enough to coat the fish and the pan
Salt and pepper

Directions
1. Brush olive oil on both sides of the fillets.
2. Season with salt and pepper on both sides.
3. Oil the baking pan and place the fish, skin side down, on pan.
4. If the fillets are thin at the ends, fold them under. Your goal is to even out the thickness of the fillets so they cook uniformly.
5. Cook about 20 minutes. When the fish is opaque and flakes, it is done.

SIDEBAR

STORAGE:

Refrigerate: 2 days

Sauce meunière (page 97)
Pan-sautéed spinach (page 131)

"Cooking demands attention, patience, and above all, a respect for the gifts of the earth. It is a form of worship, a way of giving thanks."

—Judith B. Jones

SAUTÉING

A quick and easy way to cook.

ABOUT SAUTÉING

ABOUT SAUTÉING

Sauter means to jump in French.
Food jumps in a very hot pan.

Sautéing is a quick and easy way of cooking food using a small amount of fat in a large sauté pan over high heat. This method creates a lot of flavor without taking a lot of time. It works equally well with vegetables, meats, and fish.

This method works best with thin cuts that have a large amount of exposed surface that allows them to cook quickly, resulting in moist, flavorful food. To finish off your sauté, deglaze the pan to create your sauce.

Directions

1. Heat sauté pan to high heat.
2. Add oil with high smoking point (canola, grapeseed, safflower). Let it get hot.
3. Place food in your pan.
4. Let it sear without touching for several minutes. Once food naturally pulls away from pan, it is ready to be flipped. Repeat on reverse.
5. Food cooks quickly so check for doneness to make certain you do not overcook your food.
6. Deglaze your pan with broth and finish off by whisking in a little butter and herbs to make your sauce.
   Serve.

Deglaze (page 36)
High-heat oil (page 44)

QUICK BEEF SAUTÉ
WITH ONIONS & ASPARAGUS

This quick beef sauté can be done with different vegetables. For example, mushrooms and broccoli or carrots and peppers. You can sauté the beef with salt and pepper and serve it with seared spinach.

Serves: 3
Prep time: 40 minutes
Total time: 40 minutes

Ingredients
1 lb thinly sliced beef round or sirloin steak
High-heat oil
2 cloves garlic, minced
Salt and pepper to taste
½ large onion, sliced into rings
6 asparagus stalks, ends removed and cut into 1½" pieces
½ cup low-salt beef broth
2 teaspoons soy sauce
1 tablespoon corn starch, dissolved in 2 tablespoons of water, let the cornstarch fully absorb before stirring the mixture.

Directions
1. Before slicing beef, place it in freezer for about 60 minutes.
2. Once semi frozen, you can easily slice beef into thin slices.
3. Season with salt and pepper to taste.
4. Heat a large skillet over high heat.
5. Add enough oil to coat bottom of pan. When pan is very hot, add half beef.
6. Cook until no longer red. Remove from pan and set aside; cook remaining beef, set aside.
7. If necessary add oil; cook onions until transparent and set aside.
8. Add asparagus; cook until tender, remove from pan.
9. Reheat pan, add oil if needed. Add garlic and ginger and let flavor develop, 1 minute.
10. Deglaze pan with broth: add soy sauce and cornstarch mixture. Let thicken, then return ingredients to pan, stir to coat.

SIDEBAR

STORAGE:

Refrigerate: 2 days

NOTES:

Serve with white rice

This is a flexible recipe; use your imagination and what you have in your refrigerator.

Deglaze (page 36)
Pre-Freeze meat (page 228)

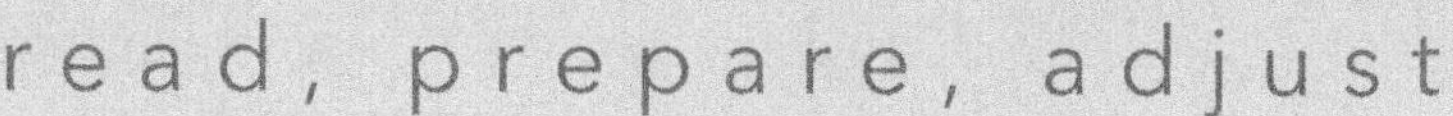

CHICKEN BREASTS
SAUTÉED

This is a quick weeknight dinner that we depend on because it's easy, tasty, flexible, and light.

Serves: 4
Prep time: 20 minutes
Total time: 20 minutes

Ingredients
Boneless skinless chicken breast; cut each in half and serve 1 or 2 per person, depending on size
2 to 3 tablespoons high-temperature oil
Salt and pepper
1 cup low-salt chicken broth, possibly more
½ cup white wine
1 clove garlic or 1 shallot, diced thin
¼ cup chopped parsley
2 tablespoons butter
1 lemon squeeze

Directions
1. Flatten and tenderize the chicken breasts by placing each breast between plastic wrap and pound it with a mallet or rolling pin. You want the slices to be ½" thick to ensure they cook quickly and evenly.
2. Sprinkle with salt and pepper.
3. In a large sauté pan, heat the oil on medium-high heat.
4. Add chicken; cook until meat separates naturally from pan. Do not pull it off; it needs to be fully browned and it will easily lift off. Flip breast and cook, as above.
5. Test for doneness; use fork to pierce chicken to see if juices run clear.
6. Remove chicken from pan, cover, and keep warm.
7. Deglaze pan, add ¼ cup broth to hot pan. Scrape bottom to dislodge the crispy bits.

SIDEBAR

VARIATIONS:

Besides using, skinless chicken breast try veal scaloppini, thin pork chops or fish fillet. This method is the same for veal, thin boneless pork chops, or fish fillets.

When cooking fish fillets, select thin fillets. Do not pound the fillets or they will fall apart.

If you don't want to make a sauce, simply add a little butter to the pan, and sprinkle with chopped fresh parsley and a squeeze of lemon.

Deglaze (page 36)

CHICKEN BREASTS SAUTÉED continued

8. Add aromatics like shallots, garlic, herbs, salt, and pepper plus ¼ cup white wine. Simmer to release flavors. You want to have about ¾ of a cup of sauce. Taste and adjust seasonings.
9. You can finish the sauce by adding a pat or two of butter and mixing it in.
10. Serve by spooning the sauce over the chicken breast, adding a pinch of parsley and squeezing some lemon over the chicken before serving. (The lemon brightens the flavor perfectly.)

SIDEBAR

DON'T FORGET!

Recipes are just suggestions. Learn from them and let yourself be inventive and creative.

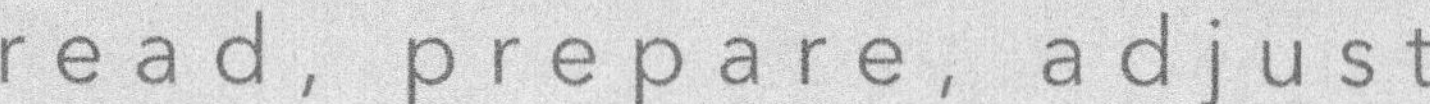

VEAL SCALOPPINI

SIDEBAR

Veal that is thinly sliced, and cooked quickly will take on the flavor of the aromatics you choose to use.

Serves: 4
Prep time: 25 minutes
Total Time: 25 minutes

Ingredients
1¼ lbs veal cutlets
Salt and pepper
1 tablespoon olive oil plus more if needed
6 tablespoons butter
½ cup white wine
1 teaspoon lemon juice
1 tablespoon capers
1 tablespoon chopped parsley

Directions
1. Pound the veal cutlets to get them very thin, ¼". Place the veal cutlet between plastic wrap or parchment paper and pound it with a meat mallet or a heavy frying pan. Reverse and pound on the reverse side.
2. Salt and pepper both sides of the veal.
3. In a sauté pan, heat 1 tablespoon oil and 1 tablespoon butter to medium-high heat.
4. Sauté veal in batches so pan stays hot and meat is able to brown. Cook about 2 minutes per side. If needed, add oil between batches. Set meat aside on a platter, cover with foil.
5. Add wine to deglaze the pan. Scrape the bottom to separate all the crispy bits.
6. Add butter, letting it melt; lower the heat to simmer, and let the butter brown.
7. Add lemon juice and capers and pour over the veal.
8. Sprinkle with parsley and serve.

Deglazing (page 36)

SAUTÉED FISH FILLETS

Sautéing fish fillets sounds harder than it is. If you follow a few basic steps you'll see it isn't hard. Flounder, halibut, salmon, and striped bass are all good selections.

Serves: 4
Prep time: 20 minutes
Total Time: 35 minutes

Ingredients
4 fish fillets
Salt
1½ lemons
1 tablespoon olive oil
6 tablespoons butter
1 tablespoon chopped parsley

Directions
1. If your fillets have skin, use a sharp knife to slice small cuts into the skin 1" apart. (This helps prevent the fillets from curling.)
2. Salt both sides of the fillets, let sit 10 minutes.
3. Heat the pan to medium-high heat. Once hot, add the oil until it is shiny.
4. Add the fillet, skin side down. Reduce heat, let it cook without turning.
5. When the flesh is almost opaque, remove the fillets from the pan and set aside.
6. Add the butter to the pan and let it cook until it turns brown.
7. Add the fillets back into the pan, skin side up.
8. With a spoon, pour the butter over the fillets.
9. Plate the fillets, skin side down, and squeeze a little lemon juice on top and sprinkle parsley. Serve with 1 wedge of lemon.

SIDEBAR

SERVE WITH:

Fish fillets are best eaten fresh. I buy just enough for my needs. Salmon, on the other hand, is good served cold. I like making more than I need so I have leftovers for lunch.

SHRIMP SCAMPI
MARK'S

This is a quick and easy shrimp dish. It is a classic and is always great to eat when you want a quick meal during the week. It's delicious served with white rice or pasta.

Serves: 2
Prep time: 25 minutes
Total time: 25 minutes

Ingredients
6 to 8 medium shrimp per person, 6 large per person
½ cup butter, divided
5 cloves garlic, minced
Salt and pepper to taste
¼ cup white wine
1 tablespoon lemon juice
2 tablespoons chopped parsley
Lemon wedge per person

Directions
1. Shell and devein shrimp if necessary.
2. In a large sauté pan, heat ½ of the butter, add ½ the garlic and the shrimp. Cook until the shrimp turns pink.
3. Turn over and cook until it is pink and no longer transparent in the center. (5 to 6 minutes)
4. Season with salt and pepper.
5. Remove shrimp and set aside.
6. Add the extra butter to the pan, melt, add the remaining garlic, white wine, lemon juice, and parsley, and simmer for 5 minutes.
7. Put the shrimp back into the pan and coat with the sauce.
8. Serve with a wedge of lemon.

SIDEBAR

STORAGE:

Refrigerate: 2 days

How to devein shrimp (page 222)

LEMON SCALLOPS

Simple, easy, and tasty. That describes this dish perfectly.

Serves: 4
Prep time: 5 minutes
Total time: 10 minutes

Ingredients
1 tablespoon butter
1 teaspoon olive oil
6 large sea scallops per person, (there are usually 20 to 30 per lb)
Salt and pepper
Lemon butter sauce
2 tablespoons butter
3 cloves garlic, minced
2 tablespoons lemon (1 lemon)
Salt and pepper
2 tablespoons chopped parsley

Directions
1. Dry the scallops with a towel.
2. Season with salt and pepper.
3. Melt butter and oil in a large skillet on medium-high heat.
4. Add scallops to skillet without crowding. Work in batches. Let scallops brown without turning over. You'll see scallops start to become opaque. When they naturally release, turn over and continue cooking until brown and opaque.
5. Set aside and keep warm.
6. Melt butter to make sauce, add garlic, cook 1 minute, stirring as garlic gets aromatic. Add lemon juice (lemon is strong so add it in slowly) and salt and pepper.
7. Put scallops back into skillet and stir to coat with sauce.
8. Place in a serving bowl, add the parsley and serve.

SIDEBAR

SERVE WITH:

Simple salad
Rice, orzo, or couscous

STORAGE:

Refrigerate: 2 days

NOTES:

Look for sea scallops; they are the large ones. The dry-packed scallops are the preferable scallops to buy since they do not contain additives or extra water to increase their purchase weight.

TACOS

I love making tacos at home. But I don't like the flavor packets that are full of chemicals. I came up with a recipe that leaves out all the chemicals. When I make up the spice mixture, I make up a large batch and store it in a sealed jar; that way it is ready when I need it. I replace the beef with turkey meat. The result is lighter and it absorbs the flavor of the seasonings better. Adding sweet or spicy turkey sausage is a great addition to the overall flavor.

Serves: 4
Prep time: 20 minutes
Total time: 45 minutes

Ingredients

1 lb turkey meat
1 lb turkey sausage, casing removed
3 or more tablespoons of the spice mixture
1 cup water
Low-salt chicken bouillon, the equivalent of 2 cubes
1 cup salsa (I like a thick and chunky medium salsa.)
1 cup cheddar cheese, shredded
8 hard taco shells or soft tortillas or both
1 cup raw white rice
1 can of black beans
Follow the chart to make the spice

Directions

1. Mix the ground turkey with the sausage in sauté pan and cook through.
2. Add 3 tablespoons of taco spice mix into the meat.
3. Add 1 cup water and simmer on medium heat.
4. Add low-salt chicken bouillon plus 1 cup of salsa.
5. Let simmer for 20 minutes, taste, add more spice mix if needed and continue simmering until the flavors meld together and the liquid has almost evaporated.

SIDEBAR

SERVE WITH:

As a salad
Serve over lettuce greens as a salad.
Add these condiments:
Yogurt or sour cream
Guacamole
Avocado
Chopped tomatoes
Chopped lettuce
Salsa sauce
Cilantro
Leftovers are great.
To increase the amount you make, double for 8.

NOTES:

Spicy turkey sausage (It isn't spicy just full of flavor.)

Do not use pre-shredded cheddar; it has a coating that prevents it from melting properly.

Remove sausage casing (page 164)
Rice (page 184)

TACOS continued

6. While the meat mixture simmers:
7. Cook the rice.
8. Heat black beans over low heat in a pot.
9. Heat soft tortilla and/or hard shells.
10. Using either type shell, layer the rice, meat, black beans, taco sauce and top with cheddar cheese.
    Serve.

TACO SEASONING			
	SERVINGS		
INGREDIENTS	1 TO 2	3 TO 4	8 TO 10
oregano	2 tablespoons	½ cup	1 cup
chilli powder	2 tablespoons	½ cup	1 cup
cumin	1 tablespoon	¼ cup	½ cup
paprika	1 tablespoon	¼ cup	½ cup
cayenne *	½ teaspoon	2 teaspoons	4 teaspoons
fennel seeds	1 teaspoon	4 teaspoons	2½ tablespoons

* Cayenne is a spicy ingredient: this mix has a nice bite, but if you don't like a lot of spice either omit the cayenne or reduce the quantity by half or more.

SIDEBAR

STORAGE:

Refrigerate: 5 to 6 days

Once seasoned and cooked, the meat can be frozen 4 to 6 months.

Rice page 185

"The greatest dishes are
very simple."

—Auguste Escoffier

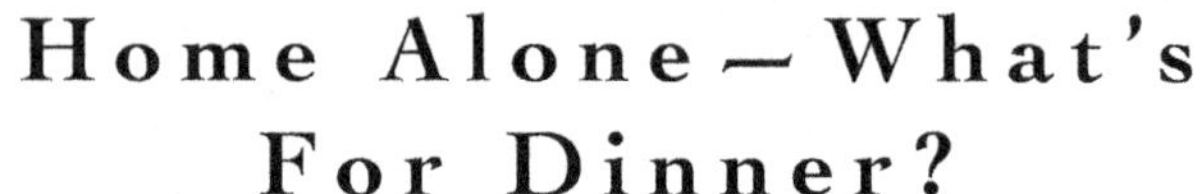

Home Alone—What's For Dinner?

It's a good question, but the real question is what kind of dinner do you plan to have?

Standing in front of an open refrigerator nibbling on leftovers? Or maybe standing over the sink eating that leftover chicken leg? I've done a lot of nibbling to satisfy my hunger without taking the time to have a meal. After all, no one is home so I don't really need to make a big production out of dinner. But I've found that it almost always leaves me feeling unfulfilled. Technically I'm full, I've squelched my hunger, but I find myself longing for something I find hard to identify.

The rest of the evening, I wander back to the kitchen looking for that illusive thing that's still missing. Maybe something sweet. Then a bit later, something salty to balance out the sweet. The point is no matter what I eat it doesn't satisfy that yearning.

It took a while for me to discover that a meal isn't just putting food into my mouth to satisfy my hunger. It is a ritual that feeds my entire being.

If I don't take the time or make an effort to prepare and serve myself a meal, I just nibble to get it over with, ignoring my emotional being who also needs to be nourished. Meal time is an opportunity to feed all of me. It is a gift we can give ourselves.

Ask yourself:
How do you welcome guests when you invite them to your home to share a meal? That is the same way you should treat yourself.

Set the table and serve yourself a meal. It doesn't have to be elaborate or complicated; it can even be Chinese food that you've ordered in. What it can't be is eaten out of the package, standing up or while you are doing something else.

I've discovered that taking the time to be as good to myself as I am to my family and friends fills me with love that nourishes my soul at the same time the food is feeding my body. When I'm done, I'm full, no longer looking for that illusive thing that was previously missing.

The bottom line: be good to yourself and eat well; you deserve it.

SOUPS

A liquid that we eat instead of drink.

ABOUT SOUPS

A liquid that we eat instead of drink.

Soup is defined as a liquid food, that can be eaten hot, at room temperature, or cold. There are three different types of soups: clear soups, thick soups, and puréed soups.

Cooking a combination of ingredients such as vegetables, meat, poultry, fish, legumes, grains, and seasonings with a liquid—usually water or broth—for either a short amount of time or many hours until the ingredients meld together and becomes a soup.

One of great things about soups is that they are flexible. It's a perfect way to use leftovers or to finish up what's left in your refrigerator to make another delicious meal.

Directions

1. To build flavor, cook aromatics such as onion, garlic, celery, and carrots in oil until they start to brown and soften. Browning caramelizes sugars in food and adds lots of flavor.
2. Add your selection of herbs and spices and cook for a few minutes to release their flavors.
3. Add other ingredients: vegetables, meat, and grain if you are using them. Add enough water or broth to cover by a few inches.
4. Cook at a simmer until all ingredients are cooked through. That can vary from minutes to hours.
5. If you are only using vegetables, you can emulsify the ingredients to create a purée, or make a creamed soup by adding a touch of heavy cream.
   Serve.

CREAM OF VEGETABLE SOUP

This recipe uses zucchini as the main vegetable but it works just as well with other vegetables. Try: broccoli, carrots, spinach, asparagus, onion, mushrooms, butternut squash, pumpkin, red peppers, or any combination of those. Changing the vegetables will alter the soup's flavor providing you an opportunity to adjust the seasonings. Taste your result and see if it needs anything to bring it to life. This is the fun part of cooking. The more you do, the more comfortable you will be experimenting.

Serves: 6
Prep time: 15 minutes
Total time: 50 minutes

Ingredients
1 medium onion, diced
1 tablespoon oil and 1 tablespoon butter
½ teaspoon salt
4 medium zucchini—6 cups cut in half and sliced
2 large carrots peeled and diced (2 cups)
Optional: 1 medium-size potato, peeled and diced
3 to 4 cups vegetable broth (or chicken broth)
Salt and pepper
Low-salt bouillon, equivalent of 2 to 3 cubes of chicken or vegetable
1 tablespoon chopped parsley

Directions
1. Heat butter and oil in a large stockpot, add onions, sauté over medium heat, and cook until they are translucent, about for 6 to 8 minutes.
2. Add zucchini, carrots potato (if you are using it), stock, salt, and pepper.
3. Bring to a boil, lower heat and simmer for 30 minutes until ingredients are very soft.
4. Use an immersion blender or kitchen blender to purée the soup until it is completely smooth.
5. Add cream and season to taste.
6. Serve hot, at room temperature, or cold.
7. Garnish with chopped parsley and serve.

SIDEBAR

SERVE WITH:

Place toasted and buttered slices of baguette in the center of the bowl and sprinkle with Gruyere cheese and chopped parsley.

STORAGE:
Refrigerate: 5 days
Freeze: 4 months

NOTES:

Optional additions to the soup:
½ cup heavy cream
Dash of nutmeg
Grated Gruyere cheese
Toasted sliced French bread

DID YOU KNOW?

There are an endless number of ingredients that you can combine to make a soup.

That's what makes soups so much fun.

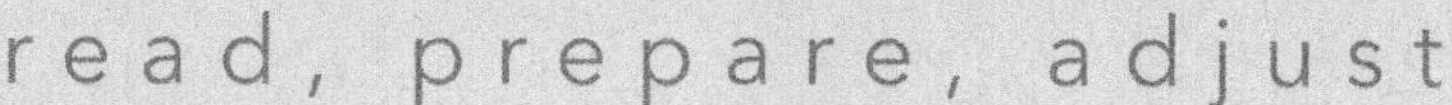

POTAGE BONNE FEMME

This is the classic French vegetable soup. Every family has their own slightly different version of this soup. Traditionally, a French dinner at home starts with a bowl of vegetable soup like this one. As with all soups, this one is especially flexible.

Serves: 6
Prep time: 10 minutes
Total time: 1 hour

Ingredients
6 tablespoons butter
1 tablespoon oil
2 cups carrots, chopped
2 cups leeks, cleaned and chopped
3½ cups diced potatoes (russet)
3 cloves garlic, diced
7 cups of water
Salt and pepper
1 bay leaf
¼ to ½ cup of heavy cream

Directions
1. Peel and chop vegetables.
2. Bring the water to a boil.
3. In a 4-quart saucepan, melt half the butter with 1 tablespoon of oil. Cook vegetables until soft but not browned.
4. Pour the boiling water into the saucepan.
5. Add the bay leaves.
6. Cook for 45 minutes, making certain all vegetables are tender.
7. Remove the bay leaf.
8. Emulsify the soup, using either a blender or an immersion blender.
9. When the soup is creamy, place it back in the pot and add the remaining butter and the cream to finish the soup.
   Serve hot.

SIDEBAR

NOTES:

Dinners in France are generally the lighter meal; at least they use to be. Soup is traditionally served as a starter and this creamy vegetable soup is often on the menu. The smell of this soup floods me with memories of family dinners.

Every family has their own version of this soup. The recipe is passed down from one generation to the next.

STORAGE:

Refrigerate: 4 to 5 days
Freeze: 4 to 5 months

LEEK AND POTATO SOUP

Also known as soupe aux poireaux pomme de terre. This soup is delicious served either hot, at room temperature, or cold. Personally, I like it any way it is served—especially with a good loaf of bread. This recipe is explained using both your stovetop and pressure cooker.

Serves: 6
Prep time: 15 minutes
Total time with a pressure cooker: 30 minutes
Total time using a stovetop: 45 minutes

Ingredients
4 large leeks—cut off the green tops and discard
4 potatoes, peeled and diced (keep the quantity of potato and leeks equal)
3 cups chicken broth
3 low-salt chicken bouillon cubes
½ cup heavy cream

Directions

1. Slice the white part of the leek in half lengthwise and then slice into ½" pieces and wash. Leeks can have lots of dirt inside that you want to remove before cooking.
2. Pressure cooker instructions: place leeks, potatoes, and 3 cups of water or chicken broth into a pressure cooker, bring temperature up to medium, and let it cook for 15 minutes.
3. Stovetop instructions: place all the ingredients into a pot and bring to a boil, reduce to medium, partly covered, and cook for 30 minutes until everything is cooked through.
4. Using either an immersion blender or a regular kitchen blender, combine all ingredients until they are emulsified.
5. If soup is too thick, add broth or water.
6. Taste soup and add bouillon cubes if you need to punch up flavor.
7. Mix in the cream.
8. Add salt and pepper to taste.
   Serve.

SIDEBAR

NOTES:

What makes this soup so great is the balance of the flavors between the potatoes and the leeks.
Don't be tempted to add more potatoes or you will lose that great flavor balance.

Try using cottage cheese instead of heavy cream. Use the immersion blender to purée the soup.

STORAGE:

Refrigerate: 4 to 5 days
Freeze: 4 to 5 months

CAULIFLOWER, FENNEL
& PARMESAN SOUP

At the farmers market, I picked up a head of cauliflower and a fennel bulb, not because I knew what I was going to make with them, but because they were in season and beautiful. As I went through my recipe notebook, I found a note with no recipe that said cauliflower, fennel, and Parmesan soup—try it! So I did. It was really good! The addition of the Parmesan made it very interesting, I now make it all the time.

Serves: 8
Prep time: 10 minutes
Total time: 50 minutes

Ingredients

1 head cauliflower; remove the stem and cut into 2" chunks
1 large bulb fennel; trim off stalks (save 1 tablespoon of chopped fronds for garnish), cut into 2" chunks.
¾ cups of grated Pecorino Romano
½ cup heavy cream
Low-sodium vegetable broth, chicken broth, or water, enough to cover vegetables by 1"
Bouillon low-salt chicken or vegetable, the equivalent of 2 or 3 cubes

Directions

1. Place chopped vegetables in a stockpot and add enough liquid to cover vegetables by 1".
2. Bring to a boil, reduce heat and simmer uncovered, approximately 30 minutes. (You want vegetables to be very soft, so add more liquid if it goes below the vegetables during cooking.)
3. When vegetables are cooked, use an immersion blender or kitchen blender to purée soup.
4. Heat soup over medium-low heat. Add cream and half the cheese, stirring to combine.
5. Taste and add bouillon to add more flavor.
6. Keep warm until ready to serve.
7. You want a nice balance of flavors. Add more cheese if needed.
8. Adjust flavors, add salt and white pepper to taste.
9. Serve soup, garnish with fennel fronds and extra cheese.

SIDEBAR

VARIATIONS:

Try using cottage cheese instead of cream in blended soups. It's my mother's trick and it's a great one. The result is a light and creamy mixture that is delicious.

You can use a pressure cooker to make this soup. Bring to high heat and cook for 15 minutes.

STORAGE:

Refrigerate: 4 to 5 days
Freeze: 4 to 5 months

NOTES:

Pecorino Romano is my preferred cheese for this soup. Put extra cheese in a bowl and pass it around.

CREAMY TOMATO
SOUP

A creamy tomato soup is always good, whether served with a grilled cheese sandwich or as a starter at a dinner party. You can't go wrong with this easy and tasty recipe.

Serves: 4
Prep time: 30 minutes
Total time: 1 hour

Ingredients
2 tablespoons high-heat oil
2 tablespoons butter
2 medium onions, diced
3 carrots, diced
1½ cups chicken broth
2 28-oz canned peeled whole tomatoes cut up (Use kitchen scissors, in can, and cut tomatoes up.)
4 tablespoons soy sauce
4 bouillon cubes or the equivalent to taste, you may add more
½ cup half and half or heavy cream
¼ cup light cream sherry, optional
1 tablespoon chopped parsley

Directions
1. In Dutch oven heat oil and butter.
2. Add onion and cook 2 minutes. Add the carrots and continue cooking to soften without browning, 5 minutes.
3. Slowly add the broth; continue to stir as it cooks.
4. Add tomatoes, bring to a boil.
5. Lower heat and let simmer 45 minutes, stirring as it cooks.
6. Take off heat, let sit 5 minutes.
7. Using an immersion blender, emulsify the soup.
8. Add 4 tablespoons soy sauce, one at a time, tasting as you go.
9. Add the equivalent of 3 bouillon cubes or more to taste.
10. Taste and adjust the seasoning with salt and pepper.
11. Add the heavy cream, blend.
12. Stir in sherry if using, sprinkle with parsley and serve.

SIDEBAR

VARIATIONS:
Adding the sherry to this soup makes it perfect for entertaining!

It is also perfect served for lunch.
Serve with a green salad and a few pieces of thinly sliced baguette, toasted, buttered, and sprinkled with grated Gruyere cheese.

STORAGE:

Refrigerate: 4 to 5 days
Freeze: 3 to 4 months—don't add the cream or the sherry if you plan to freeze the soup; add only once the soup is reheated.

EGG DROP
SOUP

This may be the easiest soup I've ever made. It is perfect when I want something that is quick and flavorful.

Serves: 4
Prep time: 15 minutes
Total time: 15 minutes

Ingredients
4 cups chicken broth
1 egg
1 teaspoon water
A dash of sesame oil
1 small scallion, finely sliced

Directions
1. Bring 4 cups of good low-salt chicken stock to a simmer. You want to make certain broth has enough flavor to stand on its own. If needed, add low-salt chicken bouillon.
2. In a small bowl, beat egg and water with a fork, making it frothy.
3. When stock is simmering, slowly pour egg in a thin stream while you are stirring broth. This is important; stirring broth is what causes the egg to break up and congeal in strands, making it egg drop soup.
4. Add a dash of sesame oil.
5. Ladle the soup into the 4 bowls, top with the scallions. Serve.

SIDEBAR

VARIATIONS:

Add spinach, mushrooms

Straciatella—The Italian version is made with chicken broth spinach and beaten eggs.

SERVE WITH:

Serve with a salad made of watercress, bean sprout, carrot, and shredded chicken salad.

STORAGE:

Refrigerate: 4 to 5 days

CUCUMBER
SOUP

I often serve this soup at room temperature in small cups as an hors d'oeuvres at parties. It's a fun break from the usual appetizers, especially if it's warm out. It is also perfect for a light lunch served with a salad.

Serves: 6 to 8, depending on the serving size
Prep time: 20 minutes
Total time: 50 minutes

Ingredients
5 cucumbers
1 small onion, chopped
1 tablespoon olive oil
1 tablespoon butter
2 tablespoons or more lemon juice; add extra just before serving
4 cups low-salt chicken broth
3 tablespoons fresh dill, chopped fine. Reserve 2 tablespoons.
½ to 1 cup yogurt to taste
Salt and white pepper

Directions
1. Peel cucumbers, slice in half lengthwise. Using a spoon, remove the seeds.
2. Grate the cucumbers and set aside.
3. Add oil and butter to stockpot. Cook the chopped onions until soft; do not brown.
4. Add cucumbers, lemon juice, and broth; bring to a boil.
5. Reduce heat, add half the dill, and simmer 20 to 30 minutes until cucumbers are soft.
6. Set aside 1 cup of cooked cucumber.
7. Purée the soup using an immersion blender or kitchen blender.
8. Add yogurt and blend until combined.
9. Add the reserved cucumber to soup to add texture.
10. Taste and adjust seasonings with salt and white pepper, lemon juice, and more yogurt if needed. Garnish with dill and serve.

SIDEBAR

NOTES:

I like serving the soup at room temperature, but I have to admit it is also good served hot or cold.

STORAGE:

Refrigerate: 4 to 5 days
Freeze: 4 to 5 months

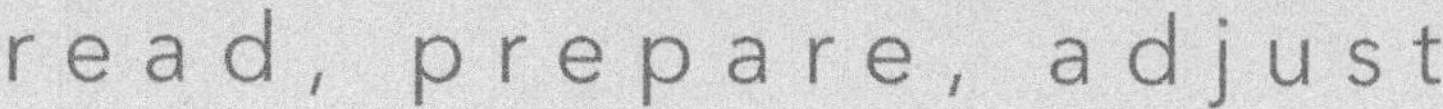

MANHATTAN CLAM CHOWDER

SIDEBAR

STORAGE:

Refrigerate: 3 to 4 days
Freeze: 2 to 3 months

This is a great tomato-based soup. The clams add a great texture and flavor to the soup. Emulsifying 1 cup of the vegetables and adding them back into the soup is a good way to thicken the soup.

Serves: 6 to 8
Prep time: 55 minutes
Total time: 55 minutes

Ingredients
1 large onion, diced
3 stalks celery, diced
3 carrots, diced
4 cloves garlic, diced or minced
1 28-oz can stewed tomatoes
1 large potato, peeled and diced into ½" cubes
Parsley: 1 tablespoon, chopped
Thyme: 2 sprigs
1 bay leaf
5 cups clam juice
2 cans whole baby clams
2 cans minced baby clams
1 teaspoon hot pepper sauce

Directions
1. Cook onion, carrots, and celery, 10 minutes.
2. Add garlic, cook 2 more minutes.
3. Add thyme and bay leaf.
4. Add potatoes, clam juice, and chopped stewed tomatoes. Bring to a boil, reduce heat to a simmer, cook 10 minutes until potatoes are tender.
5. Remove the thyme and bay leaf.
6. Remove 1 cup of vegetables and blend in mixer or immersion blender. Return the mixture to the pot.
7. Add the clams, simmer covered, 10 minutes.
8. Season with salt and pepper to taste.
9. Serve and garnish with chopped parsley.

CLASSIC BEEF & BARLEY SOUP

I've always loved this soup. The combination of the barley and the beef creates a great texture that is delicious and a comforting winter soup at its best.

Serves: 6
Prep time: 15 minutes
Total time: 2 hours

Ingredients
1 lb beef steak top round, cut into ½" cubes
1 tablespoon oil
5 cups beef broth
2 cups water
⅓ cup medium-pearl barley
1 teaspoon salt
⅛ teaspoon pepper
1 cup chopped carrots (2 large carrots)
½ cup chopped celery (1 large stalk)
¼ cup chopped onion (½ onion)
3 tablespoon minced fresh parsley

Directions
1. In a Dutch oven, brown beef in oil. Set the beef aside.
2. Add the onion, celery, and carrots and more oil if necessary. Cook on medium heat, letting them brown and begin to soften. Set aside. Discard any leftover oil.
3. Place meat back into pot with broth, water, barley, salt, and pepper.
4. Bring to a boil.
5. Reduce heat; cover and simmer for 1 hour.
6. Add carrots, celery, onion, and parsley.
7. Cover and simmer for 45 minutes or until meat and vegetables are tender.

See how easy that was!

SIDEBAR

SERVE WITH:

You won't need very much with this full-body soup.
Crusty bread and a green salad should do the trick.

STORAGE:

Refrigerate: 5 days
Freeze: 4 months

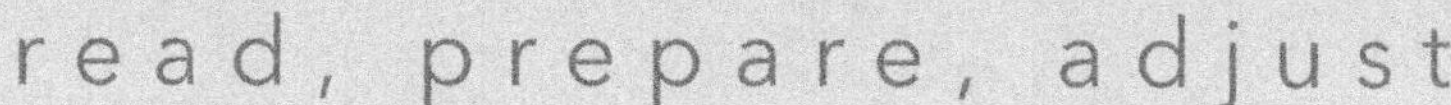

CHICKEN NOODLE
SOUP

If you want to make a classic chicken noodle soup quickly, this is a great recipe. It's my husband's recipe and we make it a lot. Serve it with a good crusty loaf of bread for a delicious light dinner.

Serves: 8
Prep time: 10 minutes
Total time: 55 minutes

Ingredients
1 tablespoon olive oil
3 large carrots, diced, 1½ cups
1½ cups diced celery
1½ cups diced onion
1 bay leaf
1 teaspoon dried oregano
1 teaspoon dried thyme
3 quarts low-salt chicken broth
1 lb boneless skinless chicken breast
Chicken bouillon (low-salt), equivalent of 3 bouillon cubes
8 oz of wide-egg noodles (see sidebar)
1 tablespoon chopped fresh parsley
Salt and pepper

Directions
1. In a Dutch oven or stockpot, add oil, carrots, celery, and onion and cook over medium heat until vegetables start to soften. Do not let them brown. Takes about 10 minutes. Turn heat down if they begin to brown.
2. Add dried herbs and continue to cook for 3 minutes.
3. Put chicken broth into pot and bring to a simmer.
4. Cut chicken breast into 1" cubes and add to broth.
5. Simmer for 30 minutes.
6. Taste soup: if it needs more flavor, add equivalent of one bouillon cube at a time; taste, and add more if needed.
7. Remove bay leaf. Add salt and pepper to taste and finish with chopped parsley.

SIDEBAR

STORAGE:

Refrigerate: 5 days
Freeze: 3 months
I freeze the soup without the pasta and add the cooked noodles after the soup is thawed and while I'm reheating the soup.

NOTES:

I like to cook the noodles in a separate pot to avoid making the soup too starchy. I put the cooked noodles into the individual bowls and ladle the soup on top.

LENTIL
SOUP

This is a hardy soup that is a meal in itself. The addition of turkey sausage adds great flavor and texture. Serve it with a loaf of French bread and enjoy! We always do.

Serves: 8
Prep time: 20 minutes
Total time: 1 hour 20 minutes

Ingredients
1 tablespoon olive oil
1 tablespoon butter
3 medium diced onion
3 large diced carrots
4 stalks diced celery
1 package spicy or regular turkey sausage, casing removed
4 cloves garlic, crushed
1 cup smoked or regular ham cubes
1 lb lentils or 2⅓ cups dried lentils (rinsed to remove any foreign particles)
10 cups water or beef broth
2 bay leaves
Low-salt beef bouillon, the equivalent of 3 cubes

Directions
1. In a large pot, heat oil and butter; add onion, celery, and carrots; cook until they start to brown and soften—about 5 minutes.
2. Add sausage and break it up as it cooks, leaving some larger chunks for texture.
3. Add crushed garlic and diced ham and cook a few minutes.
4. Add lentils, bay leaves, and 10 cups of beef broth.
5. Bring to a boil, reduce and simmer for 1 hour, stirring occasionally.
6. Lentils should be tender; add more liquid if necessary, but remember it is a chunky soup.
7. Taste and adjust seasonings. Add more bouillon for if needed, salt and pepper to taste. Remove bay leaves before serving.

SIDEBAR

NOTES:

Don't over salt the soup. Because the sausage, ham, and bouillon are salty, I don't add salt until the end to ensure I do not over salt.

STORAGE:

Refrigerate: 5 days
Freeze: 3 to 6 months
I like to freeze it in containers that are the size I will be using: 2 or 4 servings.

Remove sausage casing (page 164)

"Cooking is like painting or writing a song. Just as there are only so many notes or colors, there are only so many flavors—it's how you combine them that sets you apart."

—Wolfgang Puck

STEWS

Put ingredients in a pot, cook for hours and magic comes out–stew!

ABOUT STEWS

Put ingredients in a pot, cook for hours and magic comes out—stew!

A stew is made of chopped ingredients that are cooked in an ovenproof pot (Dutch oven) using a long, slow, even heat. It is usually started on your stove by searing the meat and the vegetables to create flavor. To finish cooking, cover the pot and place in the oven. As steam builds up, the liquid falls back into the stew, keeping it moist as it cooks. It is possible to cook the stew just on the stovetop but you need to stir it periodically to prevent it from burning. Stews can be made from all types of meats, poultry, fish, and vegetables, making it adjustable to the ingredients you have on hand.

This recipe can be made using meat, poultry, or fish.

Serves: plan on ½ lb of meat per person.
Prep time: 30 minutes
Total time: 3½ hours
Preheat oven to 300°

Ingredients
Meat cut into 1" chunks
Mirepoix, equal portions of diced onion, celery, and carrots for flavor
Liquid: broth, water, wine, or beer
Vegetables: you choose
Flavor: assorted spices
Thickener

Directions

1. Cut meat up into even-size (1 to 1½") chunks.

2. Sear the meat, brown on all sides, remove and set aside.
3. Add the mirepoix and cook until tender.
4. Deglaze with broth, wine, beer, or water.
5. Add the meat back into pan.
6. Cover the meat with liquid.
7. Bring to a boil.
8. Place Dutch oven into a preheated 300° oven.
9. Cook for 2½ to 3 hours.
10. During last hour of cooking, add other vegetables.
11. Meat needs to be very tender—you want meat to start to fall apart, fork tender.
12. Remove from oven. Adjust flavors and thicken sauce. Let juice evaporate on medium-low heat or use beurre manié or a flour slurry.
    Serve.

STORAGE:

Refrigerate: 4 to 5 days
Freeze: 4 to 5 months

Stews freeze well so make more than you need. That allows you to have a delicious meal when you're short of time.

Beurre manié (page 59)
Flour Slurry (page 60)
Mirepoix (page 120)
Deglaze (page 36)

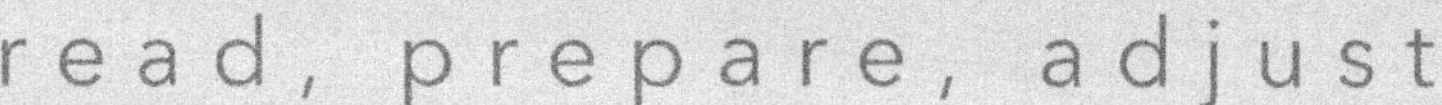

COQ AU VIN
CHICKEN WITH WINE STEW

Coq au vin is a classic chicken stew made with red wine. It is a slow-cooking dish that develops its flavors over time. Over the years I've evolved this recipe and I have to say it's delicious. One of the changes I made was to use only dark meat because it stays moist while cooking.

Don't let this recipe intimidate you. If you prepare, using mise en place, meaning that you prepare everything before starting, the recipe is easy. The flavor is well worth it.

Serves: 6 to 8
Prep time: 20 minutes
Total time: 2 hours
Preheat to 300°

Ingredients

¼ lb lean salt pork or thick bacon sliced into ½" pieces
¼ lb carrots, sliced (2 medium)
18 small white onions; frozen are good.
2 medium-size tomatoes, peeled, seeded, and sliced; a can of stewed, peeled tomatoes is okay to use.
4 lbs of dark meat chicken (I use just chicken thighs.)
1 teaspoon salt
Freshly ground black pepper
2 to 4 tablespoons brandy, warm
4 tablespoons of flour
3 cups red wine (If using pressure cooker, use only 2 cups.)
½ teaspoon thyme
1 bay leaf
2 tablespoons finely chopped parsley
½ lb mushrooms, quartered if large (about 1½ cups)
1 lb dried wide egg noodles

Directions

1. In a heavy bottom pot, sauté salt pork or bacon until fat is rendered. Do not burn. Add carrots and white onions and sauté until they start to brown without burning the bacon—about

SIDEBAR

SERVE WITH:

Wide noodles or mashed potatoes.

NOTES:

The only part of this recipe that you might find daunting is flambéing the brandy. If you follow all the steps and precautions, this is an easy process.

If you want you can omit the brandy and skip this step.

STORAGE:

Refrigerate: 4 to 5 days
Freeze: 4 to 5 months

COQ AU VIN continued

5 minutes.

2. Using a slotted spoon, remove all ingredients into a separate bowl.
3. Dry chicken pieces with paper towels.
4. Sauté a few pieces of chicken at a time in the remaining fat (if you do not have enough fat, add 1 or 2 tablespoons of oil). Sear all sides of chicken without crowding the pot and set aside when done. Continue until all chicken is done.
5. Remove all but 1 tablespoon of oil.
6. Put chicken back into pot and sprinkle with salt and pepper.
7. Flambé the brandy.
    a. Take pot off heat with lid close by.
    b. Pour warm brandy into the pot with chicken and ignite brandy.

    Note—There will be lots of flames, but as the alcohol burns off, the flames will die down and extinguish. Use the lid only if the flames get out of control.
8. Once flames are out, place pot back on medium heat, add tomatoes and cook for 3 to 5 minutes.
9. Add carrot mixture back into pot.
10. Sprinkle flour on top of mixture and mix well. Cook for 5 minutes, then add wine. Bring to a boil and reduce heat to a simmer.
11. Add thyme, bay leaf, parsley, and mushrooms.
12. Cover and simmer for 1½ hours. I usually cook it on the stove, but you can place it in oven for same time.
13. The chicken should be so tender that it starts to fall off bone.
14. Taste to adjust seasonings. If sauce doesn't have enough flavor, add equivalent of 1 or 2 low-salt chicken bouillon cubes (1 at a time) and taste.
15. Before serving taste and add salt and pepper if needed.

Start cooking the noodles 20 minutes before the chicken is ready,

To serve, place the noodles into a large bowl with the coq au vin on top. Or you can serve it in individual plates or bowls.

SIDEBAR

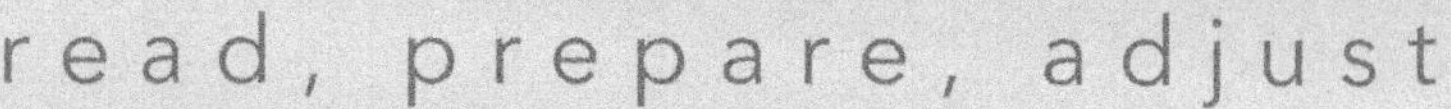

POULET A LA BASQUE

BASQUE CHICKEN

This is a classic French dish, Poulet a la Basque: Basque Chicken. This version is a one-pot meal. The rice is cooked in the same sauce that the chicken has simmered in, creating a really flavorful dish. We love it!

Serves: 8
Prep time: 15 minutes
Total time: 1 hour 35 minutes

Ingredients
3 tablespoons olive oil
4 lbs chicken, cut up into pieces (separate thigh from leg); I find the dark meat doesn't dry out as much as the white does.
6 slices of bacon, chopped into pieces
1 medium onion, thinly sliced
8 oz of mushrooms, sliced
2 turkey sausages, spicy if you can find it. Remove the casing: with the tip of a knife slice the casing and remove.
½ teaspoon fresh thyme (¼ teaspoon dried thyme)
1 bay leaf
½ cup white wine
2 green peppers, seeded and sliced
2 medium tomatoes, skin and seeds removed and chopped. (see sidebar)
2 cups chicken stock
Low-salt chicken bouillon, equivalent of 1 cube
1½ cups rice
Salt and pepper
2 tablespoons chopped parsley

Directions
1. Heat oil in a Dutch oven.
2. Braise chicken, making certain to brown it on all sides—do not crowd pan or chicken will steam. Set aside.
3. Cook bacon, add onion, mushrooms, thyme, bay leaf, salt, pepper, and sausage into pot. Brown.

SIDEBAR

NOTES:

Peeling tomatoes
Remove the skin of the tomato by cutting an X in the bottoms of the tomatoes. Drop tomatoes into a pot of boiling water for a minute. Remove and plunge them into an ice water bath. Remove and peel off the skin. To remove the seeds, cut the tomatoes in half through the center (not through the stem) and gently squeeze over a bowl.

ENTERTAINING:

One-pot meals are great for when you are entertaining. You can place the dish on the table and let people serve themselves.

Remove sausage casing (page 164)
Deglaze (page 36)

POULET A LA BASQUE continued

4. Add white wine to deglaze pan.
5. Put chicken, tomatoes, and green peppers into pan and add 2 cups of broth.
6. Bring to a boil and lower heat to low simmer. Cook for 45 to 60 minutes until chicken is cooked through.
7. Remove chicken from pot and strain broth.
8. Place chicken and strained vegetables into a bowl, cover with foil and place in a low-temperature oven 300° to keep warm.
9. Taste broth and adjust flavor. If needed, add bouillon.
10. Make sure you have 2½ cups of liquid; add broth or water if necessary.
11. Add rice to the broth, bring to a boil, cover and reduce heat to low.
12. Simmer until all liquid is absorbed, 20 to 25 minutes.
13. Taste rice and adjust seasonings.
14. To serve: Place rice in center of a serving dish. Add the vegetables around the outside and then the pieces of chicken. Add any juice that is left in bowl and garnish with parsley.

   Serve.

SIDEBAR

STORAGE:

Refrigerate: 4 to 5 days
If you make a lot you can freeze it. But do it before you make the rice. Once defrosted and heated, follow the recipe starting at step 7.
Do not freeze with rice

DON'T FORGET!

One-pot meals are easy to make and delicious to eat.

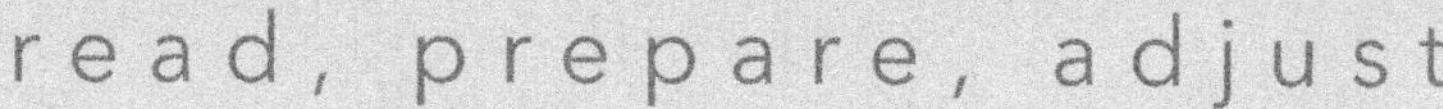

SIMPLE CHICKEN STEW

SIDEBAR

This is a simple chicken stew recipe that is not only delicious but easy to make. It's a great recipe to use as a base and improvise with your own ingredients and flavors. This is my favorite type of recipe.

Serves: 4
Prep time: 20 minutes
Cooking time: 45 minutes
Total time: 65 minutes
Preheat oven to 350°

Ingredients

2 tablespoons olive oil—enough to brown the chicken in batches
3 lbs chicken thighs, boneless and skinless, cut into 2" pieces
1 cup carrots, diced ½" cubes
1 cup celery, diced ½" cubes
1 cup onion, diced ½" cubes
3 cloves garlic, crushed
½ cup white wine
Optional: 4 oz chopped mushrooms
1 bay leaf
Sprig of fresh tarragon and sage
2½ cups low-salt chicken broth
2 tablespoons flour plus ½ cup broth or water for flour slurry
2 tablespoons chopped parsley
1 to 2 low-salt chicken bouillon cubes
1½ cups rice to be added to 3 cups water

Directions

1. In a Dutch oven, heat the oil.
2. Sear the chicken in batches. (You don't want to overcrowd the pan, or the chicken will steam and not brown.) Cook about 4 to 5 minutes per side, letting the chicken release naturally before turning. Repeat on the reverse side and set aside.
3. In the Dutch oven, add the carrots, celery, and onions (mirepoix). Add the herbs and cook until the onions start to soften and brown.

Flour slurry (page 60)
Mirepoix (page 120)
Deglaze (page 36)

SIMPLE CHICKEN STEW continued

4. Add the crushed garlic, cook 1 minute.
5. Deglaze the pan by adding white wine and separating all the browned bits stuck to the bottom of the pan with a spoon.
6. Add the chopped mushrooms if you are using them and cook until they soften and start to brown, 8 to 10 minutes.
7. Add the chicken with all the drippings and the chicken broth. Bring it to a boil.
8. Cover and place in the oven. Cook for 45 minutes.
9. After 20 minutes, start cooking the rice.
10. Add 1½ cups rice to 3 cups of water and bring to a boil. Reduce heat to lowest setting, cover pan. Cook without stirring about 20 minutes until water has absorbed.
11. Once stew has finished cooking, remove from oven and place, uncovered, on burner at medium heat.
12. Taste and adjust flavors. If needed, add chicken bouillon. Combine and taste again, and adjust.
13. If stew needs thickening, either let it evaporate on medium heat or add a flour slurry to thicken the sauce.
14. Remove the bay leaf and the large herbs before serving.
15. Serve the chicken over the rice and sprinkle with parsley.

SIDEBAR

BLANQUETTE DE VEAU

VEAL STEW

This stew is a very popular French dish. It is served with white rice and a wedge of lemon. This is the version my mother made and I like it because of its simplicity.

This type of stew is called a white stew, because nothing in it has been browned.

Serves: 6
Prep time: 20 minutes
Total time: 2 hours 20 minutes

Ingredients
1 medium yellow onion, diced small
3 carrots sliced in half and sliced into ¼" disks
½ cup flour
Salt and pepper
4 lbs veal chunks for stewing (I often buy more than 4 lbs because the meat shrinks as it cooks. For 6 people, I may buy 6 lbs of meat, knowing that I will have leftovers.)
5 cups low-salt chicken bouillon (Add more if you are using more meat; you want to just cover the meat.)
1 bay leaf
½ cup heavy cream
1½ lemons cut into wedges (one per person)
1 tablespoon chopped parsley

Directions
1. In a Dutch oven sauté the onion over medium heat. Let it get transparent without browning it.
2. Place the flour, salt, and pepper in a plastic bag and mix well. Add a handful of meat at a time and coat with flour. Continue until all veal is coated.
3. Place into pan with onions and mix well.
4. Add enough broth to cover meat and bring to a boil. Add bay leaf, reduce and let simmer for 1½ to 2 hours.

SIDEBAR

SERVE WITH:

White rice or wide noodles.
It is best served with a squeeze of lemon juice.

STORAGE:
Refrigerate: 4 to 5 days
Freeze: 4 to 5 months

BLANQUETTE DE VEAU continued

5. As it is cooking, check that you have at least 2" of liquid in pot, add more water or broth if needed.
6. When done, veal needs to be fork tender. That is important because the veal can be chewy if it isn't cooked long enough.
7. Taste the sauce and adjust the flavors with chicken bouillon and salt and pepper.
8. If the sauce hasn't thickened enough to coat the back of a spoon, use a slotted spoon to remove the veal into a bowl and cover with foil.
9. Raise the heat and continue to cook, letting the sauce evaporate, being careful not to let it burn.
10. To thicken, add a flour slurry to the sauce and continue cooking 2 to 3 minutes while it thickens.
11. Before serving, add ½ cup of heavy cream.
12. Serve, with a wedge of lemon.

SIDEBAR

THE MAGIC OF STEWS

Once you understand what makes a good stew, the ingredients you use are up to you!

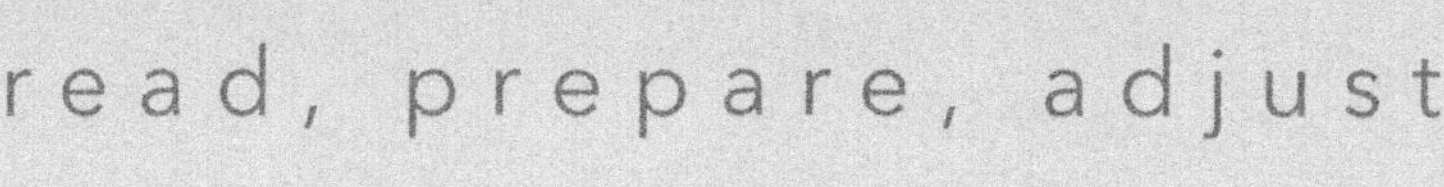

RAGOUT D'AGNEAU

LAMB STEW

Lamb was the traditional meal at Easter in our family. But the truth is that lamb is good any time.

SIDEBAR

NOTES:

If you haven't used turnips before you'll find they add a subtle flavor to stews that is delicious.

Serves: 6
Prep time: 40 minutes
Total Time: 3 hours

Ingredients

2¼ lbs lamb, cut into 3"cubes
4½ tablespoons butter
⅓ cup flour
2¼ cups beef bouillon
¾ cup onion
1 cup diced carrots
⅔ cup turnips, cut into chunks
1½ cups potatoes, cut into same size chunks as turnips
Bouquet garni (parsley, thyme and bayleaf.
Salt and pepper

Directions

1. Brown lamb on all sides, add the onion. Cook until translucent.
2. Add carrots and turnips, cook until they start to brown.
3. Dust with flour.
4. Add 1 cup of broth to make a roux, (thick paste), cook 2 minutes, then add the remainder of the broth, stirring to blend.
5. Salt and pepper to taste and add the bouquet garni.
6. Cook 1 hour.
7. Add potatoes, cook 1 to 1½ hours more until the meat is tender.
8. Remove the bouquet garni and serve.

Roux (page 60)
Bouquet garni (page 49)

QUICK & EASY BEEF STEW

Beef stew is comfort food. A version of this dish is found in many different cultures. The taste varies depending on the unique flavors added to the meat. This version is typical of American beef stew.

Serves: 6
Prep time: 15 minutes
Total time: 2 hours 15 minutes

Ingredients
4 tablespoons oil
1 medium onion, diced
2 celery stalks, sliced ¾" thick
1 clove garlic, minced
½ teaspoon oregano
1 bay leaf
1½ lbs stewing beef—chuck is your best choice
¼ cup flour
1 cup red wine
¼ cup tomato paste
1 cup beef broth
4 medium potatoes, peeled and cubed
2 carrots, sliced ¾" thick rounds
Salt to taste
Low-salt beef bouillon if needed
Beurre manié
1 tablespoon chopped parsley

Directions
1. In a heavy-bottom saucepan or Dutch oven, heat oil and sauté the beef in batches. Cook until well browned on all sides and set aside. Continue until all meat is browned.
2. In the same pot, sauté the onion, celery, and the garlic; brown about 5 minutes.
3. Add the flour, stir to combine, and cook a few minutes.
4. Combine the tomato paste and mix well.

SIDEBAR

STORAGE:

Refrigerate: 4 to 5 days
Freeze: 4 to 5 months

Stew meat can be frozen. It isn't essential but it is better if you freeze the beef before adding the vegetables. After the beef has cooked for 1½ hours, remove from stove, let it cool, and freeze in serving portions.

To finish cooking, thaw the stew, add the carrots and potatoes, and continue cooking until they are done. If the stew is thick, add water or broth to thin while cooking the carrots and potatoes.

If you want to omit the carrots and potatoes, you can serve the beef stew over mashed potatoes or wide egg noodles.

Flour slurry (page 60)
Beurre manié (page 59)

QUICK & EASY BEEF STEW continued

SIDEBAR

5. Add the meat, wine, and broth; bring to a boil, lower heat and simmer for 1½ hours, stirring occasionally.

6. Add the potatoes and carrots and cook for ½ hour until tender and the meat starts to fall apart. Taste and adjust the flavor. Add bouillon if needed.
7. If the sauce needs thickening, add either a flour slurry or beurre manié. Cook to combine and thicken the sauce.
8. Remove the bay leaf. Ladle the stew into bowls and top with parsley and serve.

BOEUF BOURGUIGNONNE
BEEF STEW WITH RED WINE

This is a classic French recipe that is full of flavor The key to this stew, as with all stews, is cooking the meat for a long time at a slow steady heat while it is steeping in a liquid taking on all that aromatic flavor.

Serves: 6
Prep time: 45 minutes
Total time: 2 hours 30 minutes
Preheat oven to 350°
Marinate 4 hours

Ingredients
3 lbs lean boneless beef chuck, cubed
1 large onion, thinly sliced
½ teaspoon thyme
1 bay leaf
1 tablespoon chopped parsley
1 clove garlic, crushed
½ teaspoon salt
Freshly ground pepper
1 cup dry red wine
2 tablespoons olive oil
¼ lb lean salt pork or thick-sliced cut bacon cut into chunks
18 small white onions (I use frozen)
2 tablespoons flour
1½ cups beef broth or bouillon
½ lb mushrooms
2 tablespoons butter

Directions
1. Place the meat, onions, thyme, bay leaf, parsley, garlic, salt, and pepper in a bowl. Combine the wine and olive oil and pour over the beef and marinate for 4 or more hours, stirring the mixture occasionally.
2. Dry beef cubes with a paper towel and put marinade aside for later.

SIDEBAR

SERVE WITH:

Wide noodles or mashed potatoes

STORAGE:

Refrigerate: 4 to 5 days
Freeze: 4 to 5 months

This stew is even better the day after you've made it. Reheat and serve.

That means it's great for entertaining.

BOEUF BOURGUIGNONNE continued

SIDEBAR

3. Place salt pork or bacon strips in a heavy casserole and sauté until fat is rendered.
4. Add small white onions and sauté until tender and browned and salt pork or bacon is crisp.
5. Remove from pan.
6. Sauté beef in hot fat (add more oil if necessary), browning well on both sides (3 to 5 minutes).
7. Sprinkle flour in pot, cook for a few minutes, and add salt pork and onions, including marinade and beef bouillon to pot. Bring to a boil and lower to a simmer, cover and cook for 2 hours or until beef is very tender. The meat needs to fall apart. You can cook stew on your stovetop at low heat or place the covered pot into your preheated oven.
8. In a separate pan, sauté the mushrooms with butter until they release their juices and begin to brown.
9. When beef is done, taste for seasonings, add mushrooms to the casserole.
10. Simmer 15 minutes to blend the flavors.
    Serve.

PROVENÇAL FISH STEW

This is a version of the fish stew I grew up eating when I lived in the South of France. The classic bouillabaisse as described by the editors of the Encyclopedia Britannica: "Bouillabaisse, complex fish soup originating on the Mediterranean coast of France, one of the glories of Provençal cuisine. Recipes for bouillabaisse abound, but the Marseilles formulation is generally acknowledged as the most authentic; it contains, besides fish and shellfish, olive oil, onions, tomatoes, garlic, parsley, saffron, fennel, thyme, bay leaf, and orange peel. True bouillabaisse must be made with Mediterranean fish, including the essential rascasse (a bony rock fish), plus whiting, conger eel, mullet, chapon, saint-pierre, and a number of others."

This doesn't mean you can't create a delicious fish stew—just not the classic Bouillabaisse. I use anchovy paste blended with garlic to add flavor to the stew. If you are not a fan of anchovies, don't worry, you won't taste them, just the wonderful savory flavor they add.

Serves: 4 to 6
Prep time: 30 minutes
Total time: 1 hour 30 minutes
Preheat oven to 400°

Ingredients
5 cloves garlic; roughly chop 4, reserve 1 clove
1 teaspoon salt
1 teaspoon anchovy paste
8 to 12 slices of good baguette; brush both sides with olive oil.
5 tablespoons high-heat oil
1 medium carrot, diced
2 stalks celery, diced
1 medium onion, diced
1 cup chopped parsley
1 fennel bulb chopped in 1" chunks
2 tablespoons chopped fennel fronds, reserve for garnish
2 8-oz bottles of clam juice

SIDEBAR

This recipe seems long, but that's only because it contains a lot of aromatics to create the wonderful flavor. Like all recipes, if you prepare all the ingredients before starting to cook (mise en place), you'll see it isn't hard at all.

You can play with the ingredients and adjust the recipe to your liking. I recommend you try this version first.

FISH STEW continued

SIDEBAR

½ cup of dry white wine
½ cup water
1 14-oz can of peeled, diced, and seasoned tomatoes with juice
1 large potato, peeled and diced
1 bay leaf
2 sprigs thyme
Optional: ¼ teaspoon saffron
1½ lbs firm fish fillets (cod, halibut, red snapper, or tilapia cut into 2" pieces.)
8 to 12 little neck clams
8 to 12 mussels
6 to 8 Shrimp and sea scallops
Optional: 2 tablespoons of pastis (Pernod or Ricard)
Optional: a slice of orange peel

Directions

1. Using a mortar and pestle, start pulverizing the garlic, add salt, and smash to make a paste. Add anchovy paste and mix well. Set aside.
2. Grill both sides of bread. Brush coat both sides with good quality olive oil, then rub with the garlic clove. Set aside.
3. In a Dutch oven or heavy bottom pot, add all the oil, onion, celery, carrots, fennel, and herbs. Sauté until they start to soften, about 10 minutes.
4. Add the garlic paste, mix well, and continue to cook, 2 minutes.
5. Add the potatoes, clam juice, tomatoes, wine, and water and continue to cook below boiling until vegetables are tender and the broth reduces, 30 minutes.
6. Taste and adjust seasonings.
7. Add the fish fillets, simmer 5 minutes covered.
8. Add the clams and mussels and continue cooking covered until the fish is cooked through and flakes easily and the mussels and clams are open, about 5 minutes. Remove any clams or mussels that haven't opened and discard.
9. Remove bay leaf and thyme. Add the parsley, taste, and adjust seasonings.

Garlic paste (page 50)

FISH STEW continued

10. Serve by putting 2 slices of bread into the bottom of a soup bowl. Add the clams, mussels, and fish fillets and pour the soup and vegetables over.
11. Sprinkle with the fennel fronds and serve.

SIDEBAR

"Cooking is the art
of adjustment."

—Jacques Pepin

7.

A SWEET FINISH

A bit of perfection is the right way to end a meal.

ABOUT SWEETS

ABOUT SWEETS

There is nothing like a little sweet to end a good meal.

Desserts are the little bit of sweet that is served following the savory part of our meal and the part that makes us feel satisfied. There is actually a reason for that good feeling we get from sugar; serotonin, the hormone that makes us happy, lifts our moods and actually helps with our digestion.

We are familiar with the negatives associated with sugar, the first being that eating sugar causes us to crave more sugar. Too much of a good thing is associated with weight gain, as well as depression. The challenge is finding the perfect balance. That means that you only eat sugar when you want it—not hidden in foods we purchase.

Harvard Health Publishing says that "Unless you consume only whole, unprocessed foods, you are bound to have added sugars in your daily diet." I don't know about you, but I want to be the one deciding where my intake of sugar comes from. I enjoy eating a good dessert after dinner a lot more than I do eating sugar hidden in drinks, morning cereals, sauces, or even health bars.

Since a little bit of sweet is a good thing, because it makes us feel better and helps us digest our meal, I've included a selection of desserts for you to enjoy.

Desserts come in many different forms and shapes: cakes, candies, cookies, custards, puddings, frozen desserts, jellies, pastries, pies, and cobblers and in moderation they are all delicious.

Let's not forget one of my favorite desserts: fruit. Fruit adds that little bit of sugar without a lot of effort, offering a lot of flexibility eaten as they are, cooked, grilled, or frozen. A piece of fruit is my choice most evenings but when I'm in the mood for something more elaborate I go to one of the recipes that follow.

LEMON MOUSSE

I love lemonade in the summer. Whenever I'm at a café in France and it's hot, I order a citron pressé. It's lemon juice squeezed into a glass with a few ice cubes, a pitcher of water, and a container of powdered sugar. You sweeten it yourself—how civilized—I can decide for myself how sour I want it and that changes depending on my mood.

In the spring I like lemon mousse because it wakes up my taste buds with a big wow. This recipe is easy but you do need to make it ahead of time so it can set up. I refrigerate it overnight before serving. That way it is ready to serve when I'm ready. The mousse should be tart so don't be afraid to add lemon juice.

Serves: 6 to 8
Prep time: 50 minutes
Total time: 8 hours 50 minutes

Ingredients
5 egg yolks, freeze the egg whites*
1 cup sugar
4 or 5 lemons, zest and reserve 1 teaspoon
Juice the lemons (after zesting) you should have about 1 cup, strain to remove pulp and seeds
1 cup cold heavy whipping cream

Directions
1. Place an inch of water in a pot.
2. Find a bowl large enough to sit on top of the pot so it doesn't touch the water. I like to use a metal bowl.
3. In the metal bowl, combine yolks and sugar, whisk until smooth.
4. Bring water to a boil, reduce heat slightly.
5. Add lemon juice and zest to yolk mixture. Whisk to combine.
6. Place bowl on top of pan, whisking continuously until the egg mixture thickens enough to coat back of a spoon, about 10 to 20 minutes.
7. Remove from heat. Cool to room temperature.

SIDEBAR

NOTES:

*Freeze egg whites either together or individually. When you need egg whites simply thaw them and use them wherever a recipe calls for egg whites.

Zest (page 70) means to remove the yellow part of the lemon skin that contains all the flavor without touching the pith, the white layer that is bitter. Use a grater or vegetable peeler to remove it.

Always zest before juicing the fruit.

Serve with raspberries or strawberries.

STORAGE:

Refrigerate: 3 to 4 days

How to Fold (page 36)

LEMON MOUSSE continued

SIDEBAR

8. With a hand mixer, beat heavy cream until it forms firm peaks; be careful to not over beat.
9. Add ⅓ of whipped cream to cooled lemon mixture, folding it in gently.
10. Add remaining whipped cream, folding until it is combined and you don't see white streaks in the mixture.
11. Pour mixture into either one large bowl or 6 to 8 small serving bowls or glasses.
12. Cover and refrigerate overnight.
13. If you've chilled the mousse in a large bowl, you can spoon it into individual serving containers.
14. Before serving, sprinkle top with a little lemon zest and serve.

CHOCOLATE MOUSSE

This is a simple but delicious chocolate mousse—rich and creamy. Most mousses use eggs but this one uses only chocolate, heavy cream, and sugar to make a delicious mousse.

Serves: 8
Prep time: 20 minutes
Total time: 1 hour 20 minutes
Refrigerate: 1 to 2 hours

Ingredients
4 oz semi sweet chocolate, broken up into even pieces
1 tablespoon butter
1 cup sugar
1 pint heavy cream

Directions
1. In a pot place 1" of water and bring to a boil. Place a heat-proof bowl over the pot, making sure it doesn't touch the water. Add the chocolate and butter, stirring as the chocolate melts.
2. Add ¾ cup of sugar and mix into the chocolate.
3. In a large bowl, pour the cold heavy cream. Using a hand mixer, beat it until it thickens and has medium peaks when you lift the beaters. Add the remaining ¼ cup of sugar, continue beating until the cream creates stiff peaks.
4. Combine the chocolate into the whipped cream by folding it in until well combined. Do not over stir.
5. Pour the mixture into a large bowl, cover with plastic wrap, and refrigerate for 1 to 2 hours.
6. Scoop the mousse into individual bowls and serve.
7. Optional: Sprinkle a few grains of finishing salts or kosher salt on top before serving. The contrast of salt with the sweet adds flavor and brings out the sweetness.

SIDEBAR

STORAGE:

Refrigerate: 4 days

SERVE WITH:

Raspberries or caramel are a good toppings for chocolate mousse.

How to Fold-in (page 36)

CRÈME CARAMEL
CARAMEL CUSTARD

This is a dessert from my childhood that I've always loved. The first time I made it, I was amazed that it worked. It seemed magical: When you pour the caramel into the custard cups, it becomes totally solid on the bottom of the cups. Yet when the custards are cooked and then cooled, they've transformed. As you remove the custard from the cups, the caramel is now liquid and pours out over the custard. I don't need to understand how it works; it just does and it's delicious.

Serves: 8
Prep time: 18 minutes
Total time: 1 hour 8 minutes
Preheat oven to 350°
Refrigerate: 2 or more hours

I make this in eight 6-oz oven-safe custard cups but you can make it in one large oven-safe bowl.

Ingredients
¾ cups sugar for the caramel
4 eggs
¾ cups sugar for the custard
3 cups whole milk
2 teaspoons vanilla
⅛ teaspoon salt

Directions
1. Have your custard cups out to be filled as soon as your caramel is ready. Or use a 1½ to 2-quart ovenproof baking dish.
2. Place ¾ cup of sugar in a heavy saucepan over medium heat and let sugar melt. I stir it with a wooden spoon until it has melted and then, without stirring, let it start to turn golden. Do not let it get too dark or burn or it will taste bitter.
3. Remove from stove immediately and pour into bottom of eight 6-oz oven-safe custard cups, dividing it evenly between them.

SIDEBAR

NOTES:

Though this may seem difficult, trust me, it is surprisingly easy to make. Make it as a treat for yourself or invite a few friends over and make it for them. They'll thank you.

Bain-marie (page 66)

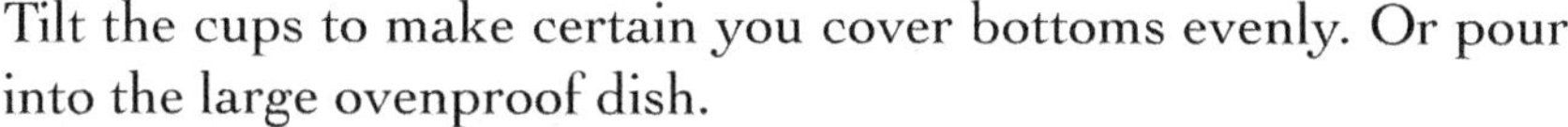

CRÈME CARAMEL continued

Tilt the cups to make certain you cover bottoms evenly. Or pour into the large ovenproof dish.

4. Optional: In a large roasting pan—large enough to fit custard cups or a baking dish—place a folded dish towel on bottom and place custard cups on top. This prevents the cups from moving around.
5. In a large bowl, stir the eggs, milk, vanilla, salt, and sugar until well mixed but don't let it get bubbly as this will alter the consistency of the custard.
6. If mixture isn't smooth, pour it through a sieve into a large measuring cup. This will eliminate any bubbles, ensuring that custard is silky smooth.
7. Pour mixture into custard cups.
8. Pour simmering water into the roasting pan, known as bain-marie, so it comes halfway up the side of the cups. (Do not use boiling water since it will cause the custard to cook unevenly.)
9. Bake in lower half of your 350° oven for 30 to 35 minutes, until toothpick inserted in center comes out clean.
10. Remove custard cups from pan and let cool on a wire rack for 1 hour.
11. Refrigerate for 2 hours or more.
12. To serve, slide a sharp knife around outside of cup. Place your plate over cup and turn it over. You may need to slightly jiggle the cup until the custard releases and the caramel sauce pours out on plate.

    Serve.

SIDEBAR

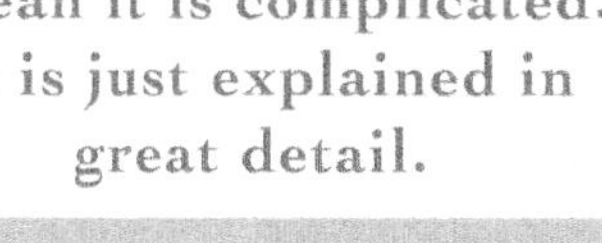

DON'T FORGET!

A long recipe doesn't mean it is complicated. It is just explained in great detail.

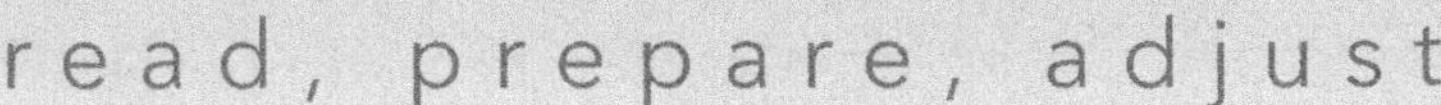

POACHED PEARS IN WINE

SIDEBAR

VARIATIONS :

Use white wine instead of red.

Ingredients
4 Anjou pears
2 cups white wine
1½ cups sugar
1 teaspoon lemon juice
1 cinnamon stick
Follow the directions for red wine poached pears.

These recipes will work equally well with other firm fruits. Try firm peaches or apples. The only thing that changes is the amount of time it will take for the fruit to become tender when poached. Test to determine when it is ready.

STORAGE:

Refrigerate: 4 days

This is a classic French dessert that takes full advantage of the fresh flavor of pears as well as the richness of local wines. I've included both a red and a white wine recipe. The results are different but equally as good.

Serves: 8
Prep time: 10 minutes
Total time: 30minutes

Ingredients
4 Anjou pears, select firm fruit
1½ cups red wine
¾ cups sugar
2 teaspoons vanilla extract
1 cinnamon stick
1 pint vanilla ice cream

Directions

1. Peel pears, cut in half, and core.
2. Combine wine, sugar, vanilla, and cinnamon into a deep pot. Bring to a simmer, add the pears, cook for 10 minutes.
3. Turn the pears over and continue cooking 10 minutes or until pears are tender when pierced with a knife.
4. With a slotted spoon, remove pears and cool.
5. Continue simmering wine until reduced by half and it becomes a syrup thick enough to coat a spoon.
6. Remove the spices.
7. Place pears into serving bowls, pour syrup over, and serve with a scoop of vanilla ice cream.

FRUIT TART

This is a great summer tart. Summer is a time when you want to take advantage of the freshness of all the available fruits. Fruit tarts are a great way to do that. I use store-bought puff pastry and add the fresh fruits to create a simple and delicious summer tart.

Serves: 8
Prep time: 35 minutes
Total time: 1 hour
Preheat oven to 425°

Ingredients
2 sheets puff pastries
I egg plus 1 tablespoon of water, well blended
4 tablespoons of apricot jam
½ cup sugar
1 tablespoon butter
5 apricots, cut open remove pit and cut into 6 slices

Directions

1. Thaw both sheets of frozen puff pastry about 20 minutes.
2. Sprinkle flour on your work surface.
3. Roll out each sheet. Cut one into about a 10" x 12" rectangle.
4. Cut the other sheet into strips of dough 1" wide; I use a ruler.
5. Place the rectangle on a piece of parchment and move to a baking sheet.
6. Using a brush, spread the egg wash 1" around the outside of the rectangle.
7. Place the strips on top of the egg wash at the edge, creating a border. Cut off any extra crust and push down gently to seal.
8. Spread 2 tablespoons of jam on the bottom of the crust.
9. Place the fruit either haphazardly across the bottom of the dough or lay it out the apricots in rows slightly overlapping.

SIDEBAR

VARIATIONS:

This tart can be made with different kinds of fruits: Italian plums, apples, pears, blueberries.

With every fruit consider adding something a little different to accentuate the fresh flavor of the fruit:
Peach tart—peach brandy or Grand Marnier
Apricot tart—apricot jam
Raspberries and blueberries are a good combination.
Try apples mixed with calvados.
Pears with Pear William are delicious.
Peaches with Grand Marnier.
The possibilities are endless; it is up to you and your taste buds.

STORAGE:

Refrigerate: 5 days
Freeze: 1 month

FRUIT TART continued

SIDEBAR

10. Cover with the rest of the jam.
11. Sprinkle with sugar and dot with slivers of butter.
12. Place into a 425° oven for 20 to 30 minutes until the puff pastry has puffed up and is golden brown. The apricots should be nice and bubbly. If needed, continue cooking until the top browns without burning.
13. Let cool before serving.

DON'T FORGET!

Once you make the pie crust, what you put in it—savory or sweet—is up to you.

BERRY COBBLER

Berry cobbler is a perfect dessert for the summer months. I make it all summer long. Try using other fruits: peaches, apricots, apples, or pears. I avoid using raspberries because they melt into the sauce.

Serves: 8
Prep time: 20 minutes
Total time: 1 hour 10 minutes
Preheat oven 375°
Use a 2-quart shallow baking dish

Ingredients
2 containers strawberries
2 containers blueberries
1 container blackberries
⅓ cup granulated sugar
2 tablespoons all-purpose flour
Topping
1½ cups flour
¾ cup sugar
¾ cup brown sugar
1 stick butter cut into ½ cubes, room temperature

Directions
1. Butter 2-quart baking dish.
2. In a bowl combine the 2 tablespoons flour and ⅓ cup sugar. Add berries and stir to coat berries evenly.
3. Pour fruit into buttered 2-quart baking dish making certain to include all sugar and flour left in the bowl. Mix gently.
4. Make topping in separate bowl. Mix flour, sugar, and cubes of butter. With your hands, blend butter into flour sugar mixture until it resembles coarse meal.
5. With your fingers, squeeze in a handful of topping, letting it crumble in chunks over berries, covering berries completely.
6. Place dish on a sheet pan to catch any drippings. Bake in upper third of oven until filling is bubbling and topping is crisp and golden, about 50 minutes.

SIDEBAR

STORAGE:

Refrigerate: 4 days.
Do not freeze: it will be too watery when thawed.

SERVE WITH:

Serve at room temperature with vanilla ice cream.

NOTE:

I always double the topping quantity recipe to make sure I have more than I need to cover the berries with lots of topping that's what makes it so good.

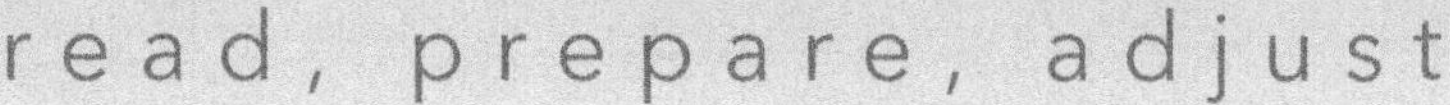

RUSTIC APPLE TART

Let's talk about rustic tarts. In France they are known as galettes; in Italy they are called crostatas. Whatever you want to call them, they are tasty and easy. You don't need a pie pan or any special techniques—this tart is freeform. Even the ingredients are flexible. And that means you can enjoy the great bounty our farmers have to offer us.

All you need to do is roll out your dough. It doesn't matter what shape—circle or rectangle. Place your ingredients in the center of your shape and fold the edges of the dough over the edge of the ingredients. This is freeform so all that really matters is that only the edge of your filling is covered. Bake till the crust is golden-brown, and the filling is bubbling. You'll have a tart that will make your mouth water. The only hard part is waiting for it to cool enough to eat.

Serves: 6
Prep time: 40 minutes
Total time: 2 hours
Preheat oven to 400°

Ingredients

For the dough:

1 cup all-purpose flour
2 tablespoons sugar
¼ teaspoon salt
1 stick very cold unsalted butter, diced
2 tablespoons ice water

For the filling:

2 lbs medium apples, either Granny Smith, Cortland, or Empire (tart apples are best)
½ cup brown sugar
¼ teaspoon salt
2 tablespoons flour
4 tablespoons unsalted butter

SIDEBAR

VARIATIONS :

This recipe is simple, delicious, and easy to make. There are two ways to make the crust: puff pastry purchased frozen, thawed and used as the recipe indicates; or regular pie crust. With a bit of practice you'll see how easy it is to make.

You can use other fruits to make this recipe: apricots, peaches, or plums. Using brown sugar will give more of a caramel flavor to the fruit. It also works well with white sugar. Try both and see what you like best.

NOTES:

This concept can be made with savory ingredients. Try a layer of caramelized onions add slices of zucchini and tomatoes, top with Parmesan and Swiss cheese cook till tender add the crust is golden.

Pie crust (page 321)

RUSTIC APPLE TART continued

1 egg plus 1 tablespoon water

Directions

For the dough:

1. Start rolling out the dough—either the puff pastry or the pie dough—about 8" round. Transfer the dough to a floured piece of parchment paper the size of your sheet pan (13" x 18"). Continue rolling until it is about 14" round shape. (Don't worry if dough overlaps parchment or if the shape isn't perfect. Remember, this is a freeform tart.) Refrigerate.

For the filling:

1. Peel and core the apples and slice into about ¼" slices, set aside.
2. In a bowl, mix the brown sugar, butter, salt, and flour together until the mixture becomes crumbly and starts to stick together.
3. In a small bowl, blend the egg and water with a fork to make the egg wash.
4. Place the apples in the center of the dough leaving a 2" edge all around.
5. Cover the apples with the brown sugar mixture.
6. Fold the outer crust over the edge of the apples. You'll need to overlap the crust, leaving the center open.
7. Brush the egg wash under the folds, pressing gently to glue them down. Brush the remaining dough with the egg wash.
8. Refrigerate 30 minutes.
9. Place the tart into the oven and bake 40 to 50 minutes. Make sure the dough is golden brown and the topping is bubbly before removing from oven.
10. Let it cool.
11. Holding the side of the parchment paper, lift the tart off the pan. Then, using 2 large spatulas, place tart on your serving plate.

SIDEBAR

NOTES:

This tart can be frozen!

For best results, freeze before baking.

Place tart in the freezer on a plate or pan to pre-freeze.

Once frozen, wrap using the parchment paper. Wrap again in plastic wrap and then in foil. Place the tart into a self-closing bag, remove excess air before closing. Label and date. Lasts 4 to 6 months.

When you are ready to bake the tart **do not thaw**.
Place in a preheated 400° oven and bake for 40 to 50 minutes. It might take a bit longer.

Freezing after baking is not optimal but can be done.

Cool the pie completely.
Wrap as above.
When you are ready to serve, thaw at room temperature.
Place in 400° oven for 20 to 30 minutes, serve.

BROWNIES

This recipe was inspired by a recipe I found years ago created by Katherine Hepburn. Over the years I have altered it to this version. I like that there is very little flour. The brownies are amazingly moist and chocolaty—delicious. I've turned them into chocolate candies by slightly under-cooking the brownies and placing a spoonful of cooked dough into fluted paper candy holders. I serve them with a cup of coffee after dinner to great delight. Everyone LOVES these.

This recipe works well to make brownies without wheat flour. I substituted a wheat-free flour with great results.

Makes: 16 2"x 2"-sized brownies
Prep time: 10 minutes
Total time: 50 minutes
Preheat oven to 325°

Ingredients
1 stick butter
2 1-oz squares unsweetened chocolate
1 cup sugar
2 eggs
½ teaspoon vanilla
¼ cup flour
¼ teaspoon salt

Directions
1. In a pan, over medium heat melt the butter and 2 squares of the chocolate. Take the pan off the heat.
2. Stir in 1 cup of sugar, add 2 eggs and ½ teaspoon vanilla, mix well.
3. Stir in ¼ cup flour and ¼ teaspoon salt.
4. Pour the brownies into a buttered and floured 8-inch square baking pan.
5. Bake for about 35 minutes.
6. After about 30 minutes, I check the brownies because I like them to be undercooked and gooey.

SIDEBAR

VARIATIONS:

Want gluten and wheat-free brownies?
It's easy: just switch out the flour for a gluten and wheat-free blend.

STORAGE :

Store the brownies in an air-tight container so they do not dry out:
4 to 5 days.

Freeze: I like to cut the brownies into 1½" squares. I place 12 squares into a freezer-safe resealable bag and freeze them. When we want to indulge in a little sweet after dinner with coffee, I just go to the freezer and take out a few and we eat them still frozen. Since they are very soft, they just melt in your mouth.

Label and date before freezing. They will last 3 to 4 months, that is if you don't eat them before.

POUND CAKE

What's better or more versatile than a good pound cake?

Pound cake is believed to have originated in the mid-18th century in Northern Europe. The name is derived from the recipe—a mixture of one-pound butter, one-pound sugar, one-pound flour, and one-pound of eggs. Thank goodness we can make the recipe in smaller quantities.

Serves: 8 to 10, makes 2 loaves
Prep time: 35 minutes
Total time: 1 hour 20 minutes
Preheat oven to 350°

Ingredients
Make sure all ingredients are room temperature
2 sticks butter, softened
2½ cups sugar
4 large eggs at room temperature
2½ cups all-purpose flour
½ teaspoon baking powder
½ teaspoon salt
1 teaspoon vanilla

Filling optional

½ cup chopped walnuts
½ cup packed brown sugar
1 teaspoon cinnamon
½ teaspoon nutmeg
¼ cup butter

Directions

1. Grease, and flour, 2 loaf pans (approximately 8½" x 4½" x 2½").
2. Sift flour, baking powder, and salt together.
3. Using a hand mixer or kitchen blender, cream the butter and sugar until light and fluffy—about 5 minutes.

SIDEBAR

VARIATIONS:

Serve with different toppings such as fruits, ice cream, lemon curd, chocolate sauce, or caramel sauce.

If you bake it with the filling, it's delicious with just a little ice cream.

STORAGE :

Pound cake freezes really well and is the perfect dessert if you have unexpected guests. Wrap it with parchment paper and then aluminum foil and then place it in a plastic bag. Freeze: 3 to 4 months.

POUND CAKE continued

SIDEBAR

4. Add one egg at a time, combine completely before adding the next egg.
5. Add vanilla.
6. Mix in flour and combine thoroughly.
7. If you are not using the filling, pour the mixture into each pan and go to step 10.
8. If you are using the filling, pour half the mixture into the pans, add half of the filling to each pan, and finish by adding the rest of the batter on top of the filling.
9. With a knife, swirl the batter in a figure eight to combine the filling with the batter.
10. Gently shake to remove any air bubbles.
11. Bake 45 minutes or until toothpick inserted into the center comes out clean.
12. Let cool 10 minutes, remove from pan and place on wire rack. Serve when cool.

CHEESECAKE

This is a really good and creamy cheesecake recipe. I make it in a spring form pan; those pans have detachable bottoms. It makes removing the cake from the pan very easy.

Serves: 12
Prep time: 15 minutes
Total time: 45 to 60 minutes
Preheat oven to 375°
Cool: 2 hours

Ingredients
Crust

12 graham crackers, crumbled
3 tablespoons sugar
½ cup melted butter (1 stick = 8 tablespoons)

Filling

Note: all ingredients should be at room temperature
3 8-oz packages cream cheese
1 cup sugar
2 tablespoons flour
1 teaspoon vanilla
¼ cup milk
3 eggs, slightly beaten

Optional: ½ teaspoon lemon zest will add a strong lemon flavor to the cheesecake. It's perfect if it complements the topping you choose.

Directions
Crust

1. Mix Graham crackers with sugar and butter.
    a. Spread a layer on the bottom of the pan and continue pressing it up the side at least 2".
2. I use a straight-edge cup to push the crust down and into the pan's edges; it works really well.

SIDEBAR

STORAGE :

Refrigerate 4 to 5 days
Freeze: 3 months
Make certain it is completely cool before freezing.
If you have room, freeze the cake before wrapping. Once frozen it is easier to wrap in plastic and then in foil.

I like to make the cheesecake the day before I plan to serve it, giving it plenty of time to cool.

VARIATIONS :

Making a fruit sauce for your cheese cake is easy:
Either strawberry or raspberries or a combination of the two.
2 cups of fruit, room temperature
If using strawberries, cut them up.
Place 1½ cups fruit in a blender with ½ cup sugar. Blend and then add the remaining ½ cup of whole fruits, to add texture.
Refrigerate sauce until ready to use.
Slice the cheesecake and place each piece on a plate and pour the sauce over it before serving.

CHEESECAKE continued

Filling

1. Blend the cream cheese, sugar, flour, and vanilla with a hand mixer or stand mixer until well combined. Make sure there are no lumps left in the cream cheese.
2. Add the milk until smooth—add lemon if using.
3. Stir in the eggs slowly until just combined to avoid air bubbles.
4. Before pouring batter into your pan tap the bowl on the counter to bring any air bubbles to the surface.
5. Bake in preheated oven (45 minutes for an 8" pan, 35 minutes for a 9"pan). Cook until the sides are puffy and the center is no longer liquid, though it will still jiggle. That's fine.
6. Take the cheesecake out of the oven and place on a wire cooling rack for 10 to 15 minutes.
7. Take a thin knife and run it around the edge between the pan and the crust.
8. Open the hinge of the of the pan and remove the sides.
9. Let the cheesecake cool completely 2 to 3 hours before refrigerating.

SIDEBAR

NOTE:

Cheese cakes have a tendency to crack but instead of worrying about it, hide it. I either top the entire cake with fruits, or slice the cheese cake and serve it on individual plates pouring the fruit sauce, as mentioned above, on top of each piece.

BUTTER BALL COOKIES!

I discovered that these cookies are delicious eaten right from the freezer!

BUTTER BALL COOKIES
A LA ELISSA

This recipe was given to me by my high school roommate and very close friend. These cookies have become a family favorite; I make them every year for the holidays—a tradition that everyone in our extended family waits for.

Makes: about 4 dozen cookies
Prep time: 30 minutes
Total time: 52 minutes
Preheat oven to 350°

Ingredients
1 lb butter
12 tablespoons confectioners' sugar (¾ cup)
4 cups flour
2 teaspoons vanilla
2 cups fine-chopped walnuts

Directions
1. Using a hand mixer or kitchen blender, cream butter.
2. Mix in all dry ingredients (sugar and flour).
3. Add chopped nuts and mix in well until you have a smooth cookie dough. (I use my clean hands to combine.)
4. Take a small amount of dough, roll it into 1" balls (do not make them larger).
5. Fill a baking sheet with balls about 1" apart.
6. Bake at 350° for about 12 minutes. (This varies with ovens so it is approximate.) Cookies will still be a light color but the bottom will have begun to brown. Remove from oven.
7. I rotate two baking sheets. While the first one is baking fill a second baking sheet and place in the oven while the first batch is cooling.
8. Remove from oven and let cookies cool for 10 minutes. Place them on a large plate until they have completely cooled. Store in a covered metal box.

SIDEBAR

STORAGE:

In a covered metal box the cookies will last 3 weeks.
Freeze: 4 months
To thaw, let sit at room temperature for 30 to 60 minutes. Store in an air-tight container.

VARIATIONS:

If you want, you can break up a bar of great quality chocolate into small pieces and mix it in. Elissa's recipe included the chocolate but I like them better without. Try both and see what you like better.

ABOUT PIECRUSTS

My mother was a harsh critic when it came to piecrusts. It had to be light, flaky, and crispy or she didn't like it. It didn't matter how great the filling was; if the crust wasn't good, the pie wasn't good. She loved anything I made with this piecrust. "C'est délicieux," she would tell me, "it's perfect!" Trust me, you'll get compliments too with this recipe and technique.

The recipe makes enough for 2 crusts or one top and one bottom. When I use a larger pan, I roll out the entire dough and cut out the size I need. What's left over, I roll back up into a ball and roll it out again to either decorate the pie by making a lattice top, or to make a freeform crust for a rustic fruit tart. If you do not need the extra dough, pat it back into a flat disk, wrap it up well, and freeze it for another time. When you want to use it, thaw the dough in the refrigerator and roll it out to make another pie.

I make this recipe in my food processor. It's quick and really easy. You can make it by hand as it's been done for generations, using a pastry blender or two forks. The result is the same; it just takes longer.

Note: This is important. Most recipes will tell you to refrigerate the dough for up to 1 hour before rolling it out. I do not do that. I have much better results rolling the dough out and placing it into the pan before refrigerating it for 1 hour. Doing it this way, the dough doesn't get overworked, resulting in a really flaky pastry.

I've explained the process in detail so the recipe seems long. Please do not be intimidated by this recipe. It is easy and so worth it because the results are delicious!

Practice makes perfect as the expression says. When I first tried making piecrusts I struggled because I found the process daunting. I'd bought frozen piecrusts for years simply because I was afraid to try making my own. I thought it was easier to just buy it. That changed when someone told me I was being silly, piecrusts were really easy and I just needed to try it—she was right!

SIDEBAR

STORAGE:

Freeze. Yes, shape it into a disk, wrap it in plastic wrap and then a freezer bag and freeze.

Thaw it before using, place in the refrigerator overnight

NOTES:

Your piecrust is the structure that holds your filling. The filling can be sweet or savory—that is up to you. What's important is that both the filling and the crust have to be good in order to have a good pie.

Some piecrusts need to be baked before the filling is added, that is called **blind baking**. Some pies, like custards, don't cook long enough for the crust to get crispy. It isn't always necessary; if the crust doesn't get golden then you know to try blind baking it the next time you make it.

Pies that do not need to be baked will need the crust to be baked completely and cooled before adding the filling.

Rustic fruit tart (page 312)

PIECRUST RECIPE
PASTRY DOUGH

Serves: 8; makes two 9" pies or one 9" bottom and 1 top
Prep time: 20 minutes
Total time: 20 minutes

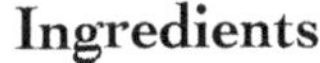

Ingredients

2½ cups flour
½ teaspoon salt
2 sticks unsalted butter, very cold cut into ½" cubes
7 to 9 tablespoons ice water

Directions

1. Place the flour, sugar, and salt in the bowl of a food processor with a steel blade. Pulse a few times to combine.
2. Add the butter, pulse until the mixture resembles coarse meal.
3. Add 3 tablespoons of ice water through the feed tube. Keep pulsing until the dough begins to gather and pull away from the wall. Continue adding more water 1 tablespoon at a time until the dough pulls away and starts to form a ball.
4. Stop immediately; don't over process.
5. Place the dough on a large piece of plastic wrap and pat into a ball. Wrap the plastic film around dough and pat it into a flat disk.
6. Remove the plastic, sprinkle your work surface, dough, and rolling pin with flour.
7. See sidebar for rolling instructions.
8. Once rolled out you need to place dough into pan. Loosely roll it onto the rolling pin and bring it over the top edge of pie plate, unroll evenly over pan.
9. Without stretching, ease dough into pan. If it breaks, don't worry, use some extra dough to patch it.
10. Cut off extra dough with knife or kitchen scissors leaving 1" overhang all around. Turn the overhang under to create a thicker clean edge you can decorate.
11. See sidebar for how to make your edge.
12. Refrigerate your dough for 30 minutes to 1 hour before baking.

SIDEBAR

NOTES :

For a 9" pie plate roll crust out to a 13" diameter.

To roll dough into a circle start in the center of the dough, with even pressure roll a few times away from you, then from the center roll toward you a few times.

Pick dough up and turn a ¼ turn and repeat rolling as above. Continue turning and rolling until your dough is ¼" or less thick and the right size for your pie plate.

To make a fluted edge place your thumb and index finger on the outside of pastry. Using index finger on other hand, press the dough to create a V; continue zig-zag edge around pie.

Position fingers

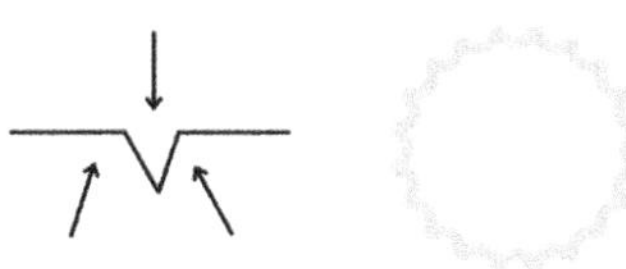

PIECRUST continued

SIDEBAR

NOTES :

You can use the tines of a fork to create a design by pressing down on the edge and leaving an imprint.

DON'T FORGET!

Any extra crust can be used to decorate the top of the pie.

Making the dough by hand

1. Cut the butter into the flour using either a pastry cutter or 2 forks until it looks like coarse meal, as above.
2. Knead small amounts of ice water into the flour mixture until it holds together into a ball.
3. Starting at step 4, above, follow directions.

Blind baking

Use this method for pies with a filling that isn't baked, such as cream pies or pies that need to start cooking before you fill and cook them. The advantage of blind baking is that the crust will have time to brown and the bottom of the crust stays crispy.

Directions

Preheat oven to 400°

1. Place dough in pie plate, finish top, and refrigerate for at least 30 minutes.
2. Using a fork, prick the entire bottom and sides of the dough to create small holes. This helps prevent the dough from puffing up.
3. Place foil or parchment paper to loosely cover the bottom and the sides of the pie. Fill with pie weights, such as uncooked rice or beans. You want to weigh the dough down so it will stay flat.
4. Bake at 400° until the edge starts to brown, about 12 to 15 minutes. Remove from oven and pull the foil or parchment with the weights out of the pie.
5. Place the pie back into the oven for another 5 minutes to cook the bottom of the crust.
6. Remove from oven and let it cool before filling.

"I love cooking. It's one of my favorite things to do. To share my parents' recipes that I grew up with is just something very special to me."

—Lance Bass

The Power of Food Passed On

Each year our families gather together,
savoring the smells and pleasures
that evoke a time when we knew
without question that the magic
we now remember was real.

Our enchantment and joy is palpable,
and we cherish it all, knowing that
we can have it year after year.

—Adeline M. Olmer

8.

IT'S YOUR TURN

Use these pages to write down your recipes.

WHY WRITE IT DOWN

"I never really cook from recipes. But the worst is when something turns out great and I can't figure out how to make it again!"
—Blake Lively

This is the section where you get to write down the recipes that you've created.

When you make a great meal, you need to be able to repeat the recipe and in my experience the only way to do that is to write it down as soon as you decide it is good enough to repeat. If you don't, it gets forgotten. Since the fun of a good recipe is to be able to savor it, it seems a shame not to be able to repeat a good dish just because you can't remember it.

Le Kitchen Cookbook replaced my many pieces of paper with notes about good recipes that I'd saved throughout the years. In it, I record what works and what needs to be adjusted the next time I make it.

Write the name of the recipe and the page number it is on the previous page so you can easily find it.

This book has become one of the most essential tools in my kitchen. I hope you will find it as usful as I have.

Enjoy.

For book bonus materials and extra videos, go to:
french-secrets.com/pages/book

write it down

Title:

write it down

Title:

write it down

Title:

Title:

write it down

Title:

write it down

Title:

Title:

write it down

Title:

write it down

Title:

write it down

Title:

write it down

Title:

INDEX

A

B

INDEX

C

INDEX

INDEX

G

H

INDEX

INDEX

INDEX

INDEX

INDEX

T

INDEX

V

INDEX

ABOUT THE AUTHOR

Adeline Olmer, a French native, is passionate about living well, enjoying good food, and sharing it with friends and family. She moved to the United States as a young girl and has had the privilege of living between the two countries for several decades. Adeline writes a weekly food and lifestyle blog, french-secrets.com

She was a co-owner of her family's iconic antique store, Antan, in Connecticut. Adeline has worked in interior design, fashion design, and has been featured in major publications including *Self Magazine*, *Cosmopolitan*, *Victoria*, *Mary Emmerling's Country*, *The Daily News*, and *The New York Observer*.

Adeline lives in Westchester County, NY, with her husband, Mark and their dog, Bentley.

Made in the USA
Middletown, DE
21 October 2021